LISTENING TO
GOD

LISTENING TO GOD

Experience His Presence Every Day

BRUCE BICKEL
& STAN JANTZ

BARBOUR
PUBLISHING

LISTENING TO GOD

Do you long to hear God's voice? Not an audible sound that only a few experience, but the still, small voice of God coming into your heart and mind, assuring you that He is ever true and always with you?

We all have a longing for something beyond ourselves, so the desire to hear God's voice and feel His presence is quite normal. But this intimate connection doesn't happen unless we're in a position to *listen* to Him. Every day, God desires to speak to us—but He needs a willing heart and an open mind so His voice can be heard. That's our first step in listening to God.

God in His grace has made it possible to hear His voice in a variety of ways: through the beauty and splendor of the natural world. . .in the Bible, His written Word. . .through the life and teachings of Jesus Christ, His only Son. . .by the power of the Holy Spirit. . .in the relationships you develop as you love and serve others. . .and through your own acts of spiritual worship. In all these ways, God is already speaking to you. All you need to do is listen.

In a small, though we hope not insignificant way, we have written this book of daily readings to encourage you to open your heart and mind to the voice of God. We have chosen seven themes—one for each day of the week—that will focus your thoughts on a particular aspect of God's voice. And we've done something rather unusual: we've written this book as if God is speaking to you in the first person.

We know that's a bold move, and maybe a little risky. But please hear us: we do not claim to speak for God. We have simply chosen a format we think will capture the personal way God loves and cares for all of us. We've been careful to present only those truths and principles that are found in God's Word, and we ask you to be open to what God has already said.

Here's what you can expect each day:

MONDAY: *God*
One of the most amazing things about God—the all-powerful, all-knowing, infinite Creator of the universe—is that He has already revealed Himself to us through His character, through the way He works in the world, and through the way He desires to relate to us. Each Monday you will hear from God concerning Himself.

Tuesday: *Jesus*

Every Tuesday you will listen to God through Jesus Christ, the most remarkable person who ever lived. Jesus is unique in human history for the kind of life He lived and the miracles He performed. Jesus came to show us God—and when He spoke, He spoke with God's voice.

Wednesday: *The Holy Spirit*

How is it possible to hear God's voice in *your* heart and mind? The answer lies in the third Person of the Trinity, the Holy Spirit. God sent the Holy Spirit so we could experience His presence every moment of our lives—as long as we are willing to listen to Him. On Wednesdays you will hear God through this very special Person.

Thursday: *God's Word*

The most popular book of all time is the Bible, God's written Word given to us so we can know Him better and discover His amazing plan for us. The Bible is more than a book. It's the grand story of God, written so we can hear God's voice—if we will just listen. On Thursdays you will hear God through His Word.

Friday: *Your Life*

Did you know that God has a plan and purpose for your life? He doesn't want to box you in and force you to follow a set of rules. He wants to show you what it means to have an abundant and flourishing life. Every Friday you will connect with God through the principles of His Word, designed to give your life the meaning you've always wanted.

Saturday: *The World*

God didn't create you to live in isolation. He wants you to live in the amazing world He made. There are both opportunities and dangers in the world: opportunities to love and serve others, and dangers from those who oppose God. On Saturdays you will hear God tell you how He expects you to relate to the world. At the same time, you'll hear His assurance that He will always be with you through every circumstance.

Sunday: *The Church*

It's only appropriate that you hear God's voice on Sundays in church. The church is more than bricks and mortar—it's the living, breathing body of believers who love and serve one another as they love and serve God. Those who are part of God's church should make it a priority to listen to God.

As you read these daily devotions, imagine that God is speaking to you personally—because He really is! As you process and ponder each day's entry, our prayer is that God will use the content of His Word to show you more of who you are even as you learn more about who He is.

In the Old Testament, a boy named Samuel heard the voice of God calling his name. It happened three times before Samuel really listened and realized it was God who was speaking. In that moment of awareness, Samuel cried out, "Speak, for your servant is listening!"

Friend, God is calling *your* name. He has many things to tell you, and all He asks of you is a willingness to listen. When you get to that point, you will hear God's voice—and it will change your life.

Bruce Bickel & Stan Jantz

I AM THE ONE AND ONLY GOD

*I am the greatest thought anyone can have
because there is nothing greater than I am.*

If there's one idea held by more people throughout human history, regardless of who they are or where they come from, it's this: God. Not everyone agrees on who or what I am, but everybody thinks about me in one way or another. Even those who deny I exist think about me. They can't help it.

Have you ever wondered why you think about me so much? I can tell you why: I really *do* exist, not as some imaginary being that people invent to make themselves feel better, but as the one and only God. You may already know a lot about me, or you may know very little. That's okay. I will meet you where you are.

Right now, as you begin this journey of listening to my voice every day, I want you to know something: I am the one who is, and who was, and who is to come, the Almighty (Revelation 1:8).

*"And there is no God apart from me,
a righteous God and a Savior;
there is none but me."*
ISAIAH 45:21

JESUS AND I ARE ONE

Everything that I am, Jesus is.

What sets your faith apart from all the other religions and belief systems in the world is not just its message, but also its Messenger—Jesus Christ, the one I sent into the world (John 3:16). You can't call yourself a Christian if you like the teachings of Jesus but reject Him as being equal to me in every way. Most of the major world religions acknowledge Jesus in some way, but only Christianity—that's the faith based on Christ—has my Son at the center. Only Christianity teaches that Jesus and I are *one*.

What do you think? What do you believe about Jesus? If you truly believe in me, then you must believe in Jesus also, because He is the visible image of who I am (Colossians 1:15).

If you haven't investigated the truth about Jesus, you have come to the right place. We're going to talk a lot about Jesus as you hear my voice on this journey—because everything I am, He is.

"I and the Father are one."
JOHN 10:30

HE, SHE, OR IT?

The Holy Spirit is not an impersonal force, but a real Person.

Because the Holy Spirit is a *spirit*, without a body or any physical form, it's only natural for you to ask if we're discussing a he, a she, or an it. Strictly speaking, a spirit would be referred to as an "it." But notice how Jesus refers to the Holy Spirit: "But when he, the Spirit of truth, comes, he will guide you into all the truth" (John 16:13).

My Holy Spirit is neither male nor female. Yet when the Bible refers to the Holy Spirit with the personal pronoun *he* instead of *it*, that's to remind you that He is a real Person, not some mysterious ghost. That means the presence of the Holy Spirit in your life is not an abstraction, but very personal and very real.

Even more important, the Holy Spirit in your life means that I live in you.

You, however, are not in the realm of the flesh
but are in the realm of the Spirit,
if indeed the Spirit of God lives in you.
ROMANS 8:9

READ AND STUDY MY WORD

*People who only read my Word usually lose interest,
but those who study my Word hunger for more.*

If you want to know me better, I have a suggestion: read my Word, the Bible. Even more, *study* my Word.

There's a difference between reading and studying the Bible. Reading is good, but it can only take you so far. You may get the general idea, but you won't understand everything. That's why merely reading the Bible is frustrating for many people. The apparent futility isn't from lack of desire or time or motivation. People lose interest when they don't understand my Word.

Don't worry if you can't grasp everything the Bible says. I don't know anybody who does, not even theologians—the people who study me for a living. Just be patient and intentional about your Bible study.

Every person I created is different, so your Bible study experience will be uniquely your own. But here are two principles that are true for everyone, principles that will help you understand my Word better: First, make every effort to learn *what* the Bible says. Then, think deeply about my Word and how you can apply it to your life (Psalm 1:2).

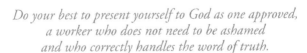

*Do your best to present yourself to God as one approved,
a worker who does not need to be ashamed
and who correctly handles the word of truth.*

2 TIMOTHY 2:15

PRAYER IS AN AWESOME PRIVILEGE

*When you talk with me through prayer,
you are talking with the Creator of the universe.*

You can communicate with people in many ways. But the best and most effective way is talking face-to-face in normal, everyday language—without formality, pretense, or hidden agendas.

The same goes for communicating with me. Though you can't see me, you can talk with me in person, and the way you do that is through prayer.

Some people have said that prayer is "conversation with God." That's true, but prayer is much more than conversation because I am much more than a person. I am *God*, and above me there is no other. No one in heaven or on earth can compare with me. So conversing with me is something you shouldn't take for granted.

Prayer is an awesome privilege. It's the way you can communicate with me face-to-face in normal, everyday language—without formality, pretense, or hidden agendas.

*I lift my eyes to you, O God,
enthroned in heaven.*
PSALM 123:1 NLT

PRAY FOR THE LOST

Your heart should break for the lost, because the lost break my heart.

If you are a follower of Jesus and you want to be like Him, you need to live like Jesus would live. You need to have the heart of Jesus, which means you need to have a heart for the lost—that is, those who are lost in their sins. Without Jesus, they have no hope.

When you study the life of my Son in the Bible, here's what you find about His heart for the lost: First, Jesus didn't come to condemn the world, but to save it (John 3:17). And Jesus is praying for everyone who will eventually believe in Him (John 17:20).

Your heart should break for people without Jesus—your friends, neighbors, coworkers, family members, even strangers. Pray for them. Ask me to help them.

I urge you, first of all, to pray for all people. Ask God to help them;
intercede on their behalf, and give thanks for them. . . .
This is good and pleases God our Savior, who wants
everyone to be saved and to understand the truth.

1 TIMOTHY 2:1, 3–4 NLT

THE CHURCH BELONGS TO ME

The church is not some human idea or invention.
The church is my idea.

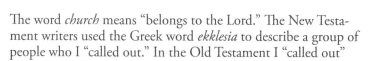

The word *church* means "belongs to the Lord." The New Testament writers used the Greek word *ekklesia* to describe a group of people who I "called out." In the Old Testament I "called out" the nation of Israel, so in a sense there was a "church" before Jesus came to earth. But the church you know today came into existence with the coming of Christ.

Jesus lived and died for the church (Ephesians 5:25), and He has promised to build the church (Matthew 16:18). Jesus began calling out people when He chose the original twelve disciples. Think of these men as a little church that experienced explosive growth on the Day of Pentecost, when the Holy Spirit first came in power to all believers (Acts 2). That first New Testament church started with three thousand people (Acts 2:41), and it hasn't stopped growing since.

If you are part of a local church, you belong to me—because I have called you out.

"I will build my church,
and the gates of hell shall not prevail against it."
MATTHEW 16:18 ESV

15

MY GREATNESS IS UNSEARCHABLE

There's nothing I can't do for you.

When you think about me, what thoughts do you have?

At this very moment, what are you picturing in your mind? An old, white-bearded man in flowing robes? A king sitting on a throne? Those are natural responses, but they aren't correct—because you're only thinking in terms of what I have made. But I have not been made, so it's impossible to describe me with mere words.

The psalm writer David (who had a way with words) said that I am *unsearchable*—that no one can fully understand who I am. That's true, but don't let that stop you from thinking about me. You should! Just remember that there are no boundaries to who I am and what I can do. That means there is nothing I can't do for you.

And here's something else to remember: even when you aren't thinking about me, I am always thinking about you.

*Great is the LORD and most worthy of praise;
his greatness no one can fathom.*

PSALM 145:3

I LOVE MY SON

As much as you love your children, I love my Son infinitely more.

If you are a parent, you know what it's like to love one of your children. You would do anything and give up everything for him or her. It's in your nature to love someone else that much—because I gave you that extra capacity to love one of your own.

But as much as you love your children, try to imagine how much I love my only Son, Jesus. First of all, my capacity to love is without limits. Love defines me, and because I am infinite, so is my love. Now think about who Jesus is—the one I sent into the world to save you so you and I could have a personal relationship.

Jesus loves you just as much as I do—so much that He gave His life for you. And when you believe and accept Jesus, I give you eternal life. But if you reject this Son I love so much, it's the same as rejecting me. So great is my love for my Son, that anyone who doesn't trust Him will feel my anger rather than experience eternal life with Jesus and me.

The Father loves the Son and has placed everything in his hands.
JOHN 3:35

THE HOLY SPIRIT COMPREHENDS ME

If you really want to know me,
the Holy Spirit will tell you all you need to know.

Remember when we discussed the difficulty of comprehending me? I can't change who I am, but I don't really want to be a mystery to you (although some mystery is a good thing). So I've made it possible for you to understand me by way of a "secret weapon." No, it's not a device or even a special program. It's a Person, my Holy Spirit, the third member of the Trinity.

Because the Holy Spirit has my nature—that is to say, He is everything I am—He can comprehend me completely, down to my deepest thoughts. And because I want you to know the plans I have for you and the salvation I have arranged for you, I have given you the Holy Spirit (John 16:13).

If you have received Jesus into your life, the Holy Spirit is in you, ready and willing to reveal more about me than you know now. Then you can understand me, experience me on an intimate level, and know all the wonderful things I have given you.

The Spirit searches all things, even the deep things of God.
For who knows a person's thoughts except their own
spirit within them? In the same way no one knows
the thoughts of God except the Spirit of God.
1 CORINTHIANS 2:10–11

I WROTE MY WORD THROUGH THE HOLY SPIRIT

When you read my Word,
you are hearing my voice.

You don't have to wait for a sign from heaven or a special inner feeling to get closer to me. Just go to my Word, and you will hear my voice.

It won't be my voice from the past, but my living, active voice that is speaking to you right now (Hebrews 4:12). Encountering my Word—whether you read it for yourself or listen to it being read—is like having a personal conversation with me. You don't have to wait for that to happen. You can hear me anytime you choose.

That's possible because of the way I wrote the Bible. I used the Holy Spirit to breathe my words into handpicked people (called prophets) so they could capture my personal message of love and hope to you. Because this same Holy Spirit lives in *you* now, you can personally experience me and know the plans I have for you every time you read my Word.

For prophecy never had its origin in the human will,
but prophets, though human, spoke from God
as they were carried along by the Holy Spirit.
2 PETER 1:21

DON'T BE PROUD

Pride sets you in opposition to me, and that's never good.

I don't talk a lot about pride in my Word, but when I do, it's always in a bad way. True, there are some good forms of pride—like when a parent is proud of a child. That's not the kind of pride we're discussing now.

Bad pride occurs when you put yourself above others. Ultimately, the highest form of pride is when you put yourself above *me*. It shouldn't surprise you that pride is what motivated Satan to rebel against me. Once, when his name was Lucifer, he was the highest ranking of my heavenly army. But pride consumed him, and he said, "I will raise my throne above the stars of God" (Isaiah 14:13). Satan wanted to be above me, so I expelled him from heaven.

People try the same thing today. They disregard me, deny me, even pretend I don't exist. They think they can live their lives without me. Essentially, they want to be above me. But I am God, and above me is no other.

So here's my advice to you: don't be proud. Pride sets you in opposition to me, and that's never good. Be humble, and I promise to show you my grace.

"God opposes the proud but shows favor to the humble."
JAMES 4:6

YOUR CITIZENSHIP IS IN HEAVEN

*Your citizenship on earth is temporary;
your citizenship in heaven is eternal.*

Do you like the world I made for you? I hope so. I created it just for you so you could enjoy a beautiful, endlessly fascinating place to live in. I know, the world sometimes can be cruel—but for the most part, it's a great place to call home.

There's only one problem with that: it's easy to get attached to the world, especially when things are going well in your life. I want you to enjoy my world, but I also want you to keep that in perspective.

You see, the world may be a great place to call home—but it was never meant as your true home. You're living in the world— that is, on earth—in a particular location in a certain country. You may even be a "citizen" of that country. That's fine, but I'd like you to remember something as you live in my world: your citizenship there is temporary.

Your true, permanent, eternal citizenship is in heaven with me. You aren't there yet, but someday you will be, in the most glorious place you could ever imagine. So you may as well think now in terms of a dual citizenship—your temporary one on earth, and your true citizenship in heaven.

*But our citizenship is in heaven.
And we eagerly await a Savior from there,
the Lord Jesus Christ.*
PHILIPPIANS 3:20

YOU ARE MY DWELLING PLACE

Thinking about where I live will change the way you live.

A lot of people have the idea that I live in churches—that the only time you can experience me personally is when you go to a certain kind of building. I'm there all right, but not because of the stained glass windows or the cross or the altar with one of those giant Bibles. I'm there because of *you*.

I don't live in buildings. I live in people. I live in *you*—if you have joined my eternal family by receiving Jesus into your life (John 1:12). In a manner of speaking, *you* are a building. In fact, you're much more than that. You are a temple where I live through the Holy Spirit.

The temple has always been a symbol of my earthly dwelling place. But now, because of Jesus and the Holy Spirit, I live in you. I know that's difficult to get your mind around, but it's absolutely true. From the time you wake up to the time you go to bed, think about where I live. If you do, it will change the way you live.

Don't you know that you yourselves are God's temple
and that God's Spirit dwells in your midst?
1 CORINTHIANS 3:16

YOU KNOW I EXIST

*People may deny that I exist,
but they can't help but think about me.*

I can't help but notice there's a huge debate over whether or not I am real.

I could understand if I had remained invisible, leaving no clues to my existence. Under those circumstances, it would make sense to be an atheist (someone who says I don't exist) or an agnostic (someone who says it's impossible to know I exist). But that's not the case. I've provided plenty of clues, starting with what's inside you.

Truth is, I've put two clues in the center of every person: First, I've given you a longing for something beyond your temporary life on earth (Ecclesiastes 3:11). Next, I've planted a "God idea" in the mind of everyone. There's no one who can't think about me, because I've made it clear that I am real.

People may suppress or even deny my reality in their lives, but they can't help but think about me. If you're already a believer, this should give you great confidence. You don't have to prove I exist because I've already done it. If you're still skeptical, trust your heart. It's a great place to start.

*They know the truth about God because
he has made it obvious to them.*

ROMANS 1:19 NLT

JESUS CAME AT THE RIGHT TIME

I'm rarely early, never late, but always right on time.

I love it when a plan comes together. I know that some television character said that, but it's my idea. Nobody executes a plan better than I do, and no one has better timing.

There's something you need to understand about my timing: it's always perfect. When you pray for things, you want them right now—but I don't come early. Before I answer, I want you to grow and mature in the middle of what you're experiencing. On the other hand, though it may seem otherwise, I'm never *late* in answering your prayers. Truth is, I am always right on time. Always.

Just look at the time I sent my Son to earth. The timing was perfect. The world was united under a single authority so the followers of Jesus could freely take His message to everyone. There was a common language, making it easier to tell people the Good News about Jesus. And people were acutely aware of their need for a liberator, even if they had different ideas about who that would be.

Jesus' coming wasn't late, nor was it early. When He came, it was at just the right time.

But when the right time came, God sent his Son.
GALATIANS 4:4 NLT

THE HOLY SPIRIT HAS EMOTIONS

Don't break my heart.
Let the Holy Spirit work in your life.

Many people have big misconceptions about me. Some think I'm a detached, disinterested deity who doesn't have emotions. But these people don't know me.

I love with an everlasting love (Jeremiah 31:3), even when you don't love me back. When you take delight in me, I generously give you what your heart desires (Psalm 37:4). Every day my mercies are new and I am always faithful (Lamentations 3:22–23). I am the God who forgives (Ephesians 4:32).

But I also have negative emotions. I am jealous when you make other things in your life more important than me. I hate sin (although I love the sinner). And my heart can be broken when you bring sorrow to my Holy Spirit.

How does that happen? When you shut Him out and prevent Him from working in your life the way He wants to. The Holy Spirit will always be part of your life, but in order for Him to move and breathe His power in you—making you the kind of person I want you to be—you need to give Him room to work.

Don't break my heart. Let the Holy Spirit work in your life.

And do not grieve the Holy Spirit of God,
with whom you were sealed for the day of redemption.
EPHESIANS 4:30

THE BIBLE IS MY WORD

*The reason the Bible is such a remarkable book
is that the Bible is my Word.*

Many people question whether the Bible is a book that I actually wrote.

Of course, I didn't write the Bible with my own hand. I did something much better: I breathed my words into more than forty trustworthy humans who then wrote down my Word in their own terms. That's why you see so much variety in the Bible. There's history, poetry, prophecy, parables, and personal letters—written over a period of sixteen hundred years. But it's all my Word.

You'll hear people question my Word, saying it's largely made up by humans to somehow make me look good. Don't believe that! How could mere human authors write hundreds of prophecies that have been fulfilled 100 percent of the time? How could so many different authors be so consistent in their writing? Most of all, how could a book written by mere mortals have such a profound effect on so many people for so long?

The answer to all these questions is me. The reason the Bible is such a remarkable book is that the Bible is my Word.

---

*And we also thank God continually because,
when you received the word of God, which you heard from us,
you accepted it not as a human word, but as it actually is,
the word of God, which is indeed at work in you who believe.*

1 Thessalonians 2:13

PRACTICE WHAT YOU HAVE LEARNED

If you want a fulfilled life, do what I say.

If you're a Christian—if you have a personal relationship with me through Jesus—you should be eager to learn all you can about me.

Imagine yourself falling in love with somebody. Wouldn't you want to know all you can about that person? It would be silly to tell him or her, "I love you, but I really don't want to know anything about you." It's no different with me. If you love me, why wouldn't you want to know me better and better? Even more, why wouldn't you want to know what I want you to do?

Having a relationship with me is more than saying you're a Christian. It's more than believing you're going to heaven someday. Being my child and a follower of my Son, Jesus, means you have a desire to know all you can about me, as well as to put into practice what you've learned.

In simple terms, being a Christian is being a "doer," not just a "hearer," of my Word (James 1:22). If you only hear me but never do what I say, your life is going to be stale and empty. But if you put into practice what I tell you, your life will be more fulfilling than you could possibly imagine.

*Whatever you have learned or received or heard from me,
or seen in me—put it into practice.
And the God of peace will be with you.*
PHILIPPIANS 4:9

PRAY FOR YOUR LEADERS

Rather than criticizing your leaders,
I want you to pray for them.

I don't like it when my people overly criticize the leaders I've put over them.

Not every leader is perfect. Many don't even acknowledge me. But most call on me during tough times, and even those who never give me credit are still accountable to me (Romans 13:1).

Rather than criticizing your leaders, I want you to pray for them. I'm talking about local leaders, national leaders, and everyone in between. Governments are my idea, put into place for your protection and well-being. If you think they are bad or corrupt, leave that to me. Ultimately, I am the one to whom all leaders must answer.

Be a good citizen, remembering who's ultimately in charge. Meanwhile—and I can't stress this enough—pray for your leaders and each another. If you do, I promise to bring you healing and peace.

I urge, then, first of all, that petitions, prayers, intercession and
thanksgiving be made for all people—for kings and all those in
authority, that we may live peaceful and quiet lives in all godliness
and holiness. This is good, and pleases God our Savior.
1 TIMOTHY 2:1–3

COME TOGETHER

When you get together,
make it a point to encourage others.

Ever heard the expression "There's strength in numbers"? The idea is that you can accomplish more with a group of people than you can by yourself.

It's true—because that's the way I created you. You are not meant to be alone, but in community. Energy, creativity, and productivity flow when you get together with others.

This is especially true when you're in community with your fellow believers. Whether you meet in a small group in a home, or you gather to worship me in song, hearing someone teach my Word in church, you will experience me in powerful and profound ways simply because you are with other members of your spiritual family.

When you get together, make it a point to encourage others. When you see others doing something good, tell them how much you like it. Your positive words will give them the courage they need to keep going.

And let us consider how we may spur one another
on toward love and good deeds, not giving up meeting together,
as some are in the habit of doing, but encouraging one another—
and all the more as you see the Day approaching.
HEBREWS 10:24–25

THE FOOL SAYS I DON'T EXIST

*It's more reasonable to believe I exist
than to believe I don't.*

Those who say I don't exist think they are so smart. In fact, they consider themselves mentally superior to people like you who believe in me, as if you don't need your brain to follow me. Nothing could be further from the truth!

Belief in me begins with knowledge. You need to have reasonable certainty that I exist before you can believe. Then you accept by faith that I want a relationship with you through Jesus. Finally, you trust me with your life, confident that I will deliver on my promises.

By contrast, unbelievers disregard the evidence for my existence from nature, from my Word, and from my Son. Not only that, they deny what their minds are telling them—that I *am* real. In place of my true story, they invent a false story that says everything you see and experience—the world around you, the people you know, all the history that's ever been recorded—are the products of blind chance rather than divine purpose.

When you think about it, who's the smart one? The person who believes in me, or the one who says I don't exist?

The fool says in his heart, "There is no God."
PSALM 14:1

ARE YOU WAITING FOR MY SON TO RETURN?

Expect Jesus to come back to earth at any time.

I'm not a big fan of people who predict the exact day Jesus will return to earth. They think they can calculate a particular date, and they get their followers all worked up. There's only one problem: nobody knows the hour or the day except for me—and I haven't told anyone.

Though you don't know the day my Son is coming back, you should expect it at any time. Jesus advises, "Be on guard! Be alert!" (Mark 13:33). You need to do what He says, because when He does return, it will be too late for people to change their mind.

For those who have trusted Jesus for their eternal future, the Second Coming of my Son will be the most exciting day of their lives. But for those who have put Jesus off, it will be the worst day imaginable.

So stay awake and keep waiting for that day!

*I wait for the LORD, my whole being waits,
and in his word I put my hope. I wait for the Lord
more than watchmen wait for the morning.*

PSALM 130:5–6

LET THE HOLY SPIRIT DIRECT YOU

When the Holy Spirit speaks to you,
don't brush Him off. Pay attention.

Like me, the Holy Spirit is a perfect gentleman. He will never force Himself on you or annoy you in any way. Like me, He will simply wait for you to call on Him for wisdom, insight, and direction in your life.

Knowing that He can help you, especially when you face difficult situations or decisions, should give you great confidence. Why go it alone when you have my power and perspective available through the Holy Spirit?

There will be times when the Holy Spirit takes the initiative, giving you a warning about a coming circumstance, either good or bad. Some people call this *intuition*—but in your life it's the Holy Spirit. For example, when you meet someone and have a sudden feeling that you should say something encouraging or do something to help, that's the Holy Spirit talking to you. Or you may be heading for a decision point and something inside you says, "Don't do it." That's the Holy Spirit.

When He speaks, don't brush Him off. Pay attention. Listen to what He's telling you.

Paul and his companions traveled throughout the region
of Phrygia and Galatia, having been kept by the Holy Spirit
from preaching the word in the province of Asia.

ACTS 16:6

MY WORD WILL TEACH YOU WHAT IS TRUE

When you read my Word,
you are encountering my truth personally.

What is truth? That's one of the most important questions you could ever ask and answer.

When you find the truth, you've found everything. Truth will never let you down because when you get to the bottom line, truth is anything that corresponds to the way things really are.

As you sort through your life, start with the biggest truth of all—then work your way down from there. And what is the biggest truth? It's me. I am the grandest reality of all.

But I'm not some abstract philosophical equation, such as God = truth. I am personal and loving. I want a relationship with you, something I've made very clear to you in my Word.

When you read my Word, you are encountering my truth personally. Everything I have said in my Word—the stories, poetry, history, prophecy, biographies of Jesus, and letters to the churches—are there to teach you what is *true*.

All Scripture is inspired by God and is useful to teach us what is true.
2 TIMOTHY 3:16 NLT

IF YOU WANT TO FOLLOW JESUS, DENY YOURSELF

Following my Son means
you are willing to give up everything for Him.

More than anything else, I want you to follow Jesus. But I don't want you to follow Him if you're planning on *adding* Him to your life, as if He's another one of your self-improvement programs.

My Son is not a program; my Son is a Person.

Following Jesus means you are devoted to Him. Following Jesus means you make Him the number-one priority in your life. Following Jesus means you are willing to give up *everything* for Him.

When Jesus called His first disciples, He asked them to do two things: First, they had to deny themselves. When you deny something, you are saying it isn't true. So to deny yourself is to admit you don't have the truth in you. But my Son does: He *is* the truth. Second, Jesus asked His disciples to take up their cross and follow Him.

My child, this is a hard saying because Jesus meant this in a literal sense. He went to the cross for you, and He expects you to be willing to die for Him. Not that you will have to—but you must be willing. That's how serious you must be if you want to follow Jesus fully.

Then Jesus said to his disciples,
"Whoever wants to be my disciple must deny themselves
and take up their cross and follow me."

MATTHEW 16:24

LIVE AT PEACE WITH EVERYONE

*Try showing a little of the peace you and I have
with everyone you meet.*

There are two kinds of peace. The most important is the peace
Jesus came to give you—peace between you and me.

This may come as a shock, but if you didn't have Jesus in your
life, you and I would be enemies. It's not because I don't love you,
because I do—more than you could ever imagine. But because
you are a sinful person, and I am wholly holy, we are at odds. In a
manner of speaking, we're at war. But when you invite Jesus into
your life, He brings peace between you and me (John 14:27).

The other kind of peace is the type you should have with everyone you encounter. I understand, there are exceptions. You may
be doing your best to have a peaceful relationship with a neighbor,
and he just won't have it. All I ask is that you *try*, showing a little
of the peace you and I have with everyone you meet.

*If it is possible, as far as it depends on you,
live at peace with everyone.*
ROMANS 12:18

Only I Know the Heart

Only I know whose hearts are fully committed to me.

Why are you so quick to judge others? I've been watching you, and I've noticed you don't hesitate to judge those who aren't my followers.

Usually, you don't even know them—but you've read about something they've done or been accused of doing. Then you blurt out something sarcastic or condemning, often within earshot of others. Don't do that. Whatever they've done, they will ultimately answer to me, not you. Besides, what behavior would you expect from someone who isn't my child?

As much as I dislike that kind of judging, there's another kind that's even worse: when you judge someone in my family. I know, not everyone who claims to be my child acts like it. They may not agree with you on every point of doctrine. But don't judge them. Help them, guide them, most of all, *love* them.

Judging is my job. Only I know those whose hearts are fully committed to me.

Nevertheless, God's solid foundation stands firm, sealed with this inscription: "The Lord knows those who are his," and, "Everyone who confesses the name of the Lord must turn away from wickedness."

2 Timothy 2:19

My Ways Are Not Your Ways

*All I ask is that you trust me
to always do the right thing.*

I know there's a big discussion going on about who I'm going to allow into heaven. Some people think I shouldn't let in evil people, while others have the opinion that anybody should be able to reach heaven as long as they're sincere. This is a good conversation to have, because it really is a life-and-death matter.

And that's why it's essential that you leave the answer to the question of heaven (and who gets in) to me.

Though my standards for heaven are perfect—just as I am—I take delight in showing mercy to repentant sinners, no matter how wicked they are. You know how some people (maybe even you) get frustrated when a governor pardons a criminal they think deserves to die? Well, you'd be surprised how many offenders I have pardoned. In fact, you probably wouldn't approve of them.

But I don't need your approval. I only want your trust. If you try to figure out *why* I do the things I do, you'll only be frustrated. All I ask is that you trust me to always do the right thing.

*Let the wicked forsake their ways and the unrighteous their thoughts.
Let them turn to the Lord, and he will have mercy on them,
and to our God, for he will freely pardon.
"For my thoughts are not your thoughts,
neither are your ways my ways."*
Isaiah 55:7–8

Jesus Is the Cornerstone

My Son alone is your trustworthy Rock and your Redeemer.

Do you ever wonder why you feel an immediate bond when you meet another Christian? It happens even though you were strangers just a moment before.

It isn't because you have something humanly in common, like sharing a hobby. When you meet another follower of my Son, you connect because you are both part of something intangible and organic. To begin with, you belong to a *spiritual* family—so you're more like siblings than strangers. You are also members of the same spiritual body: different parts functioning together with Jesus as the head.

Beyond that, you're part of a complex spiritual building, one I'm constructing for eternity. I am building this mighty living temple, stone by stone, on the foundation of the apostles and the prophets, with my Son as the Cornerstone.

Believe me, this isn't some ceremonial little brick, but a massive stone upon which the entire building rests. Because He is faithful and true, Jesus alone is worthy of being the Cornerstone. Jesus alone is your trustworthy Rock and your Redeemer.

And so the Lord says, "I'm laying a firm
foundation for the city of Zion.
It's a valuable cornerstone proven to be trustworthy;
no one who trusts it will ever be disappointed."
Isaiah 28:16 cev

THE HOLY SPIRIT TEACHES YOU ABOUT JESUS

You can know my Son personally through my Holy Spirit.

Do you ever wish you could have been around when Jesus walked the earth? Let me tell you, it was an unforgettable, life-changing experience for everyone who met my Son.

Because Jesus is everything I am in a human body, He loved everyone He met with an everlasting love. That attracted both the mighty and the weak. He showed mercy to those who despised Him. He had compassion on those who were desperate. He showed mercy to those who were without hope. Jesus healed the sick, gave sight to the blind, made the lame walk again. He taught about me in extraordinary ways, and He forgave the sins of those who needed a Savior.

If you wish you could have met my Son face-to-face and known Him heart-to-heart, I have good news for you: you *can* meet Him, and you *can* know Him. Not physically like His followers of two thousand years ago—but spiritually, through my Holy Spirit.

That's why I sent the Holy Spirit: to make it possible for you to personally experience the love, mercy, healing, teaching, and forgiveness of the living Christ.

*"But when the Father sends the Advocate as my representative—
that is, the Holy Spirit—he will teach you everything
and will remind you of everything I have told you."*
JOHN 14:26 NLT

THE WORLD'S GREATEST INSTRUCTION MANUAL

Don't live your life through trial and error.
Immerse yourself in my Word.

If you're like most people, you're too impatient to read instruction manuals. When you get a new gadget, you want to try it out immediately. And, usually, there's no harm done because you can learn the basics through trial and error. But skipping the instruction manual is a bad idea if you want to experience the full potential of your new gadget.

The same thing goes for the world's greatest instruction manual, which happens to be my Word. Because I wrote it with you in mind, my Word gives you everything you need to know to optimize your life. It would be a real shame if you lived your life without reading my perfect manual.

Don't make the mistake of living your life through trial and error. Immerse yourself in my Word. Familiarize yourself with its contents. Study its themes in detail. Memorize your favorite parts. Get to know the manual backward and forward—and you'll get the full potential out of your life.

All Scripture is God-breathed and is useful for teaching,
rebuking, correcting and training in righteousness.
2 TIMOTHY 3:16

HONOR ME WITH YOUR BODY

Think of your body as my dwelling place.

I'm going to tell you something you already know: your culture is obsessed with sex, and not in a good way.

This is nothing new. Ever since the Fall, when sin entered the world, people have been distorting this beautiful gift I designed for a husband and wife to enjoy in their marriage. What's new is the ever-increasing temptation.

When you face sexual enticements, I want you to remember two things: First, it's not a sin to be tempted. Only when you give in to the temptation do you sin against me. Second, you don't have to fight the temptation alone. I am there with you through the Holy Spirit.

In fact, here's a good way to keep your body and your heart pure: think of your whole self as my dwelling place. Every time you're tempted sexually, imagine that I am there right with you. Do you want me to see what you see? Do you want me to hear your thoughts? Do you want me to know what you are experiencing? Of course you don't.

Let me help you. When you are tempted, call on me. I will help you to honor me with your body.

Do you not know that your bodies are temples of the Holy Spirit,
who is in you, whom you have received from God?
You are not your own; you were bought at a price.
Therefore honor God with your bodies.

1 CORINTHIANS 6:19–20

ACT JUSTLY

I don't want your money or your efforts. I want you.

I appreciate it when you do things for me. I really do! But so many people seem confused about *what* they should do. They try to impress me by giving me money or property—as if I need these things. Or they try to make up for some past sin by offering to make a great personal sacrifice. Then they ask me, "Is this good enough?"

Let me make this really simple: I don't want your money or your efforts. I want *you*. Shall I be more specific? Okay, for starters, I want you to act *justly*. Now don't confuse "acting justly" with "doing social justice." That's fine, but I'm more concerned with your heart and your personal actions than I am with the kind of societal work you're doing.

Are you treating the people around you—your coworkers, neighbors, and family—fairly? Are you doing the right thing at the right time for the right reasons? And are you committed to acting justly for the rest of your life, no matter where you are?

Even if you contribute to a cause to help others in need, don't rely on the organization to do justice for you. Be the face of justice to everyone you meet.

He has shown you, O mortal, what is good.
And what does the LORD *require of you?*
To act justly.
MICAH 6:8

MY SON LOVED AND DIED FOR THE CHURCH

*Jesus promises to love you sacrificially,
even as He asks you to love one another.*

Do you want to know how much Jesus loves the church? He loves her so much that He died for her.

Notice that I use the feminine *her* to describe the church. That's deliberate. Just as a husband loves his wife, Christ loves the church. And just like a husband is willing to give his life for the bride he loves so much, Jesus willingly died for the church—which is *you*, and all true believers of all time.

When the apostle Paul wrote about husbands loving their wives, it was a bold comparison. Women weren't held in high esteem at that time, so to say that a husband would actually love his bride enough to die for her was revolutionary. But that shouldn't surprise you, because my Son was revolutionary.

Jesus came to upset the rigid rules and hierarchy people had put into place. His purpose was to break down the cultural, economic, religious, and gender barriers that existed in the first century. And He's still breaking down barriers in the twenty-first century by uniting all of His followers into one family—the church.

In the process, He promises to love you sacrificially, even as He asks you to love one another.

*Husbands, love your wives, just as Christ loved the church
and gave himself up for her.*
EPHESIANS 5:25

SEEK ME WHILE I CAN BE FOUND

I am as near to you at this moment as I have ever been.

Dear child, how I long to have a close, personal relationship with you. Not some sterile, unemotional, detached connection like two reluctant strangers—but a close relationship between two friends who enjoy being in one another's company. For this to happen, you need to take the first step. You need to make a move toward me.

This is so important that you should do it right now. Seek me out and call my name while you and I are having this conversation. I am as near to you at this moment as I have ever been. Don't put it off. Ask me to show myself to you more clearly and nearly than I ever have before.

If you have difficulty picturing me in your mind, try picturing my Son, who became human so you could identify with Him. If you ask Jesus, He will answer. If you seek Him, you will find Him. If you knock on His door, He will answer (Matthew 7:7).

Seek the LORD while he may be found;
call on him while he is near.
ISAIAH 55:6

LOOK TO MY SON IF YOU WANT TO GLORIFY ME

*Glory is very important to me,
and it's not because I need my ego stroked.*

Whenever you think of doing something—whether it's a major life decision or a simple, ordinary task—ask yourself a question: "Will this glorify God?"

Glory is very important to me, and it's not because I need my ego stroked. The reason this theme of *glory* appears about 275 times in the Bible is because every time you glorify me, your life gets better. In other words, *you* are the winner when I am glorified.

Basically, when you make me look good, you are glorifying me. And when I look good, you look good, because people recognize that you are deflecting credit away from yourself to me. To gain this benefit, you should look for ways to glorify me every day.

If you're having trouble coming up with scenarios, here's a recommendation: look to my Son. Ask yourself, "How would Jesus handle this?" or "What would Jesus do in this situation?" If you learn to process your decisions like this, you will glorify me every time.

*The Son is the radiance of God's glory and the
exact representation of his being,
sustaining all things by his powerful word.*

HEBREWS 1:3

THE HOLY SPIRIT GLORIFIES MY SON

The Holy Spirit is the presence of Jesus in you.

The Holy Spirit has always been around because, like me, He is eternal (Hebrews 9:14). And just as I am, He is everywhere at once (Psalm 139:7), living in every believer. But it wasn't always like this. The Holy Spirit didn't show His true power until Jesus came to earth.

That's because the Holy Spirit's primary role has always been to bring attention to Jesus. So the Holy Spirit appeared only sporadically in the Old Testament. Even during my Son's life on earth, the Holy Spirit didn't show Himself very often. Once Jesus left the earth, however, the Holy Spirit came in power to all believers—something He's been doing ever since.

In your life, the Holy Spirit's primary role is as a witness to my Son. Literally, the Holy Spirit is the presence of Jesus in you. I know this is hard to grasp, but in time you will understand with the help of—you guessed it—the Holy Spirit.

All you need to know now is that my Son is with me and the Holy Spirit is with you, glorifying Jesus in your life.

"But when he, the Spirit of truth, comes. . .
He will glorify me because it is from me
that he will receive what he will make known to you."

JOHN 16:13–14

MY WORD WILL TEACH YOU TO DO WHAT IS RIGHT

Other books are written to give you information.
I wrote my book to give you transformation.

Do you sometimes struggle to understand my will? Do you want to know my plans for you? Are you ever faced with a decision that requires a yes or no answer, but you just don't know what to do? Are you looking for stability in a world that is constantly changing? I have good news! I can help you with every one of these struggles if you will do just one thing: go to my Word.

Believe me, I've thought of every possible dilemma or decision you can face, and I've put the answer in my Word. It may be in the form of a story, a parable, a psalm, or a letter. My wisdom for your life may even come directly from me (you've heard of the Ten Commandments, right?). It's all there in my Word.

Other books are written to give you specific information, or a checklist for success. But that's not how the Bible works. My Word is a guidebook for living, written to transform you—from a self-centered, what's-in-it-for-me kind of person, into someone who wants to do the right thing by loving me and others.

All Scripture is inspired by God and is useful to teach us what it true and to make us realize what is wrong in our lives. It corrects us when we are wrong and teaches us to do what is right.

2 TIMOTHY 3:16 NLT

FREE FROM THE MASTERY OF SIN

Say no to sin and yes to me.

There's a war going on in your life, and I want to help you win it.

The war is between the good you want to do and the sin you keep committing. Instead of doing right, you do the things you hate. My child, this is the great struggle of the believer, and there's only one way out—Jesus.

His death on the cross, where He paid the penalty for your sin, broke sin's mastery over you. You don't *have* to sin. You have a choice every time you are tempted. But you can't do it alone. You need to constantly remind yourself that my Son has set you free so you can say no to sin and yes to me.

Are you under a heavy burden of sin and guilt? Are you too ashamed even to admit your weaknesses to me? Don't put it off any longer: confess your sins and I will forgive you (1 John 1:9). Then claim the power of Jesus in your life. Let Him live your life. Give Him control. Let Jesus take the wheel.

I do not understand what I do. For what I want to do I do not do,
but what I hate I do. . . . What a wretched man I am!
Who will rescue me from this body that is subject to death?
Thanks be to God, who delivers me through Jesus Christ our Lord!

ROMANS 7:15, 24–25

LOVE MERCY

In order to show mercy, you need to love mercy.

One of the sweetest prayers I could ever hear from you is, "Have mercy on me, O Lord." When you call on me for mercy, you are accessing my endless compassion (Lamentations 3:22). So many people perceive me only as a God of justice and judgment. But consider my mercies. They are new every morning (Lamentations 3:23).

Just as I am merciful to you—not giving you what you deserve—I want you to be merciful to others. But in order to show mercy, you need to *love* mercy. As much as you love it when I am merciful to you, I want you to look for ways to be merciful to those around you.

When someone has offended you, and you feel like responding with a biting comment or hateful thought, show mercy. When you catch yourself feeling morally superior to another person, embrace my heart of mercy and make it your own.

Remember, loving mercy is more than just acting in a merciful way—you can actually show mercy grudgingly. "Loving mercy" is developing an attitude that tells me you want mercy to characterize your life.

And what does the LORD require of you?
To act justly and to love mercy.
MICAH 6:8

I LOVE IT WHEN YOU SING TO ME

I don't just want you to think about me;
I want you to feel me.

I love music, and I love it when you use music to praise me.

When you sing to me in church, at home, or in your car, it shows you are really worshipping me. When you use music to communicate with me, I know it's coming from your heart.

That's where music starts—deep inside you. Have you noticed how profoundly music can move you? That's not by accident. Music is my gift to you so you can worship me with your emotions as well as your mind. I don't just want you to think about me; I want you to *feel* me.

Here's something else about music: when you sing an old hymn like "Amazing Grace," you are joining the voices of generations of believers. And when you sing a newer song like "Shout to the Lord," you are uniting your voice with countless other worshippers today who are directing their praises to me. Either way, you are united with a global chorus that transcends time and space.

Sing and make music from your heart to the Lord.
EPHESIANS 5:19

YOU CAN KNOW ME BY DESIGN

My creation sings like a symphony.

I hope you appreciate the world I created—because I made it just for you.

Consider how perfectly everything in the universe works together. The planets in your galaxy are in a precise orbit and rotation so life on earth is possible. The sun that gives you light and life is ideally positioned for maximum effect.

Everything on earth—from the tiniest particle to the largest ocean—is ideally designed for your benefit and enjoyment. My creation sings like a symphony from a finely tuned orchestra, making beautiful music for your benefit and my glory.

It wasn't chance that made the world. Nothing happened by accident. Everything you see—and everything you don't see—came from my hand by the power of my word (Hebrews 11:3). My signature in creation is there for all to see (Romans 1:20).

The heavens declare the glory of God;
the skies proclaim the work of his hands.
Day after day they pour forth speech;
night after night they reveal knowledge.
PSALM 19:1–2

51

THE PROMISE OF JESUS

The rebellion of the human race didn't take me by surprise.

The crowning achievement of my beautiful creation was the human race, represented by the first man, Adam, and the ideal complement I made especially for him, Eve. I had such a wonderful relationship with them. I blessed them and told them to fill the earth and manage all of its creatures and resources (Genesis 1:28). Our relationship was intimate and mutually satisfying. Everything was perfect.

But then Adam disobeyed my clear command, and sin entered the world. At that moment, everything changed. Instead of harmony, humanity would be embroiled in strife. Their labor would be a burden rather than a joy. Where once all was life, now there would be death.

I was heartbroken—but I wasn't unprepared. Right there, at that moment of rebellion, I promised Adam and Eve (and all humanity to come) an opportunity to have a personal relationship with me again. Though I didn't name Him, the promise was my Son. Someday He would come, at great personal cost and out of infinite love, as a sacrifice for sin.

"He will crush your head, and you will strike his heel."
GENESIS 3:15

I HAVE ADOPTED YOU

I am your Father. You are my child.
Nothing can ever change that.

For an orphan, there's nothing more life-changing than adoption. Think of it! An orphan is one whose parents are gone, a child completely alone and helpless. There's nothing an orphan can do to arrange an adoption by a family who will provide love, care, and protection.

In a spiritual sense, *you* were once an orphan. You were abandoned by humanity's parents, Adam and Eve, when they disobeyed me and opened the door for sin to enter the world. You were alone and helpless. Your only chance for love, care, and protection was through adoption into my family, made possible by the saving life of my Son. Because of Jesus, you became my child, with all the rights and privileges that go with being a family member.

In case you ever forget this, the Holy Spirit will bring it to your memory. I am your Father. You are my child. Nothing can ever change that.

The Spirit himself testifies with our spirit that we are God's children.
Now if we are children, then we are heirs—
heirs of God and co-heirs with Christ.
ROMANS 8:16–17

MY WORD WILL EQUIP YOU

If you immerse yourself in the scriptures,
you will discover my purpose for your life.

I have some big plans for you. Seriously, I do.

You may think I make plans just for the high-profile people who preach to thousands, or for those who venture into difficult and dangerous places to share my grace and take my Good News to those who need it most. Yes, I make their plans—but I am just as interested in you, and my plans for you are just as important.

When I saved you, it wasn't only to give you a ticket to heaven. I also wanted to set you on an earthly life journey for the express purpose of carrying out my plans (Ephesians 2:10). What kind of plans? You will find out soon enough if you stay close to me and allow my Holy Spirit to speak to you.

Most importantly, you will know my plans for you as you read and study my Word. If you immerse yourself in the scriptures, you will discover my purpose for your life, because my Word will equip you—literally, furnish you completely—to do those good things I want you to do.

All Scripture is God-breathed and is useful for teaching,
rebuking, correcting and training in righteousness,
so that the servant of God may be thoroughly equipped
for every good work.
2 TIMOTHY 3:16–17

ACCEPT ONE ANOTHER

If you want to honor my Son and please me,
have compassion on everyone.

Rejection is a terrible thing. Nobody likes it, not even me.

To be rejected is very personal, because when you're rejected, people are basically saying, "You don't have any value to me." Even more painful than being rejected yourself is to watch someone you love face rejection. That was my experience when I sent my Son to earth to be a mediator between you and me. As my prophet Isaiah put it, "He was despised and rejected by mankind" (Isaiah 53:3).

Yet Jesus never complained. He accepted and willingly sacrificed Himself for the very people who rejected Him. Though they treated Him badly, He accepted them without qualification.

I want you to have the same attitude as Jesus did. Don't base your acceptance of others—particularly other members of my family—on how they treat you. And please, don't reject someone because they possess a quality you find offensive. If you want to honor my Son and please me, have compassion on *everyone*. Love the unlovely. Receive those who aren't welcome. Most of all, accept people who have experienced rejection.

Accept one another, then, just as Christ accepted you,
in order to bring praise to God.

ROMANS 15:7

LOVE YOUR ENEMIES

*Christianity is attractive because
it's unlike anything else in the world.*

Too many of my followers want to be accepted by the world, so they do everything they can to be like the world. They adopt the world's values and attitudes, thinking that those outside the faith will be attracted to it. What a terrible and ineffective strategy!

Christianity isn't attractive because it's like everything else in the world. It's attractive precisely because it's so different. This is especially true in the way people treat each other. When someone slaps you on the cheek, the world says, "Slap him back." But I say, "Turn the other cheek." When someone cheats you out of money, the world says, "Get even." But I say, "Be generous." When someone becomes your enemy, the world says, "Have nothing to do with them." But I say, "Love your enemies."

These relational values run counter to your culture—but they are perfectly in line with my values. They are the kind of values that will attract people to you and to me.

*"You have heard that it was said,
'Love your neighbor and hate your enemy.'
But I tell you, love your enemies and pray for those who persecute you,
that you may be children of your Father in heaven."*
MATTHEW 5:43–45

DO EVERYTHING IN THE NAME OF MY SON

*My favor rests on you because of Jesus,
not because of you.*

I have a very simple guideline for you. If you follow this principle, you will be successful and you will please me in all you do. Here it is: do everything in the name of Jesus.

Does that seem difficult for you? It might be if you've never tried it, so let's start with some basics.

Whenever you pray, pray in the name of my Son. This is an easy one, because Jesus Himself suggested it (John 14:13–14). Whenever you give me thanks, thank me in the name of Jesus. Whenever you ask for my help, ask in the name of my Son. Praying in the name of my Son tells me you recognize His authority in all things. This tells me you are more interested in doing my will than your own. My favor rests on you because of what Jesus did for you, not because of anything you've done. He deserves all the credit.

One more thing. Please don't think that the name of Jesus is magical, as if I'm going to bless you just because you use it. I will bless you because you acknowledge His rightful place as the Lord of your life.

*And whatever you do, whether in word or deed,
do it all in the name of the Lord Jesus,
giving thanks to God the Father through him.*
COLOSSIANS 3:17

MY LAW IS WRITTEN ON YOUR HEART

I am the ultimate moral lawgiver.

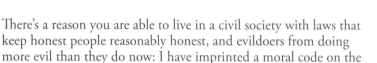

There's a reason you are able to live in a civil society with laws that keep honest people reasonably honest, and evildoers from doing more evil than they do now: I have imprinted a moral code on the heart of every person.

This sense of what's right and wrong is responsible for the laws of your land. And your inner moral compass is the reason people obey the law.

I am a moral being—the *supreme* moral being—and the ultimate moral lawgiver. Because every person bears my divine imprint (Genesis 1:27), every person bears the imprint of my morality—usually referred to as the *conscience.*

People may not always obey their conscience, but they know what's right and what's wrong. Aren't you glad you have an inner moral compass? Even more, aren't you glad your neighbor has one? You can thank me for that.

They demonstrate that God's law is written in their hearts,
for their own conscience and thoughts either accuse them
or tell them they are doing right.
ROMANS 2:15 NLT

Jesus Loves You Extravagantly

*The love of my Son knows no limits,
nor does it have any boundaries.*

I want to tell you just how much Jesus loves you. If you can grasp this, your life will change.

The love of my Son is so *wide* that it covers the whole world. There isn't one person living now whom my Son doesn't love.

The love of my Son is so *long* that it extends throughout the ages to all people who have ever lived and ever will live.

The love of my Son is so *high* that it is impossible for anyone to topple it.

The love of my Son is so *deep* that you will never fathom its meaning nor mine its riches.

Think about this love. Let it wash over you and give you comfort and strength for your life journey, no matter who you are or what you are going through.

*And I pray that you, being rooted and established in love,
may have power, together with all the Lord's holy people,
to grasp how wide and long and high and deep is the love of Christ,
and to know this love that surpasses knowledge.*

Ephesians 3:17–19

THE HOLY SPIRIT TELLS YOU WHAT'S COMING

*The Holy Spirit has signed, sealed,
and delivered His assurance to your heart.*

I love the Holy Spirit, and I hope you do as well. I sent the Holy Spirit to be a witness to the reality and the glory of my Son in your life. I love Him for that! The Holy Spirit also empowers you, gives you at least one spiritual gift, convinces you when you're on the right path, and convicts you when you're not. He's so versatile!

The Holy Spirit does something else you probably overlook, so I'm going to remind you: the Holy Spirit speaks about what is coming. I'm not talking about things in your immediate future, though He will sometimes give you warnings and confirmations. No, I'm referring to the big picture of what's to come—namely, your glorious future in heaven.

The Holy Spirit is like a deposit guaranteeing that Jesus is coming back for you, to unite you with all believers of all time, for all eternity. There's nothing you can do to revoke this promise. The Holy Spirit has signed, sealed, and delivered His assurance to your heart (Ephesians 1:13–14).

Whenever you grow weary of this world, with all of its cares and troubles, remember what the Holy Spirit is telling you.

*"He will not speak on his own; he will speak only what he hears,
and he will tell you what is yet to come."*

JOHN 16:13

MY WORD IS ETERNAL

My promises, purposes, and plans will never fail or fade.

There aren't many things you can count on in your life. Your health, your job, your finances, your family, and your relationships—all of these are subject to change. Even your very life is but a vapor when measured against the sweep of history and the vast stretch of eternity.

Are you worried about the fluctuating, temporary nature of your life? It's natural to be concerned—but it isn't necessary. You shouldn't be surprised when some things in your life change and others come to an end. Everything about your earthly existence will bloom for a while then fade and fail. It's the reality of your fallen world.

But I have not left you alone and without hope. I have given you my Word, filled with my precious promises, my purposes, and my plans for your future. This Word is eternal because I am eternal. My promises, purposes, and plans will never fail or fade. They are my everlasting gift to you.

"The grass withers and the flowers fall,
but the word of our God endures forever."
ISAIAH 40:8

DON'T BE ANXIOUS

Cast every care on me, for I care deeply for you.

My dear child, I know everything about you. I know all the ambitions and desires you have, and I am fully aware of every concern. Right now, the pressures you feel may be overwhelming you like a flood. Your heart is heavy. You wake up in the middle of the night, calling my name, hoping for relief.

As tempting as it is to give yourself over to worry and stress, I want you to give your anxieties to me—all of them. Cast *every* care on me, for I care deeply for you. Are you worried about your finances? Tell me about it. Is someone you love suffering? Pour out your heart. Has a child of yours wandered from the truth? Hold nothing back. Don't keep your worries and concerns to yourself. By faith, give them all to me.

Trust me to act in your best interest—for your good, in my time. Your circumstances may not change immediately, but you will begin to know my peace in a profound way.

Do not be anxious about anything, but in every situation,
by prayer and petition, with thanksgiving,
present your requests to God. And the peace of God,
which transcends all understanding,
will guard your hearts and your minds in Christ Jesus.
PHILIPPIANS 4:6–7

INVEST IN THE RIGHT PLACE

Whatever you do in my name will never be destroyed.

Treasure can take many forms. You may think it's money and jewelry, but I see *treasure* as much more.

Your treasure could be wrapped up in your ability to run a company or lead a church. It could be your security, your position, or your reputation. Whatever you think about day and night, whatever matters most to you, whatever you fear losing the most—*that* is your treasure. And it's all susceptible to loss and decay.

In fact, it's almost guaranteed that the earthly things you treasure will degrade over time. Occasionally, the destruction is blindingly swift, leaving you in a state of bewilderment. I'm not saying these things aren't important. I understand your need for security and esteem when you keep them in a proper perspective. But never invest your heart in these temporary pleasures.

Fix your gaze on me—in my will and my work. Whatever you do in my name will never be destroyed.

"Do not store up for yourselves treasures on earth,
where moths and vermin destroy,
and where thieves break in and steal.
But store up for yourselves treasures in heaven,
where moths and vermin do not destroy,
and where thieves do not break in and steal."
MATTHEW 6:19–20

GIVE THANKS WITH A GRATEFUL HEART

Express your gratitude for the mercies I show you every day.

You know what I'd like to see more of in your church services? Thanksgiving.

I appreciate the one day each year you set aside to give me thanks, but that seems a little inadequate. You should give thanks every time you gather with other believers to worship me.

Thanksgiving is for *your* benefit, not mine. I know what I've done for you, but I want you to recognize the ways I've caused all things in your life to work together for your good (Romans 8:28). Express your gratitude for the mercies I show you every day (Lamentations 3:23). Give thanks for everything I do for you in all situations.

No less a person than my Son thanked me in all things. Remember when He performed the miracle of feeding a huge crowd with just a small amount of food? He gave thanks.

For the miracles in *your* life, give thanks with a grateful heart.

Give thanks in all circumstances;
for this is God's will for you in Christ Jesus.
1 THESSALONIANS 5:18

WITH ME ON YOUR SIDE, YOU WILL NEVER LOSE

*If I gave up my own Son for you,
don't you think I will protect you?*

Have you ever been in an unfair fight? Well, you're in one now.

Because you are my child, you are automatically in for the fight of your life. There are many who will oppose you and some who will go far beyond simple opposition. But it isn't a fair fight—because I am on your side. Plain and simple, I will never let you lose. Whoever comes against you has to go through me first.

Do you sometimes feel as if your culture accuses you of intolerance, political incorrectness, weak-mindedness, and being out of step? Are people trying to pick a fight with you simply because your values are in line with my Word rather than the world system? If you are truly my child—and you aren't shy about telling people about it—then you are most likely experiencing opposition.

Or beyond the accusations of others, are you accusing yourself, feeling unworthy of my love? Listen to me! If I gave up my own Son for you, don't you think I will protect you and hold you securely in my arms? Trust me, you have nothing to fear. I am *with* you and I am *for* you. . .always and forever.

*What, then, shall we say in response to these things?
If God is for us, who can be against us?*
ROMANS 8:31

The Love of My Son
Is Indescribable

*The love of Jesus is so thorough and so powerful
that it will never leave you.*

It's common to view love as a passive emotion, defined mostly by feelings of attraction and affection. But that's only one part of love—and it doesn't begin to describe the quality of love my Son has for you.

Jesus' love is active and powerful, defined more by sacrifice than affection. Because Jesus willingly gave His life for you, His love is the greatest of all (John 15:13).

So great is my Son's love for you that it defies description. How do you begin to describe a love that strengthens you when you are weak, that keeps you secure during times of trouble, that comforts you when you are being marginalized, and that protects you when you are threatened?

Only the love of my Son can do all this, and I assure you that His love is so thorough and powerful that it will never leave you. Never.

*Who shall separate us from the love of Christ?
Shall trouble or hardship or persecution or famine
or nakedness or danger or sword?*
Romans 8:35

THE SPIRIT HELPS YOU REFLECT MY GLORY

*The Holy Spirit is transforming you
into someone who is more and more like Jesus.*

Usually I talk with you about giving me glory—which basically means I want you to make me look good in all you do. But there is also a glory that radiates *from* me, a glory so bright that it lights all of heaven (Revelation 21:23). Few people have experienced my glory firsthand. Moses saw it when he came into my presence to receive the Ten Commandments (Exodus 34:29). As a result, his face glowed brightly—and he had to wear a veil so the people wouldn't be terrified.

With you, my glory is different. Oh, it's still the same radiance—but when you put your trust in me you don't have to wear a veil to hide my light from others. Jesus ripped the veil in two when He gave His life for yours. The end result is that, unlike Moses, whose face reflected a fading glory, you reflect an every-increasing glory as the Holy Spirit works in your life.

I know this may be a bit tough to grasp, so I'll make it really simple: as my child, you are reflecting my glory to the world because the Holy Spirit is transforming you into someone who is more and more like Jesus.

*And we all, who with unveiled faces contemplate the Lord's glory,
are being transformed into his image with ever-increasing glory,
which comes from the Lord, who is the Spirit.*

2 CORINTHIANS 3:18

MY WORD GIVES YOU JOY

*My Word will give you joy
when you engage it with every part of your being.*

Whenever you read my Word, you should have one of three responses.

One is *intellectual*. This comes when you use your mind, seeking to understand the meaning of what I've said. The intellectual response takes study and diligence on your part and a willingness to hear skillful teachers who know how to explain the scriptures.

Another response is *volitional*, which comes when you decide with your will to do what my Word says. (The worst thing you can do is to hear my Word and never do it—see James 1:22.) The third response is *emotional*, when you feel the joy of interacting with my Word.

If you're not enjoying my Word, perhaps you don't understand it—or maybe you know what you should do, but you aren't doing it. My Word will give you joy when you engage it with every part of your being—your mind, your will, and your heart.

*Then all the people went away to eat and drink,
to send portions of food and to celebrate with great joy,
because they now understood the words
that had been made known to them.*
NEHEMIAH 8:12

WHEN YOU TEACH

*If you aren't willing to take your teaching seriously,
you shouldn't teach.*

Do you desire to teach my Word? Nothing would please me more. My church needs good teachers to help my children understand what I've said in my Word.

But if you want to become a teacher, there are some things you need to know. First, be aware that I hold Bible teachers to a higher standard (James 3:1). If you aren't willing to take your teaching seriously, you shouldn't teach at all.

On the other hand, if you are ready to work hard and be accountable, here's what I want you to do: above all, be sure your life and character match your words. Be the same person behind closed doors that you are in front of your students. Next, make your teaching clear and coherent so your students can understand. But don't do their thinking for them—lead them to discover my truth for themselves.

If you can do these things, you'll fulfill your obligation to me *and* your students.

*In everything set them an example by doing what is good.
In your teaching show integrity, seriousness and
soundness of speech that cannot be condemned.*
TITUS 2:7–8

EXPECT CRITICISM

There's no guarantee you'll have an easy life when you trust me.

My children try too hard to make the Christian life attractive.

In fact, that's why some people never completely trust me. They've been told that having a personal relationship with me is easy, that all their troubles will disappear, and that a life of health and prosperity awaits them if they just have enough faith. *I've* never said that, by the way.

So some people make a verbal commitment to me, though their heart isn't in it. After a while, they realize this life of faith is anything but easy. And they fade away.

Truth is, there's no guarantee you'll have an easy life when you trust me. Quite the opposite may be true. In fact, if you're following me with your whole heart, you should *expect* criticism, insults, and false accusations. It's a sign that you are doing what I say.

If you are suffering in any way because of me, take heart. You're taking your relationship with me seriously.

"Blessed are you when people insult you, persecute you
and falsely say all kinds of evil against you because of me.
Rejoice and be glad, because great is your reward in heaven."
MATTHEW 5:11–12

SHOW HOSPITALITY

*If you've opened your heart to me,
you need to open your heart to others.*

Church is a wonderful place for my children to gather, no matter what day of the week. But if the only place you meet your fellow believers is within the walls of your church, you're missing out on one of the joys of the Christian life: fellowship.

Sure, you can begin an acquaintance with someone by chatting in the church hall, but you'll never get to know them until you break bread together in a home—preferably *your* home.

If you've opened your heart to me, you need to open your heart to others. Practice showing hospitality to others, whether they're members of your church or neighbors in your community.

And don't confine your hospitality to people you already know. Did you meet someone for the first time last week? Invite them over for dinner. Do you know someone who has an immediate need? Does a college student need a place to live? Don't just offer to pray for them; extend a spirit of generosity and help them. Really get to know them.

Don't worry about who will meet *your* needs. If you are willing to help others, I will help you.

*When God's people are in need, be ready to help them.
Always be eager to practice hospitality.*
ROMANS 12:13 NLT

MY JUSTICE IS TRUE

*Instead of questioning my judgments,
be thankful for my mercies.*

Do you ever wonder how I can be both just and merciful? Does it seem contradictory that my justice stands against sin, yet I am filled with compassion?

I know it's hard to grasp, but you must understand that none of my personality traits contradicts another. Compassion and love flow from my absolute goodness, and my goodness is tethered to my justice. To put it another way, I could not be good if I were not also just. If I *punish* sinners, it is because they deserve it. And if I *pardon* sinners, it is because I am good.

My Son is the fullest expression of my compassion. Because He took your punishment upon Himself, my justice is satisfied and my compassion is magnified. Instead of questioning and criticizing my judgments, be thankful for my mercies as expressed in Jesus. That is why this song will be sung in heaven:

> *"Great and marvelous are your deeds,
> Lord God Almighty.
> Just and true are your ways,
> King of the nations."*
> REVELATION 15:3

THE LOVE OF MY SON IS INDESTRUCTIBLE

You aren't just a passive recipient of Christ's love,
but an active participant in it.

Love is much more than an emotion. Love is a power.

Love is what motivated me to send my Son into the world, so that anyone who believes in Him will not die, but will instead have life everlasting with me. If you believe in my Son and have received Him into your life by faith, His love is now part of your life. You aren't just a passive recipient of Christ's love, but an active participant in it.

This is an awesome truth: the indestructible love of my Son is actively working on your behalf, binding you to me for good so that *nothing* in all creation can come between us—especially those forces you can't see. Whether you know it or not, Satan is on the prowl, trying to devour you (1 Peter 5:8). On your own, you'd never stand a chance against him. But you are not on your own.

I am with you, and my love for you—as demonstrated by Jesus—is your indestructible force. It ensures that Satan's snarling lies and evil accusations will never touch you. . .and never separate us.

For I am convinced that neither death nor life,
neither angels nor demons,
neither the present nor the future, nor any powers,
neither height nor depth,
nor anything else in all creation, will be able to separate us
from the love of God that is in Christ Jesus our Lord.
ROMANS 8:38–39

DON'T LIE TO THE HOLY SPIRIT

Keep your relationship with the Holy Spirit open and honest.

All sin offends me, but there are some sins I especially detest. At the top of my list is lying.

When you lie to someone, you are deliberately deceiving them. You can't have a relationship based on a lie, even if you think the lie is "harmless." You know it's hard to stop at one lie—you need to cover your first deception, so you tell more lies. . . or simply perpetuate the original one. Sadly, people who lie soon begin to *believe* their own lies. That self-deception is bad enough—but not even the worst thing.

When you lie, you are ultimately lying to *me*. More specifically, you're lying to the Holy Spirit, who lives in you and knows everything about you. You might conceal a lie from others, but you will never succeed in lying to the Holy Spirit. He takes lying seriously because He knows how destructive it is to you, your family, and your brothers and sisters in Christ (Ephesians 4:25).

Keep your relationship with the Holy Spirit open and honest. Don't let a lie come between us.

"How is it. . .that you have lied to the Holy Spirit?"
ACTS 5:3

EXAMINE THE SCRIPTURES

*Become so skilled at handling my Word
that you can distinguish truth from error.*

I know when people misinterpret my Word. If a Bible teacher is sloppy in handling the scriptures, I am aware of it.

How about you? Do you have enough knowledge and understanding of my Word that you can tell when truth is not being taught? I'm not talking about small issues that don't affect your relationship with me, such as music styles. On those matters where I haven't made myself perfectly clear, don't have immovable opinions. Be generous with those who disagree with you.

But on those major topics that directly relate to our relationship—Jesus, the Holy Spirit, salvation, and my Word— I expect you to be well versed and accurate (2 Timothy 2:15).

Back in the first century, there was a group of people from Berea who diligently examined the scriptures to make sure my apostle Paul was teaching the truth. He didn't take offense at that—Paul *commended* them for their "noble character."

And that's the way you should be—so skilled at handling my Word that you can distinguish truth from error.

*Now the Berean Jews were of more noble character. . .
for they received the message with great eagerness
and examined the Scriptures every day
to see if what Paul said was true.*

ACTS 17:11

REJOICE IN ME ALWAYS

Rather than being a sourpuss,
you should be full of joy.

Too many of my followers complain. Not about me necessarily, but about life in general. They are negative about their jobs, they criticize their leaders, they find fault with the church. Life is just never good enough.

What terrible witnesses these people are to the world. It's one thing for an unbeliever to act as if his life is less than it should be—because it is! But when one of my followers is a chronic complainer, it reflects poorly on me.

Listen! Rather than being a sourpuss, you should be full of joy. The people you encounter, whether friends or strangers, should notice your positive attitude.

If you have a hard time mustering a smile or, if there's very little joy in your life—perhaps you aren't spending enough time with me. If you're always dissatisfied, you're not thinking enough about me. And you surely aren't spending much time in my Word.

I keep my eyes always on the LORD.
With him at my right hand, I will not be shaken.
Therefore my heart is glad and my tongue rejoices;
my body also will rest secure.

PSALM 16:8–9

The World Is Passing Away

*Fix your heart and your eyes
on things above rather than things below.*

I created the world so that you do more than just exist. I made a dazzling array of living things and a planet perfectly suited for you because I want you to flourish.

When sin entered the world, life got tougher (Genesis 3:16–19). Though it was still beautiful and functioned well, the world began to show signs of decay. As you grow older, you'll probably notice a gravitational pull toward death that steadily draws you down. It's there. And the same thing is happening to the world itself. It's passing away.

Here's a way to break free from this downward spiral: fix your heart and your spiritual eyes on things *above* rather than things below. Instead of growing attached to the world, think about me and what I want for you. When my Son prayed, "Our Father in heaven, hallowed by your name, your kingdom come, your will be done, on earth as it is in heaven" (Matthew 6:9–10), He was telling you to adopt my values and to do my will right now where you are.

I have you on earth for a reason—to witness to the world of my love and grace. But never forget that I also have a place for you in heaven.

*The world and its desires pass away,
but whoever does the will of God lives forever.*

1 John 2:17

YOU ARE PART OF ONE BODY

*The body of Christ thrives
as each part functions according to its purpose.*

There's a simple reason I chose to use the human body as an analogy for the church: you are more familiar with your body than anything else in your experience.

You may not know in exact detail how every part of your body functions, but you are very aware of their work and interaction. You know that if any one part *stops* working—a hand, a leg, an eye, a baby toe—your entire body notices.

The same principle applies to the body of Christ. Like the parts of a human body, the members of the church are interconnected and interdependent. As the human body thrives with each part functioning according to its purpose, so the church operates best when each person uses his or her spiritual gift for the benefit of the entire body.

Some parts of the body (such as the eyes) get more attention, while others (like the pancreas) are forgotten—but every one is important. In the same way, some roles in the church have a higher profile, while others go unnoticed. But all are essential.

*Just as a body, though one, has many parts,
but all its many parts form one body, so it is with Christ.*
1 CORINTHIANS 12:12

I AM SLOW TO ANGER

My nature and my desire are to be compassionate and gracious.

Do you think of me as quick tempered?

If so, that may explain your reluctance to do mighty things for me. You're like the servant who buried some money his master had asked him to invest. Why? He was afraid his master would be angry if he lost the money. The master became angry, all right—but only because this particular servant didn't trust him (Matthew 25:14–30).

Now picture you and me in that kind of relationship: I've given you gifts, resources, and opportunities, and I expect you to invest what you have to advance my work on earth. If you trust me and make an effort, I'll be generous in my help and encouragement. If you make mistakes, I won't be angry. My nature and my desire are to be compassionate and gracious.

But if you needlessly squander what I've given you—if you sit on your gifts and don't use them because you haven't made my kingdom your priority—then I will be angry. But you really have to push me there. That process is a slow one.

"The LORD, the LORD, the compassionate and gracious God,
slow to anger, abounding in love and faithfulness."
EXODUS 34:6

THE VIRGIN BIRTH

*My Son was born holy and remained holy
so He could be acceptable to me.*

I am a God of miracles. That shouldn't surprise you, because I am a supernatural being—and by definition, a miracle is a supernatural occurrence.

Most of my followers don't have a problem believing "big" miracles, such as my creating the universe out of nothing (Hebrews 11:3). But one of my "small" miracles—Jesus being born of a virgin—gives them trouble. Why is that?

Everyone is familiar with childbirth in one way or another—so maybe it's tough for you to imagine how Jesus could have been conceived by anything other than human means. But that's why it was a miracle. It was inconceivable!

And it was necessary. Since the human race is infected with a sin virus—inherited both physically and spiritually—Jesus could not have been sinless if He was born the natural way. He had to be conceived *supernaturally*, by the Holy Spirit, in order to be fully human yet without sin.

My Son was born holy through the virgin birth, and He lived a perfect life so you and I could have a relationship (Romans 5:18–19).

*"How will this be," Mary asked the angel, "since I am a virgin?"
The angel answered, "The Holy Spirit will come on you,
and the power of the Most High will overshadow you.
So the holy one to be born will be called the Son of God."*

LUKE 1:34–35

80

THE HOLY SPIRIT GIVES NEW LIFE

When you receive Jesus by faith,
I breathe new life into you through the Holy Spirit.

Do you remember the story of Nicodemus? He was a member of the Pharisees, a very influential religious group that gave Jesus a lot of trouble. Nicodemus wanted to learn from Jesus, so he came to my Son at night to ask some questions. Jesus carefully explained that anyone who wanted to experience my eternal kingdom had to be "born again." And the only way to be born again, Jesus said, was to be born of the Holy Spirit (John 3:3, 7–8).

Nicodemus was astonished, and he pushed Jesus to explain how someone could be born a second time. Jesus patiently told him that humans can only produce human life—and only the Holy Spirit can give new, spiritual life.

When you receive Jesus by faith, I literally breathe new life into you through the Holy Spirit. I turn you into a new person with a new spiritual nature—and a new destiny (2 Corinthians 5:17).

Jesus replied, "I assure you, no one can enter
the Kingdom of God without being born of water and the Spirit.
Humans can reproduce only human life,
but the Holy Spirit gives birth to spiritual life."
JOHN 3:5–6 NLT

81

MY WORD WILL NOURISH YOU

My Word contains the basic nutritional building blocks of your faith.

Are you a spiritual baby?

Don't take offense. There's nothing wrong with being a baby, spiritually speaking. Every Christian starts there. Nobody who is born again begins the new life as a full-grown spiritual adult. Everybody starts at the beginning, like a newborn who needs to be fed and cared for.

Like a baby, a newborn believer needs nourishment—and there's nothing that nourishes like spiritual milk. When I mention "milk" for a spiritual newborn, I am referring to the foundational principles of my Word. These are the basic nutritional building blocks of the faith that every baby believer needs: the truth about me, my Son, the Holy Spirit, my Word, and what you need to know to grow.

Here's something else to keep in mind: newborn babies don't question the basic elements of their food—they just long for the milk they need. In the same way, a newborn believer doesn't need to know every ingredient of my Word. Just take it in so you can begin the process of spiritual maturing.

Like newborn babies, crave pure spiritual milk,
so that by it you may grow up in your salvation.
1 PETER 2:2

A SWEET PERFUME

When I adopt you as my child,
you take on the sweet fragrance of my Son.

I created you with many special abilities, including your five senses. You can taste, touch, see, hear, and smell.

Of these, your sense of smell is often the least appreciated, yet it's this sense that can give you remarkable pleasure. Without your sense of smell, your sense of taste would be limited. But when you combine taste and smell, you're able to enjoy an almost limitless array of flavors and fragrances.

I enjoy fragrance, too—especially the sweet aroma of my Son's sacrifice for you (Ephesians 5:2). But the sweet perfume doesn't end there. When I adopt you as my child, you take on Jesus' fragrance as I use you to tell others about Him.

Often, your words aren't even necessary. Just as a beautiful fragrance compels people to find its source, the aromatic example of your life—your love for me and your compassion for the lost—will be enough to draw others to me.

But thanks be to God, who always leads us as captives
in Christ's triumphal procession and uses us to spread the aroma
of the knowledge of him everywhere.
2 CORINTHIANS 2:14

THE SMELL OF DEATH

You should expect to be offensive to some people.

As you imitate my Son in your life, I will use you to spread the Good News of what my Son has done for the world. For those who are drawn to me, your life will have a sweet aroma. But to those who resist me, you're going to stink. Your aroma will be foul, pungent, and offensive.

Don't be surprised—and don't take it personally. In fact, you should *expect* to be offensive to some people. That's not because you're obnoxious, but because the message about me is a challenge to their philosophy of life. Honestly, your words of truth are a message of life to the living, but a message of death to the dying. And who is dying? Anyone who refuses to listen to me.

Listen! This is why my followers are often the object of skepticism and ridicule. The words they speak (and the lives they live) are an affront to those who have turned up their noses to me.

For we are to God the pleasing aroma of Christ
among those who are being saved and those who are perishing.
To the one we are an aroma that brings death; to the other,
an aroma that brings life. And who is equal to such a task?
2 CORINTHIANS 2:15–16

JESUS IS THE HEAD OF THE BODY

My Son fits and forms all members of His church into a single body.

I've been telling you about the body of Christ and the members of my church who complement one another with their spiritual gifts. Every member of the body is important; no one is expendable.

What I haven't told you is this: while there are many of you who are hands and feet for the body, and others who are eyes and vocal cords, there is only one *head*. That's my Son.

Jesus is uniquely qualified to lead His body, comprised as it is of a large group of individuals from a wide range of cultures and locations. Have you ever wondered how you can meet a complete stranger, yet immediately feel a common bond when you discover you're both my children? The reason for that connection is Jesus, who fits and forms all members of His church into a single body of believers, united in purpose and in love for each other.

We will grow to become in every respect the mature body
of him who is the head, that is, Christ. From him the whole body,
joined and held together by every supporting ligament,
grows and builds itself up in love,
as each part does its work.
EPHESIANS 4:15–16

I AM HOLY

Set your heart and mind on my holiness.

My child, I am going to take you to the highest heights for a moment. Long after you've heard my voice today, I want you to set your heart and your mind on this majestic thought: I am holy.

I know, you've heard that a thousand times. Many times, you've sung the chorus that declares my holiness in my three Persons: Father, Son, and Holy Spirit. But from now on, I want you to break free of a shallow familiarity with those words, and let a fresh vision of my holiness fill your being.

There is a danger in this: if you let my Spirit fill you, opening your thoughts to my unique, unapproachable, incomprehensible holiness, you are going to be traumatized by your own sinfulness. Dwell on your own depravity for a moment, just long enough for your heart to break—then let my Spirit capture your thoughts and give you a new and profound appreciation for this truth: you can immerse your unholiness in the deep love of Jesus and His precious life given for you.

That is where you must seek refuge—for when you are safe in His arms, I will see His holiness covering you.

And they were calling to one another:
"Holy, holy, holy is the Lord Almighty;
the whole earth is full of his glory."

ISAIAH 6:3

BY HIS BLOOD

*Only the blood of my Son will purify your heart
and cleanse your conscience.*

Listen to me today—I am going to tell you a mystery that is so great you'll completely miss it if you don't think about it deeply. The only way for your sins to be forgiven is by the blood of my precious and holy Son (Hebrews 9:22, 26, 28). This is hard to understand, and many in your world shake their heads, calling Christianity a "bloody" religion.

Don't shy away from this reality! Under my old agreement with my chosen people, I required ceremonial cleansing through the sacrifice of select animals by a priest. But you are now under a new agreement based on my Son—who is the perfect sacrifice for your sins. By His punishment and death you are healed, and by His blood you are washed whiter than snow (Psalm 51:7).

You don't have to *work* to make yourself good enough for me—following a set of rules and rituals will never cleanse you. Only the blood of my Son will purify your heart and cleanse your conscience so you can be from sin and guilt.

*How much more, then, will the blood of Christ,
who through the eternal Spirit offered himself unblemished to God,
cleanse our consciences from acts that lead to death,
so that we may serve the living God!*
HEBREWS 9:14

THE HOLY SPIRIT GIVES YOU LIFE

You owe the very life you have to my Spirit.

I created the heavens and the earth, but I didn't do it alone.

All three Persons of my being—Father, Son, and Holy Spirit—were involved. I created everything through my Son (Colossians 1:16), and my omnipresent Spirit hovered over the waters, brooding like a protective eagle over its unhatched eggs (Genesis 1:2). Then, when I created the first human beings, Jesus and the Holy Spirit were with me, guaranteeing that all humanity would bear our divine imprint (Genesis 1:26–27).

My child, you owe the very life you have to my Spirit, who breathed life into Adam (Genesis 2:7), and who now gives you life. Every once in a while, as you take a breath, think about the reason you live: it is the Holy Spirit who gives you life. He is my breath poured into you.

> *"The Spirit of God has made me;*
> *the breath of the Almighty gives me life."*
> JOB 33:4

THINK DEEPLY

Thoughtfully engage your heart and mind with my Word.

I have given you my Word as a guidebook for life. If you follow the Bible, you will never go wrong.

At the same time—please hear me on this—my Word is much more than a spiritual blueprint or set of instructions. It is living and breathing because when you read it, the same Holy Spirit who inspired the prophets is willing and ready to breathe my Word into you.

But know that you can't catch a little of my Word here and there, in between your other activities. You have to sit still, in a quiet place, free from distractions. You need to consciously invite the Holy Spirit to inspire you through your own reflection as you pore over my Word. Even if a passage is familiar to you, dwell on it. Pause and pray over it verse by verse.

This is what meditation is truly about. Not mindless mutterings, but a thoughtful mind-and-heart engagement with my Word.

Blessed is the one who does not walk in step with the wicked
or stand in the way that sinners take or sit in the company of mockers,
but whose delight is in the law of the LORD,
and who meditates on his law day and night.

PSALM 1:1–2

BE HOLY

*Devote yourself to me as you set yourself apart
from sin in every area of your life.*

I hope you like to be stretched and challenged to become a better person than you are now.

I think you do, because I've built a desire to excel into every person. Unfortunately, there's nothing *you* can do to meet the challenge I give you today: be holy.

Of course, I don't expect you to be perfect like me, because that's not possible. I cannot *impart* my holiness to you. However, I can *impute* my holiness to you through the precious blood and sacrifice of my Son. What I mean to say is this: when I see you, I think of Christ's holiness as being your holiness. Apart from Jesus, you are far from holy.

When I tell you, "Be holy as I am holy," here's what I want you to do: get intimately acquainted with my holiness. Search the scriptures for verses and passages on my holiness, starting with my prophet Isaiah's response (Isaiah 6:5–7). Devote yourself to me as you set yourself apart from sin in every area of your life.

Don't try this alone. You can't do it. Invite the Spirit of holiness to fill you with Christ's love so you can know what my holiness is all about.

But just as he who called you is holy, so be holy in all you do.
1 PETER 1:15

HOW BEAUTIFUL ARE THE FEET

Are you willing to tell others about me,
no matter who they are or where they live?

In the first century, when my Son and His followers walked everywhere to spread the Good News, their feet were worn and dirty. They weren't very attractive. Yet when the apostle Paul writes about those who share my message of salvation and reconciliation, he says they have "beautiful feet."

How about you? Do you have beautiful feet?

Are you willing to tell others about me, no matter who they are or where they live? What about your neighbor, the one you chat with but have never invited into your home? How about that coworker going through a tough time, the one who doesn't even know you're a believer? And there's that relative who's searching for truth and would love to hear from you. How will they ever know about me the way you do unless you tell them?

You don't have to travel overseas to share the Gospel. There are plenty of lost souls in your own backyard. Use your feet to reach them. All you have to do is take the first step.

How, then, can they call on the one they have not believed in?
And how can they believe in the one of whom they have not heard?
And how can they hear without someone preaching to them?
And how can anyone preach unless they are sent? As it is written:
"How beautiful are the feet of those who bring good news!"

ROMANS 10:14–15

DO THIS IN REMEMBRANCE OF ME

The elements of communion are a sign that my Son is with you.

Today I'm going to tell you about communion, one of the sacred ceremonies (called *sacraments*) I want you to observe.

When you hear the word *communion*, you probably think of the Lord's Supper—and that's exactly right. However, there's also a sense of the term *communion* that implies a close relationship.

In fact, your relationship with my Son (and with one another) is at the heart of the Lord's Supper. First, when you participate in a communion service at your church, you are remembering the body of Christ that was broken for you (symbolized by the bread) and the blood of Christ that was shed for you (pictured by the wine). These "elements" are a visible sign that my Son is with you—and when you join others in the body of Christ to observe communion, it's as if you are gathering around a Thanksgiving table, celebrating together the death and resurrection of my Son in His sacrifice for you.

Is not the cup of thanksgiving for which we give thanks a participation in the blood of Christ? And is not the bread that we break a participation in the body of Christ? Because there is one loaf, we, who are many, are one body.

1 CORINTHIANS 10:16–17

MY NAME IS HOLY

Just as I am holy, my name is holy and awesome.

Many of my followers hold to a misconception—that taking my name "in vain" is equal to using it as a swear word. That's part of it, but the third of my Ten Commandments is much more comprehensive. (By the way, if you're in the habit of saying, "Oh my God," I advise you to stop unless you're directing *worship* to me.)

Just as I am holy, my name is holy and awesome (Psalm 111:9). If you recall, my Son taught you to begin praying to me with the words, "hallowed be your name" (Matthew 6:9). Because of the greatness of my name, anything you do that dishonors it is taking it in vain. And if you claim to love my Son or call yourself a Christian (which is taking on my Son's name as part of your identity), then live in disobedience to His commands, you're taking the name of the Lord in vain.

My name is holy. Don't misuse it. The name of my Son is holy. Don't dishonor Him.

"You shall not misuse the name of the LORD your God,
for the LORD will not hold anyone guiltless who misuses his name."
EXODUS 20:7

MY SON IS YOUR SHEPHERD

I want you to fully appreciate what the Shepherd does for His sheep.

My Son is your Shepherd, and you are His sheep. You may have a hard time relating to this analogy, especially if you live in town. You've probably never seen a shepherd at work, so I'm going to give you a little background. I want you to fully appreciate what the Shepherd does for His sheep.

The Shepherd is the ultimate caregiver. He knows and loves His sheep intimately. He protects them from extreme weather, debilitating disease, and predators who would love to devour the sheep. The Shepherd knows the terrain ahead—the hills and valleys and rocks and streams. He feeds His sheep and knows where to find good water.

When the sheep need to rest, the Shepherd finds a green pasture where they can graze safely. He removes all fearful influences so the sheep can lie down.

And when it's time for the flock to move on, the Shepherd guides them. He knows the way, because He's been there before. If any sheep wanders off, away from the flock, the Shepherd will search and search until that sheep is found and brought back to safety.

The LORD is my shepherd, I lack nothing.
He makes me lie down in green pastures,
he leads me beside quiet waters, he refreshes my soul.
He guides me along the right paths for his name's sake.

PSALM 23:1–3

THE HOLY SPIRIT IS EQUAL TO ME

Just as my Son is equal to me in every way,
so is the Holy Spirit.

I've already told you that the Holy Spirit is more than a power, a force, or an "it." The Holy Spirit is a *Person*, with all the qualities that define personhood. He has an intellect, a will, and emotions.

Just because the Holy Spirit is, well, *spirit*, you shouldn't view Him as anything less than a Person. I am spirit, and when you worship me and relate to me personally, you are doing so in the Holy Spirit.

Just as my Son is equal to me in every way, so is the Holy Spirit. Simply put, the Holy Spirit is fully God. He has all of my divine qualities: He is all-powerful, all-knowing, and present everywhere. And He is just as much a part of your Christian life as my Son and I are.

That's what theologians mean when they say the Christian faith is a *Trinitarian* faith. When you believe you can be saved and have a relationship with me by trusting Jesus, it is the Holy Spirit who makes it possible for you to be born again.

"How is it. . .that you have lied to the Holy Spirit. . . ?
You have not lied just to human beings but to God."

ACTS 5:3–4

Week 13
THURSDAY
God's Word

MY SON IS THE THEME OF MY WORD

Jesus is the living Word who fulfills my written Word.

Every great book has a great theme—a unifying and compelling idea that permeates the work. The theme of *Moby Dick* is man against nature. The theme of *Mere Christianity* is understanding and living the Christian life.

What about my Word? Do you know its unifying idea?

It shouldn't surprise you that the theme of my Word (the greatest book in the world) is the greatest theme of all: Jesus.

There is no more unifying and compelling person in the world than Jesus. He permeates every part of my Word with His divine presence. Indeed, He is the living Word that fulfills my written Word.

In one respect, the Bible is *my* story—from creation to the end of the world—the account of how much I love you and want a relationship with you. But in another way, my Word is the story of *Jesus*, who appears in all sixty-six books—not necessarily by name, but always for who He is: the one I sent to demonstrate my love.

Whenever you read and study and meditate on my Word, remember Jesus.

But these are written that you may believe that Jesus is the Messiah, the Son of God, and that by believing you may have life in his name.
JOHN 20:31

LISTEN TO MY SON'S VOICE

When your Shepherd calls for you, listen and follow Him.

My Son is your Shepherd, and you are His sheep. Do you know much about sheep? You should, because that knowledge will give you a greater appreciation for your Shepherd.

No domesticated animal is as helpless as sheep—yet they are among the most stubborn of all creatures. No matter how long a particular shepherd has cared for them, they don't always trust him. They are prone to wander. And it's when they wander that they fall into trouble.

Here's another instructive thing about sheep: for safety, they're kept in a pen at night. Often, sheep of different shepherds are kept in the same pen. In the morning, when the shepherd calls for his sheep, only those who belong to him will follow him out of the pen to form a flock.

When your Shepherd calls for *you*—through the message of my Word and the witness of the Holy Spirit in your life—listen to His voice. You already know it. Just trust and follow Him.

"My sheep listen to my voice; I know them, and they follow me.
I give them eternal life, and they shall never perish;
no one will snatch them out of my hand."

JOHN 10:27–28

YOU CAN OVERCOME THE WORLD

*My commands are designed to keep you
from being lured away from me by the world.*

——————◆——————

Those who do not believe in me by faith live under a misunder-standing: that following me is a pain, a burden. They assume (incorrectly!) that following me means keeping a long list of rules, a set of regulations that sucks the fun out of life. Nothing could be further from the truth.

Listen! If you truly love me, you'll also love my children—those who are in the family of faith, just like you are—and you will gladly do the things I've told you to do in my Word. These aren't rules and regulations as much as they are principles for spiritual success. I've given these principles so you can thrive.

My commands are also designed to keep you from being lured away from me by the world and all those things in it that stand against me. People in the world's gravitational pull don't have the ability to break free. But *you* can—because of your faith in my Son.

——————◆——————

*In fact, this is love for God: to keep his commands.
And his commands are not burdensome, for everyone born of God
overcomes the world. This is the victory that has overcome the world,
even our faith. Who is it that overcomes the world?
Only the one who believes that Jesus is the Son of God.*

1 JOHN 5:3–5

JESUS WANTS YOU TO BE BAPTIZED

Baptism is the way you show others that you belong to my Son.

Today I'm going to tell you about baptism, one of the sacred observances (called *sacraments*) I want you to observe.

Jesus wants His followers to be baptized. It's not required for salvation, but it is an important part of your faith—because it makes your association with my Son public. It's the way you state before witnesses that you belong to Jesus. As such, baptism is a natural part of the Christian experience.

Whenever baptism occurs in the Bible, it takes the form of a person being immersed in water. There's an instructive symbolism in that: when you accept my Son as Savior, your old nature dies (pictured by going under the water) and you become a new person in Christ (pictured by coming out of the water).

With this explanation, spend a few minutes considering your own experience with baptism. Is there anything you need to do to bring honor to my Son?

Then Jesus came to them and said, "All authority in heaven and on earth has been given to me. Therefore go and make disciples of all nations, baptizing them in the name of the Father and of the Son and of the Holy Spirit."
MATTHEW 28:18–19

LOVE DEFINES ME

Those who refuse to love don't know the first thing about me.

I have many qualities and characteristics, none of which contradict another. And I don't exist in a vacuum—every aspect of my personality is important to *you*.

If there's one quality that best defines me—if you had to pick just one of my many attributes to grasp and make your own—it would be *love*. I am fundamentally and essentially love. My infinite love flows from the eternal reality of my being.

I exist in community—Father, Son, and Holy Spirit—and I created you to be in community with me. My love overflows to you, as demonstrated by the way I've sacrificed for you. The fullest expression of my love is my Son.

If you know and love me, you will love others in community. If you don't love, it's because you don't know me.

Dear friends, let us love one another, for love comes from God. Everyone who loves has been born of God and knows God.

1 JOHN 4:7

JESUS IS THE I AM

To call Himself I AM put Jesus in the realm where only I exist.

My followers sometimes refer to me as *Jehovah*. That's a name derived from my most common name, *Yahweh*, which comes from the Hebrew *YHWH*, meaning "Lord." But to simplify things for you, I've given you my most defining name: *I AM*. This means I always have been and always will be. It tells you that I am always present and near to all who call on me. Always.

Everything about my name also applies to my Son. Jesus is *Yeshua* (meaning "the one who saves"), Jesus is Lord, and Jesus is *I AM*.

When my Son made this claim for Himself, He both astonished and enraged His listeners. By this pronouncement, Jesus said He existed in the eternal present—before Abraham, the father of the Jewish nation, was even born. To the unbelievers in the crowd, the claim was blasphemous, because Jesus was claiming to be God. To call Himself I AM put my Son in the realm where only I exist, apart from time and space, yet very much connected to it.

Listen! The implications of this astounding claim are profound. When you embrace my Son by faith, you are putting your trust in *almighty God*.

"Very truly I tell you," Jesus answered,
"before Abraham was born, I am!"
JOHN 8:58

THE HOLY SPIRIT LOVES

When my Holy Spirit's fire burns in you,
your potential becomes your reality.

Every person has great potential—but you, my child, have more potential than most.

As my adopted child, you have my power in you through the Holy Spirit. That's not an easy concept to grasp, and some believers go through their entire lives without realizing the power of that potential.

In scripture, the Holy Spirit is often described as a fire—one that fills you with my presence, passion, and purity. But this fire isn't always flaming. Too often, it's neglected and reduced to a pile of embers, awaiting the breath of the Holy Spirit to stoke the faint glow.

When my Holy Spirit's fire burns in you, your potential becomes your reality. He kindles your heart and draws out your love for me and for your neighbor. He prompts you to pray for those who need it. The Holy Spirit will do this if you give Him room in your life, and refuse to quench His presence, passion, and purity.

I urge you, brothers and sisters, by our Lord Jesus Christ
and by the love of the Spirit, to join me in my struggle
by praying to God for me.
ROMANS 15:30

I HAVE SECRETS

I know everything about you,
but you will never know everything about me.

I know you intimately—and I want you to love me intimately in return.

But this cannot be an even exchange. While I know everything about you, down to the number of hairs on your head (Luke 12:7), you will never know everything about me. For one thing, my greatness is beyond your comprehension (Romans 11:33). But there's another reason you will never know everything about me: I have secrets.

Don't be upset. Let me explain: I have secrets because there are certain things about me you aren't yet mature enough to understand. In time, as you grow in your spiritual life, you'll come to know some of my secrets. Others will have to wait until we're together in heaven.

But I can tell you this for sure: I have revealed enough about myself for you to obey my Word. This is critical for your spiritual health and effectiveness, for when you obey my Word you are doing my will.

Don't long to know my secrets. Strive to do my will.

The secret things belong to the LORD our God,
but the things revealed belong to us and to our children forever,
that we may follow all the words of this law.

DEUTERONOMY 29:29

COMMUNION AND COMMUNICATION

*Your communion with me is
the beginning of my communication with you.*

Everybody wants to hear from me, and I'm glad to speak through many means. You just have to be willing to listen.

In some ways, listening to me is *active*. It requires preparation and a willingness to pay attention. This part of listening is hard—it takes work. Think of listening in a school classroom, knowing you'll have to answer detailed questions later. I know that can exhaust you!

In another way, though, listening to me is *passive*. It requires a willingness to surrender to me in complete trust, allowing the words of my message to wash over your weary soul. This is what happens when you are in *communion* with me rather than merely *communicating*.

Don't get me wrong: I enjoy it when you talk with me. But sometimes I want you just to sense me, experience me, and commune with me *without words*. When you find this place, real communication begins.

*"If you remain in me and my words remain in you,
ask whatever you wish, and it will be done for you."*

JOHN 15:7

I LOVE THE WORLD

*My love for people is so great
that it's nearly impossible for you to fathom it.*

My child, I'm going to tell you something that may surprise you: *I love the world.*

When I say "world," I don't mean the physical earth itself. I mean all the human beings who populate the wonderful planet I designed and created. My love for people is so great that it's nearly impossible for you to fathom it.

The entire weight of my Good News rests in the most famous of declarations, made in the dead of night by my Son to a sincere seeker. In the verse you know as John 3:16, the essence of my story is told: though my human creation rebelled against me and became my enemy, I loved people to the degree that I was willing to give up my one and only Son. Through Him, any person—man or woman, slave or free, Jew or Gentile—could once again have an intimate, eternal relationship with me as Father and friend.

John 3:16 is no children's verse, yet it's simple enough for a child to understand. It isn't overly complex, yet scholars have studied it for centuries. Plainly, simply, this is the summary of who I am and what I've done for you:

*For God so loved the world that he gave his one and only Son,
that whoever believes in him shall not perish but have eternal life.*

JOHN 3:16

YOU MAY HAVE THE GIFT OF KNOWLEDGE

*When you exercise the discerning gifts,
stay focused and have a humble heart.*

All spiritual gifts are given by my Holy Spirit to strengthen and benefit the Christian community.

You have at least one spiritual gift, and it has nothing to do with your education, your position in the church, or your natural abilities. Think about it: a person may have a very ordinary job, yet possess an amazing ability to discern truth from error. That person isn't necessarily smarter than anyone else—the Holy Spirit has gifted him or her with the ability to know when a book, a blog, or a speaker is faithful to my Word.

Or what about the person with a knack for bringing perspective and balance to a particular situation—perhaps when two people are in sharp disagreement? This is the gift of wisdom. On occasion, you may suddenly have a unique and useful insight about a person or situation, something you could never have known except for a spiritual gift of knowledge.

This kind of spiritual gift—knowledge, wisdom, or discernment—is nothing for you to brag about. When you exercise the discerning gifts, stay focused and have a humble heart.

*There are different kinds of gifts, but the same Spirit distributes them
. . . . To one there is given through the Spirit a message of wisdom,
to another a message of knowledge by means of the same Spirit.*

1 CORINTHIANS 12:4, 8

I Am the I Am

I will always be your Provider,
your Shield, your Rock, and your Lord.

I have many names, but there's one that stands out—the name most commonly used in the Old Testament. Let me explain what it means when you see my name in capital letters like this—Lord.

There's a name behind "Lord": the Hebrew YHWH, which you may know as Yahweh.

To understand the meaning of Yahweh, go to the Old Testament where I spoke to Moses from the burning bush. At that dramatic moment—as I gave Moses an assignment that scared the daylights out of him—he asked for my name. I told him, "I AM WHO I AM," or simply "I AM." At first, that may not sound like much—but the implications of my name are enormous. "I AM" means that I exist independently of anything else. Nothing made me; there is nothing behind me. I simply *am*: I always have been and I always will be.

"I AM" also means I will never change. I will always be your Provider, your Shield, your Rock, and your Lord. Most importantly for you, my Son—your Lord and Savior—is also I AM. Everything that I AM, Jesus is.

God said to Moses, "I am who I am.
This is what you are to say to the Israelites:
'I am has sent me to you.'"
Exodus 3:14

Be Like My Son

You can never be exactly like Jesus,
but you can imitate Him as you take on His attitude.

You can never be exactly like my Son, but I want you to try anyway.

What Jesus did for you was so extraordinary that He is the only one who could ever have accomplished it. Think about it! Though my Son is equal to me in every way, out of love and obedience He set aside His divinity and took on human form—not as a king or warrior, but as a lowly servant. His whole purpose in coming to earth was to die in your place.

Though He was sinless and innocent, Jesus died a humiliating, painful death designed for the worst criminals. This was not easy for Jesus—and it was excruciating for me. At the moment of His death, Jesus carried the load of your sin—the sin of all humanity before and after you. So black and awful was this burden (and so pure is my holiness) that I turned my back to Him. But it was only for a moment, and only so He could turn His face to you.

You can never be exactly like Jesus, but you can imitate Him as you take on His attitude of extreme love and service. Go ahead. Try it. It will change your life.

In your relationships with one another,
have the same mindset as Christ Jesus:
Who, being in very nature God. . .made himself nothing
by taking the very nature of a servant.
Philippians 2:5–7

MY SPIRIT IS A FIRE

The presence of the Holy Spirit in your life should be like a fire.

Because fire is an important symbol in my story, you need to understand what it means. I appeared to Moses in a burning bush (Exodus 3:2), showing the power of my presence. I led my people through the wilderness as a pillar of fire (Exodus 13:21), demonstrating the blessing of my guidance. The Bible describes me as "a consuming fire" (Hebrews 12:29), indicating the reality of my omnipotence.

Fire is also a dramatic picture of how my Holy Spirit works. When John the Baptist announced the coming of my Son, the Messiah, he said Jesus would baptize "with the Holy Spirit and fire" (Matthew 3:11). Then, after my Son ascended to heaven following His death and resurrection, the Holy Spirit—in the form of "tongues of fire"—came upon the believers, giving them power to share the Good News of my Son with all nations.

In your life, too, the presence of the Holy Spirit should be like a fire. For one thing, it will ignite your passion to love and serve me and others in the name of my Son. For another, the Holy Spirit will purify your life, cleansing you of sin and refining you into the person I want you to be.

*They saw what seemed to be tongues of fire
that separated and came to rest on each of them.
All of them were filled with the Holy Spirit.*

ACTS 2:3–4

YOU'RE IN MY BOOK

When you read any part of my story,
you're going to find yourself in the plot.

In many ways, my Word is like a great novel. The author is world famous; the plot is a page turner, dealing with the classic themes of beginnings, loss, and redemption; the hero has to go through many trials before paying the ultimate price; and, in the end, the good guys win!

Of course, there are some differences between my Word and a great novel. For starters, my Word isn't fiction—it's entirely true. And the hero is a real Person who died and rose again, who will someday return to complete the Book's ending.

Beyond that, there's one more thing that separates my Book from anything else ever written: you're in it! Not by name, but by virtue of who you are. As author of the Bible, I've set up the plot. I know what's going to happen, and the fact is that I've written the story with you in mind.

When you read any part of my story, you're going to find yourself in the plot. Why? Because you know the Author, and the Author knows you.

From one man he made all the nations,
that they should inhabit the whole earth;
and he marked out their appointed times in history
and the boundaries of their lands.
God did this so that they would seek him and perhaps
reach out for him and find him.
ACTS 17:26–27

DIRECTION AND CHARACTER

*I am more interested in building your character
than giving you direction.*

Everybody wants to know my will. It's by far the number-one question I get from people in their prayers: "Lord, what is your will for me?"

Of course, the question isn't usually that general. People pray things like, "Lord, should I take this job?" or "Father, do You want me to go on this missions trip? If so, I need two thousand dollars."

I hope you know me well enough to believe that I always want what's best for you—and that may not always coincide with what you *want*. I might make you wait. But in the end, your Father knows best.

While you're waiting, there's something you can do for me: work on your character. As much as you want direction for your life, I want you to build character. Certainly, those decisions about vocation, ministry, and money are important—but you'll never make decisions in line with my will if your *character* is lacking. So work on it. Become a character-driven person.

*"The LORD does not look at the things people look at.
People look at the outward appearance,
but the LORD looks at the heart."*

1 SAMUEL 16:7

I CREATED THE WORLD

Everything you see comes from me.
I made it out of nothing, and I did it for a reason.

Please become very familiar with the first verse in my Word.

In those ten words, I reveal three very important truths: The universe had a beginning. I created everything at the beginning. And I existed before that beginning.

Here's what these world-changing ideas mean to you personally: *everything* you see comes from me. I didn't use existing materials to create the world. I made it out of nothing, and I did it for a reason.

I created the world with and for a purpose: that it could be inhabited by the people I made in my image. That's you! You are unique in all my creation because you are specially made to have a relationship with me. You can enjoy me. . .forever!

As pleasant as it may be to live in my world, you should never forget that I created you to experience a glorious life with me beyond the physical universe. I am your Creator. I am your Father. I am your friend.

In the beginning God created the heavens and the earth.
GENESIS 1:1

YOU MAY HAVE THE GIFT OF FAITH, HEALING, OR MIRACLES

Don't ignore these gifts, but don't seek them, either.

Certain gifts of the Holy Spirit are a little mysterious. Three gifts I want to tell you about today fall in that category: faith, healing, and miracles.

You may have a hard time understanding these gifts because they are subject to abuse. When they're combined—as in "faith healing" or "healing miracles"—some people turn the idea into a racket.

I don't want anyone's abuse of these gifts to cause you to ignore them. They're very important! Take faith, for example. Everyone who believes in me needs faith, but sometimes a special *gift* of faith is required for a specific need. The best place to see this gift in action is where the Gospel is being presented for the first time. Healing still happens, but not necessarily by faith healers—rather, by the gift of my Spirit for a special purpose in someone's life.

Don't ignore these gifts, but don't seek them, either. The Holy Spirit is picky about who gets them, and when.

There are different kinds of gifts, but the same Spirit distributes them . . . . To another faith by the same Spirit, to another gifts of healing by that one Spirit, to another miraculous powers.

1 CORINTHIANS 12:4, 9–10

113

I AM THE TRUE ORIGINAL

I have always existed as the true, one-and-only God,
who is like nothing else.

There are few things in life you can truly call "original." Most things are copies.

In other words, most things are derivatives of something that came before them. A work of art—a painting, a poem, a song—may be called "one of a kind," but it will always bear some resemblance to something that preceded it. Even *you* are a copy in certain respects—connected as you are to your parents and grandparents. You resemble them because you share the same genes.

Being a copy is nothing to be ashamed of. It's the way I designed the world—I put a familiarity throughout that links all things and points to me as creator.

There is one thing in this world, though, that is not a copy—it's a true original. Actually, it's not a thing, it's a Person: *me*. I have always existed as the true, one-and-only God, and I am like nothing else. I created all things, and I have chosen to relate to everything I have made—including you.

I am the one and only—and I love you like you're my one and only.

"I am God, and there is no other;
I am God, and there is none like me."
ISAIAH 46:9

JESUS IS ALL-POWERFUL

I want you to be amazed at my Son's power.

When He was on earth, my Son was truly a man, with all the emotions and characteristics of a human being. He cried, He rejoiced, He felt sorrow and pain—and He died. Jesus was even tempted, so there would be nothing in your experience that He has not personally known.

But Jesus was also *deity*, which means He had all the characteristics and powers that I have. One time, when Jesus was in a boat on the Sea of Galilee with His disciples, a terrible storm arose. The wind and waves were so fierce that the disciples feared for their lives—while Jesus slept. In a panic, the disciples woke Jesus and begged Him to save them. So my Son scolded the storm as a father would correct an out-of-control child, and immediately there was peace.

Imagine having the power to simply speak to a storm and make it obey. Jesus' disciples were amazed, asking, "Who is this?"

I want *you* to have that same reaction to my Son's power. Never forget: He is human like you—but He is also the almighty God.

He replied, "You of little faith, why are you so afraid?"
Then he got up and rebuked the winds and the waves, and it was
completely calm. The men were amazed and asked, "What kind of
man is this? Even the winds and the waves obey him!"
MATTHEW 8:26–27

THE BAPTISM OF THE HOLY SPIRIT

When you surrender your life to Jesus,
the Holy Spirit makes you into a new person.

I have already told you about water baptism, the symbolic sacrament that shows you belong to my Son. But there's another kind of baptism—the kind by which you are saved—that happens *before* water baptism. Yes, a baptism before baptism. Let me explain:

When the religious leader Nicodemus asked my Son to tell him how a person could be "born again," Jesus said a second birth was possible by the Holy Spirit (John 3:4–8). The apostle Paul expanded on this very important job that only the Holy Spirit can do: when you surrender your life to Jesus, the Holy Spirit makes you into a new person by cleansing you and giving you the supernatural ability to break off your love affair with sin. You still have the capacity to sin, but with the Holy Spirit's work in your life, you can resist sin's lure (Galatians 5:16).

That's what the baptism of the Holy Spirit does. It gives you a break from the old life, a new beginning—and automatically integrates you in my family, the body of Christ.

For we were all baptized by one Spirit so as to form one body—
whether Jews or Gentiles, slave or free—and we were
all given the one Spirit to drink.

1 CORINTHIANS 12:13

MY WORD IS TRUE

*Because I am incapable of lying,
everything in my Word is true.*

Many people read my Word like this: they pick and choose what they want to believe and apply to their lives. If they disagree with a passage—usually relating to my disapproval of sin—they just ignore it.

But there's no way you can *deny* what I've said in my Word. You can ignore it, you may not understand it, but you cannot declare my Word untrue.

Tell somebody what I've just told you, and you'll probably get some pushback. But you don't have to back down because it's not your Word, it's *mine*. And since I am incapable of lying (Titus 1:2), everything I say in my Word is true. That should give you tremendous confidence (and conviction) when you read it.

So what are you waiting for? Read my Word. Study my Word. Believe my Word because it's *true*.

*God's way is perfect. All the LORD's promises prove true.
He is a shield for all who look to him for protection.*
PSALM 18:30 NLT

BE KIND TO EACH OTHER

*Kindness is a serious intention
that needs to be taken seriously.*

There's way too much anger, bitterness, slander, and hurtful language within my family. Now, I expect that from the people of the world. They don't know any better. But when my own children fight with each other, it grieves my heart.

Listen! Get rid of all that maliciousness. There's just no place for it. It's damaging, both to the recipient of your words and to you. In fact, it's *worse* for you. Who do you think I'm going to hold accountable?

I know that, most of the time, you don't mean it. But when somebody says or does something to irritate you, you just go off. Don't let that happen. Catch this tendency in advance, before it catches you. Instead of harboring negative thoughts, nurture kindness.

Kindness isn't for lightweights. It's a serious intention that needs to be taken seriously. Kindness and love motivated my Son to have mercy on you and save you when you were opposed to Him. I expect you to have that same attitude, even to those you consider enemies.

Be gracious. Be good. Be kind.

*Be kind and compassionate to one another, forgiving each other,
just as in Christ God forgave you.*
EPHESIANS 4:32

DON'T WORRY ABOUT YOUR LIFE

Trust me to help you.
But first you have to get rid of worry.

Worrying is one of the easiest things to do. Though it accomplishes nothing and can even lead to physical problems, many people embrace Worry like it's a long-lost friend. They invite him in, give him a place to sleep, feed him, and never ask him to leave—though Worry just lies around and doesn't lift a finger to help.

Can I give you some practical advice? Throw the bum out! Tell Worry there's no place in your life for him. Of course you're facing challenges right now—but do you think Worry is going to help? He'll only drag you down, so get rid of him. Instead, trust *me* with your challenges and concerns.

Do you think I don't know your needs? Do you think I won't take care of you today and tomorrow and the day after that? Change that thinking. Trust me to help you. But first you have to get rid of Worry.

"So do not worry, saying, 'What shall we eat?'
or 'What shall we drink?' or 'What shall we wear?'
For the pagans run after all these things,
and your heavenly Father knows that you need them."
MATTHEW 6:31–32

YOU MAY HAVE THE GIFT OF TONGUES

*When it is exercised properly,
the gift of tongues is a beautiful thing to behold.*

All spiritual gifts are given by my Holy Spirit for the building up of the body of Christ—and every one of my children has at least one such gift.

In His wisdom, the Holy Spirit distributes gifts across the spectrum of believers, matching them up with a special supernatural ability so they can serve one another. So how does the gift of tongues fit into this pattern?

When you hear the phrase "speaking in tongues," are you suspicious? Don't be. Like any gift, this one is subject to abuse—but when it's exercised properly, the gift of tongues is a beautiful thing to behold.

Most of the time, this is a supernatural ability to speak in a language you don't already know. Sometimes the gift expresses itself in a private prayer language known as praying "in the spirit" (1 Corinthians 14:15 NLT).

Whatever you do, don't try to force the gift of tongues. It is a gift, not a trick. It's for the building up of the body of Christ, not that you can impress others.

*There are different kinds of gifts,
but the same Spirit distributes them. . . .
To another speaking in different kinds of tongues,
and to still another the interpretation of tongues.*

1 CORINTHIANS 12:4, 10

I AM SPIRIT

*I am completely unique and different
from any other kind of existence.*

The essence of my being is that I am spiritual. I don't have flesh and blood like you do, but I'm not composed of pure energy, either. Don't think of me as having size or dimension. Because I am not at all material, I'm not even infinitely large—I am immeasurable. There aren't "parts" of me in various locations in the universe. I am everywhere at the same time.

Through the ages, people have tried to compose images of me. They're all wrong, misleading even—giving people false ideas about me, like I'm a kindly grandfather type in a white beard or a vengeful judge with fire coming out of my fingertips.

Forget about trying to picture me. I've actually forbidden that (Exodus 20:4). Instead, just think of me as *spirit*—completely unique and different from any other kind of existence. But don't hold me at arm's length, either. I'm not a ghost, and I'm not nothing. I am a personal being who invites you to join me, worshipping in my spirituality, lifting you out of your ordinary physical existence into the extraordinary realm where I dwell.

*"God is spirit, and his worshipers must worship
in the Spirit and in truth."*
JOHN 4:24

MY SON HAS A BODY

*Jesus went through all the stages of life,
just like you have.*

I know how difficult it is for you to relate to me personally. Though there is ample physical evidence for my existence, I am spirit and therefore invisible. As much as you try to imagine me, you can't. So don't even try. Rather, when you have an urge to picture me in some physical form, imagine Jesus.

I don't mean that Jesus is in your imagination. My Son is a very real, historical figure who was born and lived as a human being. In one sense, He was just like you, with a human body.

Why was it necessary for Jesus to live as a human? So you could identify with Him. My Son wasn't some privileged prince who never mixed with everyday people. He was born in a barn and grew up as a carpenter's son. He went through all the stages of life, just like you have. He developed physically and gained knowledge. Everything you experience, He experienced—except for sin. But He certainly understands temptation.

Because Jesus lived as a human, you can, too. Because He died and rose again in a human body, so will you. Because He ascended into heaven in a body, you will, as well.

*And the child grew and became strong;
he was filled with wisdom,
and the grace of God was on him.*
Luke 2:40

MY SPIRIT LAUNCHED THE CHURCH

On that day, the community of believers
known as the church was born.

The role of the Holy Spirit is first and foremost to point to my Son. While Jesus interacted with people on earth—healing them, teaching them, loving them—the Holy Spirit stayed in the background. He showed up when Jesus was baptized (Mark 1:9–11), but otherwise the focus was on my Son.

After thirty-three years of life on earth, Jesus was crucified, then rose from the dead, just as my Word tells you (1 Corinthians 15:3–8). Forty days after His resurrection, my Son ascended to heaven, leaving His followers behind—but not alone. Ten days after Jesus ascended into heaven to be with me, the Holy Spirit came upon the believers in a spectacular display of wind and fire.

You should have seen it! At that moment, the Holy Spirit filled those first Christians, uniting them in the spiritual body of my Son. On that day, the community of believers known as the church was born, launched and empowered by the Holy Spirit. And since then, every person born again has automatically become a member of that universal body.

When the day of Pentecost came, they were all together in one place.
Suddenly a sound like the blowing of a violent wind came from
heaven and filled the whole house where they were sitting. They saw
what seemed to be tongues of fire that separated and came to rest on
each of them. All of them were filled with the Holy Spirit.

ACTS 2:1–4

If You Love Me, Obey My Word

*Loving me by staying faithful to my Word
should become second nature.*

There are at least four kinds of love you can have. You can express affection, such as "love" for a pet dog. You can love your fellow human beings ("brotherly love") in that you have a common bond with them. Then there's sexual love, which is my gift to you within the framework of marriage.

The highest love is the love I have for you—a sacrificial love that only wants what is best for you. As you mature spiritually, this kind of love should also grow in you.

You should love *me* this way—even though "wanting the best" for me isn't really necessary, as I already have everything I need. But I do want you to give me your best, starting with staying faithful to my Word.

Your love for me should be such that doing what I want you to do becomes second nature. If that sounds difficult, don't panic. Ask my Son to help you. He'll take whatever burden you have so you can freely love me by obeying my Word.

*In fact, this is love for God: to keep his commands.
And his commands are not burdensome.*

1 John 5:3

OVERCOME EVIL WITH GOOD

The crowd treats enemies like enemies.
I want you to treat your enemies like friends.

Do you want to stand apart from the crowd? Would you like to change the way people perceive you? Here's how: conquer evil by doing good.

I know, that's counterintuitive for human beings. Typically, when somebody wrongs you, the first response is payback. That's the way the world works. To most people, revenge is a form of justice.

Don't fall for that idea. When someone wrongs you, don't respond in kind. If payback is due, let *me* handle it. Your job is to hold your temper, to look for ways to be extra nice. Seriously!

You want to stand apart from the crowd, don't you? Well, the crowd treats enemies like enemies. I want you to treat your enemies like friends. When your neighbor gives you fits, invite him over for dinner. When a coworker makes your life miserable, be generous to a fault.

Do this, and one of two things will happen: either you'll win "your enemies" over, or they'll feel so ashamed that they'll change their ways. Either way, you win—and I'm pleased.

Do not be overcome by evil,
but overcome evil with good.
ROMANS 12:21

THE GOLDEN RULE

Do something nice for someone
before they have a chance to be nice to you.

My Word contains a number of phrases the whole world uses—usually without understanding their origins. Here's a popular phrase: "Do to others what you would have them do to you" (Matthew 7:12). You call it the "Golden Rule." This little saying speaks volumes about the way I want you to treat others, including those who aren't in my family of faith.

The Golden Rule came from Jesus—and notice how He made it a *positive* statement. Other religions say it like this: "Don't do to others what you don't want done to you." For example, if you don't want another driver to yell at you, you wouldn't aggravate him by your own reckless driving. That's fine, but it really misses Jesus' point.

My Son wants you to do more than avoiding things that harm others. He wants you to do something positive before they have a chance to do something for you. Honestly, it's much easier to refrain from doing something harmful than it is to initiate something beneficial. Restraint takes discipline, but generosity requires planning.

"So in everything, do to others what you would have them do to you,
for this sums up the Law and the Prophets."
MATTHEW 7:12

YOU MAY HAVE THE GIFT OF TEACHING, PASTORING, OR EVANGELIZING

Don't overlook these gifts,
and don't assume you need to be well known to use them.

There's a tendency to put pastors, teachers, and evangelists on a spiritual pedestal. Pastors can gain enormous popularity, Bible teachers can have huge followings, and evangelists are known to fill large arenas.

For a moment, I want you to put aside every conception you have of pastors, teachers, and evangelists. Forget that many of them are held in high esteem. I want you to think of these positions not as talents, but as spiritual gifts—which they are! And I want you to realize that *you* could have one of these gifts.

You don't have to lead a church to be a pastor. You may have the gift of caring for and protecting people in a special way—which is the primary role of the pastor as shepherd. A teacher correctly handles my Word (2 Timothy 2:15). A seminary degree is nice, but it's not a prerequisite to teaching. Do you have a knack for sharing my Good News with people who haven't heard it quite that way before? You may have the gift of evangelism.

Don't overlook these gifts, and don't assume you need to be well known to use them.

So Christ himself gave the apostles, the prophets, the evangelists,
the pastors and teachers, to equip his people for works of service,
so that the body of Christ may be built up.
EPHESIANS 4:11–12

I AM INVISIBLE YET VISIBLE

The way for you to see me is to become more and more like me.

No one has ever seen me. I can tell you that for sure (John 1:18).

Yet I have shown myself to many people. I am invisible yet visible. Another way to put it is this: you will never be able to see my total essence (which is spirit), but it is possible to see something of me through visible things.

Of course, the people living when Jesus walked the earth saw me—because my Son is my visible image (Colossians 1:15). "Anyone who has seen me has seen the Father," Jesus said (John 14:9).

But what about people who lived before and after Jesus? What have they seen? Moses used to talk with me "face to face, as one speaks to a friend" (Exodus 33:11). Yet Moses never actually saw my face, because I am spirit. So what did Moses see? He saw my *glory*, which is the radiance of my being.

As for you, don't go looking for me in sunsets or newborn babies. Beauty and wonder flow from me, but I'm not beauty and wonder. The way for you to see me—to experience my presence in your life—is to become more and more like me.

By faith [Moses] left Egypt, not fearing the king's anger;
he persevered because he saw him who is invisible.

HEBREWS 11:27

JESUS WAS TEMPTED JUST LIKE YOU

When you are tempted, you can call on my Son,
who understands what you're going through.

I'm going to share a mystery with you concerning the temptation of my Son.

You are aware that Satan tempted Jesus for forty days, focusing on His physical, emotional, and spiritual dimensions (Luke 4:1–13). Jesus resisted by quoting my Word. So thorough were these temptations—along with more ordinary ones throughout His life—that I can truly say He was tempted in *every* way you could possibly be tempted. Yet He never sinned.

Because Jesus is divine, He could *not* have sinned. Technically, as God, my Son could not even be tempted (James 1:13). But He was tempted, and the pressure was real. How can that be?

Here's the mystery. Though Jesus is God, He is also fully human—and as a man, He experienced temptation in the same way you do. Jesus' divine nature prevented the possibility of giving in to temptation, but His human nature allowed Him to *experience* temptation.

Do you see the significance of this mystery for you? When you are tempted, you can call on my Son—who truly experienced what you're going through, and who now offers you power to resist.

For we do not have a high priest who is unable to empathize with our weaknesses, but we have one who has been tempted in every way, just as we are—yet he did not sin.

HEBREWS 4:15

THE HOLY SPIRIT MAKES YOU ONE

*Make an effort to preserve the unity
you have with all members of my family of faith.*

As my child, you are part of two families. One is earthly—your
mother and father, siblings, aunts, uncles, grandparents, and
cousins. You have a common heritage and a connection by blood.
Then there's your spiritual family—your brothers and sisters in
Christ who are connected by *His* blood, united into one body by
the Holy Spirit.

Though you will always have a bond with members of your
spiritual family, disagreements and disputes will occur. But you
can minimize the strife in my family if you follow a few simple
guidelines.

First, make an effort to preserve the unity you have with all
members of my family of faith. Don't instigate disputes; be a
peacemaker. Next, remember the common hope you share with all
my children—the hope of your salvation in my Son—and what
that means to you both now and forever. Finally, keep in mind
that you all share the same Father—and I want my kids to get
along as best they can.

*Make every effort to keep the unity of the Spirit
through the bond of peace.
There is one body and one Spirit. . .one Lord, one faith, one baptism;
one God and Father of all, who is over all and through all and in all.*
EPHESIANS 4:3–6

BLESSED ARE THOSE WHO KEEP MY WORD

Every day when you wake up,
turn your heart and your thoughts to me.

How I long to bless you! To be *blessed* is to be happy—not a happiness that comes from momentary pleasure, but the deep, abiding joy that only happens when you rest in my grace and feel my presence.

My grace is unconditional, but my blessing depends on you. Every day when you wake up, turn your heart and your thoughts to me. Immerse yourself in my Word as routinely as you take your morning shower. As you read and meditate on the words and phrases of scripture, think how they apply to your relationships and responsibilities, your work and your play.

Enter into your day as a blessed person, because you first consulted my Word—then resolve to obey it. Today won't be perfect for you (no day is), but it will be filled with purpose, as you walk in my Word and my will.

Blessed are those whose ways are blameless, who walk
according to the law of the LORD. Blessed are those who
keep his statutes and seek him with all their heart—
they do no wrong but follow his ways.

PSALM 119:1–3

OBEY ME FOR YOUR OWN GOOD

My rules, whether you like them or not,
make your life better.

There's no question that I've given you a lot of instructions to follow and commands to obey.

Some say I've laid down far too many rules—that I should just let people do what they want. The problem is that people tend to do what they want anyway, with or without me. It's in their nature to rebel against my rules and go their own way (Isaiah 53:6). But it's in *my* nature to correct you, giving you rules for life and a game plan that works in your best interest.

To better appreciate my rules, imagine watching a game without rules. Take football, for example. Football is governed by hundreds of rules that are administered by referees. Imagine if football were played without rules and without referees to enforce them. Would you watch a game like that, where every player did whatever he wanted? Of course not—it would be a silly, chaotic, unproductive mess.

In the same way, I don't want to watch you play the game of your life without rules. That's silly, chaotic, and unproductive. My rules, whether you like them or not, make your life better.

"Whether it is favorable or unfavorable,
we will obey the LORD *our God. . .*
so that it will go well with us."
JEREMIAH 42:6

DON'T FEAR THOSE WHO CAN ONLY KILL THE BODY

Others may be able to take your physical life,
but your spiritual life belongs to me.

Have you ever thought that believing in me could cost you your life?

That was a real threat in the first century when the church began and Christians started professing their faith. Persecution—both by the state and religious leaders—was commonplace. Many people were put to death for proclaiming allegiance to my Son.

Through the centuries, persecution of those who follow my Son has been steady. Even now, persecution in the world at large is growing worse. In many places, you are free to worship me without reprisal—but in others, worship is actually dangerous. Three-fourths of all religious persecution in the world today is directed at those who follow my Son.

So what does this mean for you? For one thing, you should pray for your brothers and sisters who suffer for their faith. The only way to keep evil at bay is to call on me. I won't eradicate the evil—it's not yet time for that—but I will restrain it. You can also pray for courage that if you ever face a situation where your own life is at stake, you would not be afraid.

Others may be able to take your physical life, but your spiritual life belongs to me. And that's the life that matters most.

"Do not be afraid of those who kill the body but cannot kill the soul."
MATTHEW 10:28

YOU MAY HAVE THE GIFT OF SERVING, GIVING, OR MERCY

I expect all of my children to be sensitive to the needs of others.

I want to tell you about one more group of spiritual gifts—the ones involving the way you serve others.

The gift of *serving* can take many forms, but people with this gift have a sensitivity to know exactly how they can be of help to others. More important than just *knowing* what to do, this gift empowers people to spring into action and get the job done.

The gift of *giving* has nothing to do with an amount that you give—it involves an unusual sensitivity to special needs, along with an overwhelming generosity with whatever means I've given. Those with this gift really give!

I expect all my children to be sensitive to the needs of others—you should be available to comfort them in times of trouble and discouragement. But many people are oblivious to these needs, or they see the distress in others and aren't able to muster a desire to help. A person with the gift of *mercy* has both the desire and the willingness to help—and it's never a burden.

We have different gifts, according to the grace given to each of us. If your gift is. . .serving, then serve. . .if it is giving, then give generously. . .if it is to show mercy, do it cheerfully.
ROMANS 12:6–8

134

NATURE PRAISES ME

When you praise me, you are joining the symphony of creation.

I love it when you praise me. Your acknowledgment of the way I work in your life—of all the benefits you receive from being my child—is like music to my ears. Keep it up! Not as a way of flattering me, so I'll be even nicer than I already am. . .but to remind yourself that you and I have a personal relationship.

Let me tell you something about praise: it's contagious. When you've been at a big public event—a concert or a ball game—you can't help but join in when the crowd starts applauding or cheering. When you praise me, think of being part of a crowd—or even better, being a player in a grand, global symphony where the players are the heavenly hosts of angels, the sun and the moon, and every living creature on earth. Can you hear them, all joining together in a cascade of praise?

All of nature declares my greatness and beauty, my precision and care. When you praise me—whether alone or in a chorus—you join the symphony of creation. May you be energized and inspired by the part you play.

Praise the LORD from the heavens; praise him in the heights above.
Praise him, all his angels; praise him, all his heavenly hosts.
Praise him, sun and moon; praise him, all you shining stars.

PSALM 148:1–3

IF JESUS IS KNOCKING, OPEN THE DOOR

Unless your heart is in it,
you will never experience the abundant life Jesus promises.

Today I want to address those who tell others that they follow my Son—but who, in reality, are just going through the motions. This is for those people who *want* to love me with all their heart, soul, mind, and strength—but the love isn't there and they don't know why. This message can change anyone's life, if they're willing to accept it.

You can give me all the "lip service" you want, but unless your heart is in it, you will never experience the abundant life Jesus promises (John 10:10). I know your heart, and I know why you haven't given me your full attention and commitment. The world and its pleasures are a distraction, and they've divided your loyalties and your love.

There's only one way to fix that situation: respond to my Son's persistent knocking on your heart's door. Can you feel it? It's a still, small voice whispering in your ear. It's a *tap, tap, tap* on your heart, urging you to open the door and let Jesus in completely.

Stop playing games. Listen to my Son's voice. Invite Him into your life.

"Here I am! I stand at the door and knock.
If anyone hears my voice and opens the door,
I will come in and eat with that person, and they with me."
REVELATION 3:20

THE HOLY SPIRIT HELPS YOU IN YOUR WEAKNESS

You can't feel "strong and courageous" all the time.

I love it when you join the chorus of praise from my created world and the household of faith—but I'm aware there are going to be some groans amid the singing.

Just as fury occasionally interrupts nature's harmony, trials will sometimes punctuate the joys of your life. You can't feel "strong and courageous" all the time. At times, you'll be overcome by weakness.

Don't be discouraged! Not only is it normal to have feelings of inadequacy, it is beneficial. When everything is going well and you're on top of the world, your dependency on me decreases. But when weakness and discouragement creep in, you and I get a lot closer. That's why the apostle Paul could say, "When I am weak, then I am strong" (2 Corinthians 12:10). He knew from personal experience that when you have nothing left in the tank, I will fill it up with my Holy Spirit.

When problems and stress overwhelm you, sapping your strength, my Holy Spirit will help you—and not only in the specific challenge you're experiencing, but in every part of your life.

In the same way, the Spirit helps us in our weakness.
ROMANS 8:26

KEEP MY WORD IN YOUR HEART

If purity is your goal, don't pursue purity.
Pursue me and my Word.

Living a pure life isn't easy. It's especially difficult with all the distractions and temptations available in your time and society.

And you know what? Immoral behavior isn't restricted to sex or substance addictions. Your purity can be challenged at work and even at church as you're confronted by the lure of power and status.

Everyone has passions and ambitions—so how do you live a clean life? The answer is very simple, yet incredibly profound: when you awaken in the morning, before you're confronted with a hundred images, decisions, and temptations, fix your eyes and heart on me and my Word. Let me into your mind, using the same routine you follow when you get ready for work. Bring me into your day as soon as possible.

If purity is your goal—and I hope it is—don't pursue purity. Pursue me. Delight in my Word. Do that each day and purity will follow.

How can a young person stay on the path of purity?
By living according to your word. I seek you with all my heart;
do not let me stray from your commands.
I have hidden your word in my heart that I might not sin against you.

PSALM 119:9–11

TAKE JOY IN YOUR TRIALS

The world says avoid trials if you can;
I say rejoice when trials come.

There's so much about your life with me that is contrary to the way the world works. The world says to take revenge when others wrong you; I say to love your enemies. The world says to work on your outward appearance; I say develop your interior life. The world says avoid trials if you can; I say rejoice when trials come.

My advice is often opposed to the so-called wisdom of the world, and for a good reason. My focus is always on the *process* of developing your character, whereas the world usually focuses on end result. But you'll never get the results that you and I want if you skip the race and try to go directly to the finish line. If you want to win, you need to compete—and if your goal is victory, pain will be part of the journey.

I am interested in results, but not those acquired on the cheap. Be willing to pay the price. When you experience difficulties, welcome them as integral to the process of spiritual maturity. More than anything else in your life, trials will bring you closer to me—so take joy in them. They are worth any amount of suffering you have to endure.

Consider it pure joy, my brothers and sisters, whenever you face trials of many kinds, because you know that the testing of your faith produces perseverance.

JAMES 1:2–3

TAKE ME SERIOUSLY

You have a relationship with the living God.
Honor me and show me respect.

Most people have no idea what it means to *fear* me. Fearing me has nothing to do with being afraid of me—but everything to do with honoring me and showing me respect.

Let me give you a dramatic example: Once when the disciples were in a boat with my Son, a terrible storm came up, threatening to swamp the boat. After Jesus quieted the storm with a simple command, His followers were instantly filled with *fear*. They asked each other, "Who is this?" (Mark 4:41). They weren't *afraid* of Jesus—but they were filled with an overwhelming sense of awe.

Hear me on this. You don't believe in and serve an imaginary god or powerless idol. You have a relationship with the living God who created the universe with a simple command. Now I offer you healing and true freedom through your glorious Lord and Savior, Jesus Christ. Show me respect. Honor my name. Take me seriously.

That's what it means to fear me.

"But for you who fear my name, the sun of righteousness
shall rise with healing in its wings. You shall go out
leaping like calves from the stall."
MALACHI 4:2 ESV

SHOW RESPECT FOR MY CHURCH

Don't be drawn into a spirit of cynical doubt that can cause divisions.

Have you noticed these days that more people are willing to openly mock the church?

The visible church—that is, all those who claim to follow me—is not perfect. It's made plenty of mistakes. But it is still *my* church, and it grieves me when people disrespect it.

I understand some of the criticism. When someone who claims to be my child does something foolish (like setting a date for my Son's return), you should expect cynics to speak out. But when some of those same scoffers turn their derision to me and to the true church—that is, all real believers—be on guard. Don't be drawn into a spirit of cynical doubt that can cause divisions.

It's one thing to have a healthy skepticism of man-made doctrines that don't mesh with my Word (such as date setting). It's quite another thing to question an established truth found in my Word (such as the return of my Son). Know how to tell the difference.

*These are the people who divide you,
who follow mere natural instincts
and do not have the Spirit.*

JUDE 19

You Can Count on Me

Be grateful that I am not like you,
for I keep every promise and fulfill all my covenants.

In many ways you are like me. Because I created you in my image (Genesis 1:26–27), we share some of the same qualities. Although my capacity in each is infinitely greater than yours, you have a certain ability to imitate me. You can love and show compassion to others just as I do. You even share in my power to create, turning thoughts into something tangible like a painting or a building.

In other ways, we are *nothing* alike. Because you're human—and a fallen one at that—you have the capacity to lie. I do not. In your actions, you can be unpredictable. I do not change. And then there's the matter of making promises and covenants. You really intend to keep the promises you make, but you sometimes fail. Sadly, it's your nature.

But hear me on this: be grateful that I am not like you, for I keep every promise and fulfill all my covenants. I may not follow your timetable, but I never take back what I have promised. You can count on me to act on my Word every time.

"God is not human, that he should lie,
not a human being, that he should change his mind.
Does he speak and then not act? Does he promise and not fulfill?"
Numbers 23:19

JESUS CLAIMED TO BE GOD

Jesus could not have been clearer about His deity.

I want to clear up a lingering misconception about my Son.

Through the centuries since He walked the earth, many people have doubted His divinity. And it's not just the skeptics who question Jesus. Some *theologians* say my Son was just a man who said wise things and helped people, but never declared He was God. They say this claim of deity was foisted on Him by biblical writers and church leaders who wanted Him to be someone He wasn't.

This is a ridiculous argument because Jesus demonstrated His deity in *many* ways—through His miracles, His fulfillment of dozens of prophecies, and ultimately through His resurrection. He is not the same Person as me, but He has the same essence and nature. You have to be willfully ignorant or in rebellious denial to come to any other conclusion.

As for my Son never saying He was God? It's true that He never made the statement, "I am God." He didn't have to—His life was enough to show that He is. Never forget, though, that Jesus did say that He and I are *one*. He couldn't have made a clearer statement about His deity.

"I and the Father are one."
JOHN 10:30

THE HOLY SPIRIT
GUARANTEES YOUR SALVATION

The presence of the Holy Spirit in your life
is proof that you belong to me forever.

If there's one question my children ask more than any other about their spiritual life, it's this: "How do I know I'm saved?"

It's a legitimate question, because it goes to the heart of what salvation is all about. If you think you are saved by your own efforts (that's the way every other religion operates, by the way), then of course your assurance is going to waver. How do you know whether or not a particular sin is going to disqualify you from eternal life with me? The answer is that you don't—not if you think your eternal destiny depends on *you*.

On the other hand, if you believe my Word—which says your eternal destiny depends on me and the work of my Son on your behalf—then you can rest in the knowledge that if you've trusted Jesus by faith there's *nothing* you can do to lose your salvation.

Just to put an exclamation point on that statement, the Holy Spirit is your guarantee that you belong to me for eternity. Think of Him as a notarized signature on the contract you and I have. The presence of the Holy Spirit in your life is binding proof of your salvation.

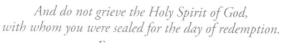

And do not grieve the Holy Spirit of God,
with whom you were sealed for the day of redemption.
EPHESIANS 4:30

MY WORD WILL STRENGTHEN YOU

*Recalibrate your life around the precision
and the promises of my Word.*

My child, I know your sorrows. Your heart grows weary when you or someone you love faces a severe health challenge. Your soul is burdened by the weight of economic concerns. Sometimes you feel as if you're lying facedown on the ground with no one to lift you up.

That's nothing to be ashamed of. Don't be embarrassed, and don't try to mask your feelings. Open your heart to me—your heavenly Father—who loves you so much. Ask me to give you strength and grace, not just for your present circumstances but for your entire life's journey, as well.

When you feel off-kilter, a little out of sync, you've lost touch with my Word. But you can always recalibrate your life around the promises of scripture. Though you change, I never do—nor does my Word.

Through your trials, sometimes by your own foolish actions, you can get offline and lose touch with me. Plug in to my Word again—and I will provide the strength you need to face your challenges and correct your actions.

*I am laid low in the dust; preserve my life according to your word. . . .
My soul is weary with sorrow; strengthen me according to your word.*

PSALM 119:25, 28

DON'T LEAN ON YOUR OWN UNDERSTANDING

I know what's coming on the road ahead—
both the obstacles and the opportunities.

Most of my children have a spiritual stubborn streak. Though you have all my wisdom and resources at hand, you'll often insist on making decisions based on your *own* wisdom and resources.

Sometimes your decisions are sound, but occasionally you miscalculate—your judgment betrays you. Then you come running to me, and, of course I want to help you. But you'd do so much better if you consulted with me *before* you make an important decision.

Why take a chance? Why not trust me with those decisions that really matter? I know what's best for you. I know what's coming on the road ahead—both the obstacles and the opportunities. And I will always work with you, not against you.

I expect you to use the mind and judgment I gave you, but don't depend on your own abilities to the exclusion of mine. With me as your guide, you'll navigate through all of life with the greatest skill.

Trust in the LORD with all your heart
and lean not on your own understanding;
in all your ways submit to him,
and he will make your paths straight.

PROVERBS 3:5–6

I Won't Put Up with Your Pride

If you think you are great,
I will bring you down.

Pride is such a sinister emotion. It cuts across race, gender, and economic class. Even nations can be full of pride—and just as I will bring down individuals whose hearts are pitched against me, I will topple leaders and countries.

Look around you: when you see regimes fall and officials exposed in their arrogance, I am behind it. I put those rulers and governments in place, and I can remove them.

In light of that, consider yourself for a moment. Are you putting faith in your own ability to secure the future? Have you spent so much time building protections around yourself and your family that you've neglected me? Do you derive your self-worth from the company you work for or the enterprise you lead? Do you value your partnerships with human agencies more than your relationship with me? Are you relying on your own experience and wisdom rather than mine?

I won't put up with that for long. Though I am great, I identify with the humble. If you think you are great, I will bring you down.

"The pride of your heart has deceived you. . .who say to yourself,
'Who can bring me down to the ground?' Though you soar like the
eagle. . .I will bring you down," declares the Lord.

Obadiah 3–4

147

KEEP YOUR BAGS PACKED

The Christian life has always been characterized by movement.

When you're tempted to coast, I have a message for you: get off the couch! This life of faith I've called you to experience was never meant to be enjoyed from your living room. There are people everywhere who need your touch.

The Christian life has never been and will never be static. It is characterized by movement. Just before He ascended to heaven to be with me, my Son commissioned His followers with this command: "Go into all the world and preach the gospel to all creation" (Mark 16:15). For two thousand years, that's the way it's been: followers of Jesus Christ taking His saving message to every corner of the globe.

Those who feel called to carry the Good News overseas—even for a season—should go. Those who aren't called to travel should open their eyes to "the world" in their own communities. The nations are at your doorstep, and the needs around you are staggering.

It doesn't matter where you go. Just keep your bags packed and be ready to move.

Again Jesus said, "Peace be with you!
As the Father has sent me, I am sending you."

JOHN 20:21

I Am Being Patient

I am definitely coming back, and it will be sooner than you realize.

There are two ways to look at the return of my Son to earth on a day only I know (Matthew 24:36).

One approach is to view me as being slow, almost like I'm asleep at the wheel. You look around, realize how bad things have gotten in the world, and figure it's time for me to come back and take care of business, so to speak. This was the attitude of first-century Christians, who wondered why I wasn't rescuing them from the persecution they experienced. My "delay" made them fret.

The other approach is to conclude that I probably won't be coming back for a while, at least not in your lifetime. So you're tempted to become complacent.

Let me suggest a third—and much more correct—view of my return.

Yes, it seems like I'm long overdue. But from my eternal perspective, there's no such thing as a delay. If it appears that way to you, it's only because I'm being gracious and patient, allowing more people to turn to me.

As for complacency—well, that's just a bad idea. I am being patient, but I'm definitely coming back, and it will be sooner than you realize. Don't act like it's never going to happen. Live as though my return could come at any time.

The Lord is not slow in keeping his promise,
as some understand slowness.
Instead he is patient with you, not wanting anyone to perish,
but everyone to come to repentance.

2 Peter 3:9

MY SON IS AT MY RIGHT HAND

*Right now, my Son is in my presence,
in human form, representing you.*

Let me tell you something you may not know about Jesus: He has not always been in human form, but He has always existed as my Son.

Jesus became human when He was conceived by the Holy Spirit. In perfect obedience, He grew and learned and lived on earth, performing miracles, fulfilling every prophecy made about the Messiah. After Jesus finished His work on the cross—bearing your sin and the sin of all humanity—I raised Him back to life. And I elevated Him above everything so that everyone would confess that He is Lord (Philippians 2:9–11).

Jesus was raised in a new, resurrected body. Then He ascended to heaven so He could be at my right hand, exalted for the sufferings that brought you and me together.

Right now, my Son is in my presence, in human form, representing you. And if that's not enough, He is also keeping the universe going by the power of His will (Colossians 1:16–17). My Son does all of this for you and for my glory.

*The Son is the radiance of God's glory
and the exact representation of his being,
sustaining all things by his powerful word.
After he had provided purification for sins,
he sat down at the right hand of the Majesty in heaven.*

HEBREWS 1:3

THE HOLY SPIRIT GAVE MY SON WISDOM

My Son accomplished the plan I authored
and the Holy Spirit applied.

Jesus existed before He took on human form, but my people didn't know Him. They should have known *about* Him, though, because the prophets wrote of some very specific qualities and characteristics of the one they knew as the coming Messiah. They knew what family He would come from, and they were aware that my Spirit would bestow on Him all the fullness of the Godhead.

According to the prophets, this "Branch" from David's royal family would have complete wisdom and understanding of all I asked Him to do. He would have the courage and power to carry out His work of redemption. And He would have complete knowledge of my glorious plan to save you—along with a determination to do my will.

This is why my Son was the perfect sacrifice for you. He was both willing and able to accomplish the plan I authored and the Holy Spirit applied.

A shoot will come up from the stump of Jesse;
from his roots a Branch will bear fruit.
The Spirit of the LORD will rest on him—
the Spirit of wisdom and understanding,
the Spirit of counsel and of might, the Spirit of the knowledge
and fear of the LORD—and he will delight in the fear of the LORD.
ISAIAH 11:1–3

DIRECT YOUR HEART TO MY WORD

You will do nothing of significance unless your heart is in it.

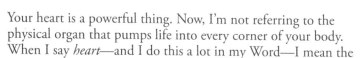

Your heart is a powerful thing. Now, I'm not referring to the physical organ that pumps life into every corner of your body. When I say *heart*—and I do this a lot in my Word—I mean the control center of your emotions and deepest desires.

Just as you carefully monitor your physical heart for optimum health, you must guard your spiritual heart, "for everything you do flows from it" (Proverbs 4:23). Simply put, you will do nothing of significance unless your heart is in it.

A wandering heart will lead to inappropriate thoughts, and inappropriate thoughts will inevitably lead to inappropriate behavior. That's why it is vital to turn your heart toward my Word. Where your heart looks, so will your eyes. Wherever your heart leans, so will your life.

> *Turn my heart toward your statutes*
> *and not toward selfish gain.*
> *Turn my eyes away from worthless things;*
> *preserve my life according to your word.*
> PSALM 119:36–37

MY VOICE TAKES MANY FORMS

Be ready to hear my voice in any number of ways.
Don't rule out anything.

The most common way you will hear my voice is through my Word. But there will be times when I use other means to instruct, comfort, correct, and encourage you.

I may use a mature and wise believer to give you counsel—and this person doesn't even need to talk to you directly. You could read something in a book or a blog, listen to a recording, or hear a sermon—and something in your heart will awaken because of the insight of those words. You may not even know the person, but you'll feel as if he or she is talking to you personally. Listen. . . that could be my voice!

And then there are those unusual, perhaps once-in-a-lifetime, occurrences when I come speak out of the blue, using something so unusual that it hardly seems possible. Once in the Old Testament, I spoke to a man named Balaam through his *donkey*—because he refused to hear me in any other way. I'll use whatever means it takes.

As for you, don't *expect* me to talk to you in miraculous ways. But don't rule out any possibilities, either.

But he was rebuked for his wrongdoing by a donkey—
an animal without speech—
who spoke with a human voice
and restrained the prophet's madness.

2 PETER 2:16

LIKE A THIEF IN THE NIGHT

Until my Son returns, let your hope be displayed before everyone.

There's a big outcry these days against suffering, evil, and injustice—and why I don't do anything to stop them. Atheists like to say I don't exist, because a) an all-loving God would not allow suffering and evil, and b) an all-powerful God would be able to stop them. Even some of my own children are troubled by my apparent lack of interest in the bad things happening on earth.

Just because I haven't dealt with suffering and evil doesn't mean I don't want to. And it certainly doesn't mean I can't. As I've explained before, I am being patient, giving people more time to turn from their sinful ways.

I *am* going to deal with suffering and evil when my Son returns like a thief in the night. Until that happens—and you know it will—watch and pray. Live a pure and blameless life. And let your hope be displayed before everyone.

But the day of the Lord will come like a thief.
The heavens will disappear with a roar;
the elements will be destroyed by fire,
and the earth and everything done in it will be laid bare.

2 PETER 3:10

BE LIKE-MINDED

When it comes to essential beliefs about me, be like-minded.

You don't have to agree with your fellow believers all the time. But I want you to share the same core convictions.

Though everything in my Word is important for your life, not everything is essential for salvation. Genesis 1:1 *is* essential: you must believe that I am the Creator of the universe—or your faith has no basis in truth. You can't be my child if you don't believe in me as Creator. But it's not necessary to believe that I created the universe in a specific time period, whether six days or six billion years. The essential belief is *who* created; the nonessential belief is *how long* it took.

You're going to have healthy discussions over nonessential matters like the "how long" of creation. Diversity of opinion here is fine as long as you show love and respect for others in my family.

But when it comes to those essential beliefs that concern the truth about me, my Son, and my Holy Spirit—along with the means of your salvation and the return of Christ—you need to be like-minded.

Make my joy complete by being like-minded,
having the same love, being one in spirit and of one mind.
PHILIPPIANS 2:2

155

DO I EVER CHANGE MY MIND?

*In my character I do not change,
but I can change my mind because of my mercy.*

I have made it very clear in my Word that I do not change (see 1 Samuel 15:29 and James 1:17). Knowing this should give you confidence to trust me in the details of your life.

But does my unchanging nature mean I never change my mind? Not at all. Because my relationship with you is dynamic rather than deterministic, I do change my mind on occasion. It's never on a whim, but always in response to the prayers and pleas of those whose hearts align with mine.

Many times in scripture you'll read how I relented and did not bring a judgment against certain people. Moses humbly prayed on behalf of his people, and I changed my mind. Hezekiah sought my favor and I decided to withhold the disaster I had pronounced. Jonah learned that I sometimes relent from sending calamity.

Here's *your* takeaway: in my character I do not change. You can always depend on my faithfulness and love. But when it comes to impending judgment—when my people repent—I can change my mind because I am full of mercy.

*"I knew that you are a gracious and compassionate God,
slow to anger and abounding in love,
a God who relents from sending calamity."*

JONAH 4:2

JESUS KNOWS WHAT'S IN YOUR HEART

An intention of the heart is just as real as an action of the body.

As one of my human creations, you have many qualities and abilities that set you apart from other living creatures. You have a spiritual dimension that gives you a sense of me. You are self-aware and possess an internal moral compass. Of all living things, humans alone communicate with me. You are indeed special!

At the same time, there are certain things you *can't* do—even if you think otherwise. For example, it's impossible for you to know the true motives and inclinations of any other person, even your closest friend. You humans are very guarded when it comes to your hearts.

I, however, do know what's in the heart of every person—and so does my Son. Whatever hidden thoughts and intentions you have, whether you act on them or not, are known by Him. In fact, as far as Jesus is concerned, an intention of the heart is just as real as an action of the body. Knowing this, commit your heart to my Son. Lay before Him your fears and temptations, your dreams and desires—everything that makes you who you are.

But Jesus would not entrust himself to them, for he knew all people.
He did not need any testimony about mankind,
for he knew what was in each person.

JOHN 2:24–25

NO EXPIRATION DATE

Because Jesus conquered death for you,
there's no expiration date on your life.

Everything about your earthly existence has an expiration date.

Look at the labels on the food you purchase. There's a "Not Good After" warning on most items because they are perishable. Even so-called "permanent" things made by humans are susceptible to decay over time. And then there's your own life (and the lives of every living thing on the planet). Little by little everything is *dying*. That's part of the curse of humanity's sin over the earth.

And that's why your personal relationship with me is so amazing: because Jesus conquered death for you, there's *no* expiration date on your life. You will live forever with all three Persons of my Godhead: your heavenly Father, your blessed Savior, and your constant Comforter.

All that we are and everything we have ever done for you will last throughout eternity. I will always love you, the blood of Jesus will always cover you, and my eternal Spirit will always be with you.

How much more, then, will the blood of Christ,
who through the eternal Spirit offered himself unblemished to God,
cleanse our consciences from acts that lead to death,
so that we may serve the living God!
HEBREWS 9:14

MY WORD GIVES YOU FREEDOM

My commands free you to live the way I desire you to live.

Do you want to experience true freedom? Of course you do, but you don't know how to find that apart from me. Before you met me and the two of us became friends, you were a slave. Not, of course, in the literal sense of being indentured against your will. No, you were a slave to something much worse: sin.

Before my Son paid the price to purchase your freedom from sin, you had no choice but to serve the desires of your sinful nature. You tried to escape on your own, but it was useless.

But because Jesus has redeemed you from sin's dominance, you have a new master and are now free to follow a new pattern for your life—a pattern I designed for your benefit and blessing. When you follow commands in my Word, you are able to explore every dimension of your freedom in Christ. My commands, far from restraining you, free you to live the way I desire you to live—and become the person I designed you to be.

I will keep on obeying your instructions forever and ever.
I will walk in freedom, for I have devoted myself
to your commandments.
PSALM 119:44–45 NLT

I CAN ALWAYS HEAR YOU, BUT SOMETIMES I DON'T

*When you harbor sin in your heart,
there is a barrier between us.*

This book is primarily about *you* listening to *me*. But let's swap places for a moment and consider this question: What about *me* hearing *you*?

Are you confident that I listen to you every time you call? Certainly, I always hear you when you pray, even when your heart is so heavy you don't know how to pray. I always hear you perfectly, and I especially delight in the prayers of the upright, who live before me with integrity and pure hearts. I am so taken with their prayers that I rush to answer, sometimes before they even ask (Isaiah 65:24).

But there are times when I do not *listen* to your prayers. When you harbor sin in your heart, there is a barrier between us—not a barrier to your salvation, but a barrier to your communication. The only way to remove this barrier and reopen the lines of communication is this: confess your sin to me. I will faithfully forgive you and restore to you the joy of your salvation (1 John 1:9).

*Surely the arm of the LORD is not too short to save,
nor his ear too dull to hear. But your iniquities have separated
you from your God; your sins have hidden his face from you,
so that he will not hear.*

ISAIAH 59:1–2

You Are the Light of the World

Before people shrouded in darkness can see my light,
they need to see yours.

Before my creation, before there was anything in the universe, there was emptiness and darkness. So it's no wonder my first command was meant to fill that void and dispel the darkness, making life possible: "Let there be light." The sun became the centerpiece of my creation, and it was good.

But it wasn't long before sin entered the world, bringing with it a *spiritual* darkness. The sun could never penetrate this blackness, but my *Son* did. He is the light of the world, giving life to all who believe in Him (John 1:4; 8:12).

Just as Jesus is *the* light, I am calling you to be light in the world, too. Through your life and your witness, the radiance of my glory—which shines fully through my Son—will likewise shine through you. Don't hide your light. When you have the chance to mention me, don't be shy. When you are tempted to conform to the world, let the light of Jesus brighten your actions instead. If you have an opportunity to dispel the darkness of misunderstanding, be a beacon of truth.

Before people shrouded in darkness can see my light, they need to see yours.

"You are the light of the world."
Matthew 5:14

DON'T SHOW FAVORITISM

At the foot of the cross, the ground is level.

Many practices can undermine the effectiveness of your church, but there's one so subtle it's often overlooked: favoritism. It may not sound so bad, but favoritism goes against everything I have taught you in my Word about loving your neighbor. Love makes no distinction between people, while favoritism singles out one person or group over another.

Listen! When my Son told you to love your neighbor, He meant you should reflect His love to *all* around you, not just those who are wealthier, better looking, or more socially connected. There is no difference between people. In Christ, all are worthy of my love and grace. At the foot of the cross, the ground is level.

I expect you to have this same attitude, especially when you gather with my family at church. Don't discriminate. Don't show favoritism. I want you to treat all people the way I have treated you.

My brothers and sisters,
believers in our glorious Lord Jesus Christ
must not show favoritism.
JAMES 2:1

KNOWING ME SHOULD BE YOUR HIGHEST GOAL

*There's another dimension to knowing me
that goes far beyond head knowledge.*

The most important thing for you is knowing me.

On the surface, this may seem a simple idea. After all, you "know me" in the sense that you know *about* me from reading my Word or hearing a preacher. That's good! I want you to learn all you can about me so your thoughts of me will be based on objective truth, rather than mere speculation.

But there's another dimension to knowing me that goes far beyond head knowledge. This dimension is where I want you to go. This should be your highest goal, a kind of knowing that is based on a deep, abiding trust. This only comes from repeated experience with me, when you have felt my presence and seen me work in your life.

What I desire—more than anything else—is for you and me to be so close that when you face a challenge or decision, an obstacle or opportunity, you will automatically think of me and trust me. These are the times when you truly *know* me.

*This is what the LORD says: . . . .
"Let the one who boasts boast about this:
that they have the understanding to know me,
that I am the LORD, who exercises kindness,
justice and righteousness on earth,
for in these I delight," declares the LORD.*

JEREMIAH 9:23–24

The Cost of Following My Son

*Have you made a decision to give Jesus
absolute preeminence in your life?*

A lot of people say they love my Son—but not all of them really
follow Him.

This is nothing new. When Jesus walked the earth, huge
crowds pursued Him. One time Jesus told a particularly large
group of people that they should put aside everything and everyone else—even their families—if they wanted to follow Him. Not
many were willing to do that then, nor are many willing to do that
today.

How about you? Are you just *saying* you follow my Son, or
have you made a conscious and heartfelt decision to give Him
absolute preeminence in your life? Before you answer, consider
the cost of what it truly means to be His follower: Jesus demands
you to put aside everything else in your life, even your dearest
ambitions and the people you love the most. He expects you to be
willing to give your life for Him—that's what He means when He
says, "Take up your cross."

This is no symbolic request. Jesus wants His followers to be
willing to pursue Him to the death. Are you willing to go that far?
That is the most important question you could ever ask yourself.

*Then he said to them all:
"Whoever wants to be my disciple must deny themselves
and take up their cross daily and follow me."*
Luke 9:23

HOW TO KNOW YOU'RE REALLY MY CHILD

*If the Holy Spirit is controlling your life,
you are my child.*

I know—sometimes you wonder if you are truly one of my children.

It's an important question to ask yourself, but it's also an easy one to answer. You can know for sure that you are my child if the Holy Spirit is controlling your life. How do you know that? Consider this: What do you think about all day? Are your thoughts dominated by selfish-ambition, pride, criticism, and lust? Is your life filled with turmoil rather than peace? If these things dominate your daily thinking, then you are being controlled by your sinful nature, not my Holy Spirit.

On the other hand, if your thoughts are focused on me and others, hoping for the best outcome in all situations; if you direct your ambitions to help others and advance my kingdom; if your heart is full of love rather than lust; and if you have a feeling of peace despite the pain in your life, then the Holy Spirit is controlling you, giving you the confidence you need to know you are my child.

*But you are not controlled by your sinful nature.
You are controlled by the Spirit if you have the
Spirit of God living in you.
(And remember that those who do not have the
Spirit of Christ living in them
do not belong to him at all.)*
ROMANS 8:9 NLT

THE COMFORT OF MY WORD

When you are anxious, remember my precious promises.

I know how easy it is for you to get discouraged. The cares and concerns of the world are many, and it may seem as if they're getting worse. When you suffer affliction or opposition, I understand your discouragement. But I don't want you to give up hope, which happens when you try to fix own your problems rather than trust my promises.

Here are two ways to shift your thinking away from your problems and toward my promises: First, remember my past faithfulness to you. My history with you is a great template for the future. Second, go to my Word—early and often. When you anxiously toss and turn at night, remember my precious promises. When you wake up in the morning, pierced with problems, let my Word bathe you in healing hope. Bookmark those verses that give you comfort in times of trouble. Commit them to memory so you can bring them to mind throughout the day. Trust me in this: my Word will comfort you.

*My comfort in my suffering is this: Your promise preserves my life. . . .
I remember, LORD, your ancient laws, and I find comfort in them.*

PSALM 119:50, 52

DO NOT MINIMIZE YOUR PAIN

I care about your hurts, no matter how insignificant they may seem.

With all the pain and suffering in the world, you may think your own problems don't amount to much. When you know someone battling cancer or grieving a death, you consider your own spiritual aches and pains rather insignificant. So rather than bringing all your needs to me, you hold some back, thinking I'm preoccupied with more important matters.

Listen: that is a completely wrong idea of the way I work. I'm not like corporate CEOs or national presidents, so focused on top-level problems that they have little time for mundane affairs. I am God! My capacity to deal with every single problem of every one of my children at every moment in time is infinite.

There's no priority system with me. You don't have to take a number and stand in line. You can tell me anything, no matter how small, and I will listen. So don't minimize your pain. Tell me what you need. Rather than keep yourself sick with worry, pour out your heart and give me your hurts. I care about them all, no matter how small.

*"They do not cry out to me from their hearts
but wail on their beds."*

HOSEA 7:14

I PUT GOVERNMENTS IN THEIR PLACE

When they work as they should,
governments are a blessing to all citizens.

My followers commonly criticize their government and its leaders—especially if the political party they support is not in the majority. If your criticism is constructive, leading those in authority to rule more fairly and with greater compassion, then by all means do what you can. But criticism is misplaced if it only undermines the authority of your leaders.

Whether or not you agree with those in authority, never forget that they would not be in power unless I allowed it. Government is my gift to you for your own good and safety. When it functions as it should, government is a blessing to all citizens. When certain leaders fall to corruption, it's because of the individual, not the office. So while you may oppose the politician, you must respect the position and obey the laws.

You may experience a time when the law forces you to disobey me. If that's in your lifetime, you must follow me above all else—and trust me to take care of you.

Let everyone be subject to the governing authorities,
for there is no authority except that which God has established.

ROMANS 13:1

SUBMIT TO YOUR SPIRITUAL LEADERS

*Your pastors and elders are not your bosses,
but they are your shepherds.*

I have put governmental leaders in place for your benefit and protection, but when it comes to your spiritual welfare, I've established a different structure of authority.

Many of my followers miss this important principle. They do well in submitting to civic laws and regulations, but when it comes to my church, they operate like they're completely autonomous, answerable to no one. Don't let this be true of you! When you become part of my church, I want you to submit to the spiritual leaders I have put in place.

Your pastors and elders have been called to lead you, and they are answerable to me for this, both for the truth of their message and the integrity of their character. Your pastors and elders are not your bosses, but they are your shepherds, entrusted by me to care for you in every dimension of your life.

Pray for them, encourage them, and submit to them so they can be more effective in their calling. And remember, when you submit to your spiritual leaders, you are submitting to me.

*Have confidence in your leaders and submit to their authority,
because they keep watch over you as those who must give an account.
Do this so that their work will be a joy, not a burden,
for that would be of no benefit to you.*

HEBREWS 13:17

LEARN TO HEAR MY VOICE

If you want me to speak to you,
slow down and make time to listen.

Most of the time nature praises me with wonder, majesty, and beauty. But sometimes the elements of earth roar with a fury that can unsettle even my most faithful followers—causing them to seek me in ways they never do when things are calm.

In the same way a major disaster gets people thinking about me, the storms of your life will have the same effect. When things are going well, you're inclined to ignore me. But when troubles come you are most interested in what I have to say.

The thing is, it's not my style to shout above the calamities of your life. It's much more likely that I'll come alongside you with a gentle, soft voice—and you won't be able to hear unless you are quietly paying attention.

If the turbulence in your life is caused by your own nervous activity, you may need to step off the treadmill to be able to hear my voice. If you want me to speak to you, slow down and make time to listen. Create space for me to work.

After the wind there was an earthquake,
but the LORD was not in the earthquake.
After the earthquake came a fire, but the LORD was not in the fire.
And after the fire came a gentle whisper.

1 KINGS 19:11–12

MY SON IS PLEADING FOR YOU

*Because of Jesus, you can come before my sacred throne
with boldness and assurance.*

Because I am in your corner, you have no reason to fear anything (Romans 8:31). There's nothing people can ever do to you, there's no disease that can ever defeat you, and there's not a disaster on earth that can destroy you—if I am on your side.

As if that were not enough to offer you a future and a hope, I went over the top to demonstrate my love and care for you: I gave up my Son for you. Jesus is the reason you can experience me personally, and because He is now at my right hand, you can literally stand in my presence through His saving life.

You see, Jesus saved you once and for all when He died for you, but His work didn't stop there. My Son continues to save you by pleading for you in my presence. Think of it! Jesus is referring to you by name, telling me that you are worthy of my love and loyalty. Because of Jesus, you can come before my sacred throne with boldness and assurance—not in your person, but in His (Hebrews 4:16).

Thank my Son for what He's done for you in the past, and for what He continues to do for you now.

*Who then will condemn us? No one—
for Christ Jesus died for us and was raised to life for us,
and he is sitting in the place of honor at
God's right hand, pleading for us.*
ROMANS 8:34 NLT

Week 24
Wednesday
The Holy Spirit

THE HOLY SPIRIT HELPS IN YOUR RELATIONSHIPS

*When you consider the options,
it should be clear which is the better way of life.*

When it comes to your relationships with your family, friends, neighbors, coworkers, and even strangers, there are two ways you can go: You can follow your old sinful nature and live in selfishness and occasional conniving, punctuated by a few random acts of kindness. Or you can live according to your new life in the Spirit—which means your life will be characterized by patience, kindness, and goodness.

Consider the difference when you're in charge versus when my Holy Spirit is in control—there's really no contest. In my Spirit, rather than being stingy with time and attention, you have a patient, generous attitude. Instead of dismissing others with unkind comments or thoughts, you deliberately treat people fairly—even when they're rude to you. And rather than ignoring people who irritate you, you go out of your way to help them.

Weighing the options, it should be clear which is the better way of life. So what are you waiting for? Ask the Holy Spirit to produce His fruit in your life and your relationships.

But the fruit of the Spirit is. . .patience, kindness, goodness.
Galatians 5:22 esv

MY WORD WILL GIVE YOU GOOD JUDGMENT

*If you lack judgment and wisdom,
all you have to do is ask, and I will help you.*

A sure sign of a mature person is good judgment. A child does silly, foolish things because of immaturity, but an adult is expected to be a skilled decision maker. What about you? Do you have good judgment, especially when it comes to spiritual matters? Some people are heroes in their profession because of business acumen or athletic abilities, but when it comes to spiritual discernment, how *wise* are they?

If you lack judgment and wisdom, all you have to do is ask— I will help you (James 1:5). I will arrange encounters with wise believers so you can see what spiritual maturity looks like. I will give you spiritual discernment through my Holy Spirit (1 Corinthians 2:14–15). Most often, I will speak to you through my Word, where you will find everything you need to develop spiritual judgment.

You don't have to remain spiritually immature, lacking wisdom and understanding. My Word is at your disposal.

---

*Teach me knowledge and good judgment,
for I trust your commands.*
PSALM 119:66

LIVE BY FAITH, NOT BY SIGHT

This is what faith is all about—
trusting me even when you can't see me.

Every person exercises faith every day.

When you drive your car down the highway, you have faith that the other drivers are going to obey the rules of the road. When you go to work, you have faith that your boss is going to pay you. If you want to live a normal life, you need faith—which is simply trusting others to do what they say they will do.

Just as you must have faith in the practical affairs of your life, you also need faith in your relationship with me. When you believe me by faith, you are in effect trusting me to do what I say I will do.

Really, even before you place faith in what I will do, you need faith to believe I actually exist. That was the case of Thomas, one of Jesus' twelve disciples, who wouldn't believe my Son had been raised from the dead until he saw the evidence. Jesus graciously accommodated Thomas, who believed on the spot.

You don't have the advantage Thomas had of seeing my Son in the flesh. That's why Jesus told him, "Because you have seen me, you have believed; blessed are those who have not seen and yet have believed" (John 20:29). This is what faith is all about—trusting me even when you can't see.

For we live by faith, not by sight.
2 CORINTHIANS 5:7

DON'T GET TIRED OF DOING GOOD

When you do good, I'm the only one you need to impress.

Here's something I want you never to forget: I saved you to do good works (Ephesians 2:10). Notice I didn't say, "I saved you *by* good works." As good as you think you are, you fall far short—even on your best day—of my perfect standard. But that doesn't mean you aren't any good. You were made in my image, remember? It's just that that goodness has been corrupted by sin.

When you agree with me—that you need my help to be truly good—I save you because of your faith in Jesus. Then you have both the ability and the freedom to do good things for me. Now, listen: I didn't save you just so you could be with me in heaven. I saved you so you could also do good on earth.

Doing good has its own rewards, but you may be discouraged when you don't get the thanks or recognition you think you deserve. Don't worry about that. I'm the only one you need to impress, and you can count on me to recognize your good deeds at the appropriate time.

Let us not become weary in doing good,
for at the proper time we will reap a harvest if we do not give up.
GALATIANS 6:9

PREACH MY WORD

People don't just want head knowledge.
They want to hear from your heart.

Today I want to talk with pastors and teachers—though everyone else can listen in, too.

Some of you have a calling to preach and teach my Word in a church. Some are Bible study leaders for small home groups, some are teachers entrusted by ministries with educating others in my Word. Whenever you open the scripture for others, you are taking on a serious responsibility—which is why it's important to follow a few basic guidelines.

First, always be prepared. Spend time in my Word yourself before you teach it to others. Let the passage you're using for your sermon or Bible study seep into your own life so it becomes a part of you. People don't want just head knowledge from you; they can get that online or from a book. Students of my Word are hungry for authentic teaching that comes from your heart.

Second, a tougher one—don't sugarcoat my Word. If the text calls people to change their ways (and it usually does), tell it like it is.

Finally, don't put yourself above your students. You are their guide, not their taskmaster. Come alongside them with encouragement and love.

Preach the word; be prepared in season and out of season;
correct, rebuke and encourage—with great patience
and careful instruction.

2 TIMOTHY 4:2

I LOVE YOU BUT I DON'T NEED YOU

Though I don't need you, I love you for who you are—
not for what you can do for me.

Many people have certain ideas about me, ideas that may or may not correspond to reality. For example, you may see me as a God who loves you so much I was willing to give up my only Son so we could have a personal relationship. That is absolutely true. But if you also see me as a God who needs love in return—who needs to be worshipped and glorified—that is absolutely *not* the way it is. I do want you to love me, and I do want you to glorify me. But that's for *your* benefit, not mine.

Because I am God, I am the first of everything. Nothing caused me and nothing came before me. I was the one who brought everything into existence, and everything exists now because of me. Think about that: when it comes to our relationship, I don't *need* you—but I love you for who you are, not for what you can do for me.

Honestly, that should make you appreciate me even more. I don't need you and I don't have to love you, but I do. . .more than you'll ever know.

"The God who made the world and everything in it. . .
is not served by human hands, as if he needed anything.
Rather, he himself gives everyone life and breath and everything else."
ACTS 17:24–25

MY SON IS YOUR ADVOCATE

My Son and I are talking about you in my heavenly throne room, and it's all good!

Under the Old Testament's rules, my priest would come before me once a year to plead forgiveness of sins on behalf of my people. Animal sacrifices were offered in the earthly tabernacle as a symbol of purification. Aren't you glad *you* don't live under that system?

As the one and only High Priest, my Son pleaded forgiveness for your sins by offering His own perfect life on the cross. It was a once-and-for-all event that replaced the old system. No longer does an earthly priest ask me to forgive your sins. You *are* forgiven—and in my eyes, I see the perfection of my Son in your life.

But there's more: Jesus is in my presence right now, representing you and telling me your needs. In effect, He is your advocate, speaking to me in support of you.

This should give you an amazing confidence as you go through your day: you aren't alone. My Son and I are talking about you in my heavenly throne room, and it's all good!

For Christ did not enter a sanctuary made with human hands that was only a copy of the true one; he entered heaven itself, now to appear for us in God's presence.

HEBREWS 9:24

THE INSIDE FRUIT OF THE SPIRIT

This spiritual fruit is intended to nourish you from the inside out.

When you orient your life around my Holy Spirit, He reveals the full array of His spiritual produce, called "fruit." You don't get just *some* of these tasty character qualities—you get them all. These three are intended to nourish you from the inside out:

Faithfulness is different than faith. To be faithful means you "can be fully trusted" (Titus 2:10). You are a person of your word as well as a person of my Word.

Gentleness is a quality of those who manage their strength for the benefit of others, like a wild horse that's been tamed.

When you display *self-control* in your life, you are the master of your thoughts and actions. Really, the Holy Spirit is in control. Essentially, you and my Spirit operate with one mind and a single purpose—to honor me in all you do.

When these qualities well up from inside you, your actions and attitudes show the world that you are my child.

But the fruit of the Spirit is. . .faithfulness, gentleness and self-control.
GALATIANS 5:22–23

PUT YOUR HOPE IN MY WORD

*I want you to put your hope in my Word
as strongly as you are hoping for my return.*

You are living in difficult days. The pressures of your life, the concerns of the world, and the failure of leadership weigh on you. But remember that I am with you always, on this day and every day from this point forward. Whatever anxieties and cares you have, give them to me (1 Peter 5:7). If I know when a sparrow falls, you can be sure I know everything you're going through, down to the smallest detail.

I am aware you struggle with waiting for me to take care of your anxieties and cares. When you long for something of value, it seems like the payoff will never come. That's the way it is with the greatest reward of all—that day when I will dry every tear, heal every hurt, and make all things new again.

Until that day comes—and you know it will because I never break my promises—I want you to put your hope in my Word as strongly as you are hoping for my return. I'm not trying to deflect your hope, but simply redirect it to the assurances and instructions I have written for you. If you can do this, your circumstances will never undermine your confidence—and you will have the hope you seek.

*My soul faints with longing for your salvation,
but I have put my hope in your word.*
PSALM 119:81

PERSISTENT PRAYER

You can be a prayer warrior,
but it is not something you can do haphazardly.

Have you envied someone who was a "prayer warrior"?

The term is appropriate for a follower of mine who has developed his or her prayer life to a greater degree than most others. A warrior shows great energy, courage, and persistence in battle, and that's exactly what prayer warriors do. They know all believers are facing spiritual warfare, so they pray with great energy, courage, and persistence.

You can be a prayer warrior, but it is not something you can do haphazardly. Praying with effectiveness and power takes a commitment to do my will. It takes a desire to develop your relationship with me to such an extent that you know my heart.

When your prayers seem weak and ineffective, it's because your faith is weak and ineffective, too. Prayer warriors express the desire that my perfect will is done in their lives, whatever their own preferences might be. And they continue to pray even when it seems I am not responding—knowing that I *will* answer at the appropriate time, in a way that far exceeds their expectations.

The prayer of a righteous person is powerful and effective.
JAMES 5:16

YOU ARE A PRIEST

My Son calls you to be a priest by representing Him to others.

I've already mentioned priests and the office of the priesthood. In the Old Testament, priests represented the people before me because the people couldn't approach me directly. When my Son continued the office, He became the ultimate Priest by His victory on the cross. Because His representation is perfect, once-and-for-all, and eternally satisfying, you can come directly into my presence without fear (Hebrews 4:16).

But that's not the end of it. Now that my Son, the High Priest, is in heaven with me, continuing to represent you, He wants you to return the favor. That's right—when you trust Jesus by faith to be your perfect representative, He invites you to join Him in His priestly work. In effect, my Son calls you to be a priest by representing Him to others.

This shouldn't surprise you. The very fact that you are called a "Christian" implies that you identify with Christ. Take identification one step further and *represent* Christ—by telling everyone you meet how wonderful He is.

Your role as priest is already official in my eyes. Why not make it official in your life?

But you are a chosen people, a royal priesthood, a holy nation, God's special possession, that you may declare the praises of him who called you out of darkness into his wonderful light.

1 PETER 2:9

PURSUE GODLINESS

*Rather than giving in to greed and lust,
actively pursue godliness.*

As a member of the royal priesthood, and a representative of my Son to everyone you encounter, you have a special responsibility to act in a way that sets you apart from the world. Just as you expect your church leaders to live with integrity and faithfulness to their call, I expect *you* to live in a manner that shows the world you belong to me.

People are often trapped by their own foolish desires, especially when it comes to money, sex, and power. As for you, I want you to run from these things—and run like you mean it! Rather than giving in to greed and lust, actively pursue godliness. In other words, be very intentional about being like the Person you represent.

Don't whine in the tough times—show the world that you are depending on me to get you through. When others criticize you for choosing faithfulness to me over the world's standards, be kind and gentle in your words and actions. Your faith should be vibrant as you demonstrate your love for others and for me.

*Pursue righteousness and a godly life,
along with faith, love, perseverance, and gentleness.*
1 TIMOTHY 6:11 NLT

NOTHING IS TOO HARD FOR ME

*All the power needed to do what I want
rest in my own infinite being.*

My child, when you feel weak and inadequate, when you slip into times of discouragement and disillusionment, when there's nothing you can do to lift yourself out of the pit, remember this: I am almighty God. I created the heavens and the earth and I keep all of nature in perfect balance for your benefit. Many people look to the vastness and beauty of creation as the ultimate power, but they should be looking at me.

All power in the universe is at my command. I direct the courses of planets, while at the same time paying close attention to the affairs of humanity—from the poorest peasant to the richest king. And you know what? I do it all effortlessly.

Because I am self-sufficient, I depend on nothing for my strength. And my power never diminishes. All the power needed to do what I want rests in my own infinite being. Nothing is too hard for me!

When you pray, communing with me, you are intimately connecting with almighty God. There's nothing I can't do—and there's nothing you can't do with me.

*"Ah, Sovereign LORD, you have made the heavens and the earth
by your great power and outstretched arm.
Nothing is too hard for you."*
JEREMIAH 32:17

JESUS WANTS YOUR BURDENS

My Son will help you shoulder your load.
He invites you to rest in His loving arms.

Sometimes you find it difficult to identify with my awesome power. My greatness and my infinite strength are beyond measure, impossible for you to fully comprehend. As a result, like you're forgetting the power of the sun when it's hidden behind the clouds, you often overlook me. You don't always remember that my power is there for you. But it is.

So when you find yourself under the weight of too many burdens, when you crave just a little relief from the pressures you feel, look to my Son. He has all my power, but He expresses that might gently.

Through Jesus, you have my infinite power at your disposal. But if all you need right now is a little rest from the weariness of your day, my Son will help you shoulder your load. He invites you to rest in His loving arms.

Jesus has already emptied Himself on your behalf. Don't you think He's more than willing to exchange His strength for your weakness? Just give your burdens to Him.

"Come to me, all you who are weary
and burdened, and I will give you rest.
Take my yoke upon you and learn from me,
for I am gentle and humble in heart,
and you will find rest for your souls.
For my yoke is easy and my burden is light."
MATTHEW 11:28–30

I HAVE PUT A NEW SPIRIT IN YOU

This new life of yours is not like your life before,
thanks to the Holy Spirit.

When you surrender your life to me, something truly miraculous happens. You aren't just a conquered person with a new master. When my Son redeems you from the slave market of sin, you become a new person because I literally regenerate you. That means I make alive what had been dead, by exchanging your earthly, corrupted spirit with my heavenly, incorruptible Holy Spirit.

In your natural, human state, you are inclined to rebel against me. Really, you once viewed me as your enemy. But not after the Holy Spirit makes you into a new person (2 Corinthians 5:17). You now have a new heart and a new way of thinking. Rather than wanting to pursue sin, you have a desire to follow me.

This new life of yours is not like your life before. In every dimension of your being—spiritually, emotionally, mentally, even physically—you are different, thanks to the Holy Spirit.

"I will give you a new heart and put a new spirit in you;
I will remove from you your heart of stone
and give you a heart of flesh.
And I will put my Spirit in you and move you
to follow my decrees and be careful to keep my laws."

EZEKIEL 36:26–27

MY WORD GIVES YOU LIFE

*Each morning, wake up with a spiritual appetite
that only my Word can satisfy.*

Reading my Word is nothing like reading an ordinary book. Oh, the words and pages may look like other volumes. In fact, my Word may be so familiar to you that you take it for granted. Some of my children go days, sometimes weeks, without feasting on my Word. I am disappointed when you ignore me like this, but not for any effect it has on me. I'm saddened by the harm and hurt it does to *you*.

When you don't take in my Word each day, it's like a hungry man forgetting to eat. When that hungry man does take physical nourishment, he'll reap the benefits. So it is with you and the nourishment of my Word.

Each morning, you should wake up with a spiritual appetite that only my Word can satisfy. Once you've eaten, remember how good it tastes. The more you feast at the table of my Word, the more you'll realize how delicious and satisfying it is.

*I will never forget your precepts,
for by them you have preserved my life.
Save me, for I am yours; I have sought out your precepts.*
PSALM 119:93–94

I'M LOOKING FOR A FEW GOOD PEOPLE

*I'm looking for those who are willing
to step up and serve me without equivocation.*

My child, let me tell you how I am building and populating my kingdom.

Many people have the impression that I am desperate for new recruits—so I let in anybody without qualification. While it's true that no one has a strong enough resume to satisfy my entrance requirement (nothing short of perfection will do), Jesus covers my expectations completely. That's why you need Him to replace your blemished record with His perfect one.

Because of my Son, whoever wants to enter into my eternal kingdom may. But when it comes to finding those people who want to serve me with completely committed hearts, I get pretty selective. I'm looking for those who are ready to follow me without equivocation—people like the prophet Isaiah, who responded to my question, "Whom shall I send?" by responding immediately, "Here I am. Send me!" (Isaiah 6:8).

My eyes will not rest until I find such people. I will search the entire world for them. Are you are such a person?

*"For the eyes of the Lord range throughout the earth
to strengthen those whose hearts are fully committed to him."*

2 CHRONICLES 16:9

PUT ON MY ARMOR

Don't go into battle unprotected.
You don't stand a chance on your own.

I am God and above me there is no other. There is no one strong enough to offset my goodness.

Satan is completely wicked and very powerful—but He is no match for me. Though he tries with all the force and fury he can muster, he can never win. In fact, he's already been defeated by my Son's death on the cross.

Satan's final doom is fixed and sealed. But until that day comes, he is your biggest enemy, roaming the earth, looking for victims to devour (1 Peter 5:8). He has marshaled his demonic forces in an all-out assault against the entire world population. He's confusing those who have not yet found me, and he's constantly tempting and accusing my children. So strong are Satan's schemes that you can rightfully say you are in a full-blown war with the powers of darkness.

Because I love you, nothing can separate you from me. But you need to protect yourself from Satan's assaults. How? Put on my armor, custom designed by me for your safety and success. Don't go into battle unprotected. You don't stand a chance on your own.

Finally, be strong in the Lord and in his mighty power.
Put on the full armor of God, so that you can take your stand
against the devil's schemes.
EPHESIANS 6:10–11

I Love to Call People Out

I have called you out of the world,
away from sin and into my grace.

You know it: for my followers, living in the world is challenging.

Physically, the world is a beautiful place, perfectly suited for humans to flourish. But spiritually, the world presents an array of temptations and wicked scenarios that can discourage even the strongest of my children. That's why I've always been in the business of calling people *out* of the world and *into* my family. Rather than feeling scattered and isolated in a world that hates them, my children have the opportunity to gather together as my people and my church, where I will provide for them spiritually.

I called Noah and his family out of the world to be a remnant of righteousness (Genesis 6:5–8). I called Abraham out of the world to be the father of a new nation that would bless all people through my Son (Genesis 12:1–3). And now I have called *you* out of the world, away from sin and into my grace, to become an active member of the body of Christ.

"Assemble the people before me to hear my words
so that they may learn to revere me as long as they live in the land
and may teach them to their children."

Deuteronomy 4:10

I KNOW WHAT'S GOING ON

I know everything about you,
and my knowledge never works against you.

Theologians use the word *omniscience* to describe what I know. In a word, I know *everything*, and I don't mean just the things going on at any given moment. My omniscience means I know all that *can* be known about every possible thing, event, creature, person, or nation.

Not only do I know everything that has happened in the past, is happening now, or will ever happen in the future, I also know every contingency of everything that *could* have happened. I know every relationship and emotion, every mystery and secret, every detail of every scientific law, everything natural and supernatural, everything that is to be known about good and evil, heaven and hell.

Make no mistake: I know everything about you, too. Your deeds, thoughts, intentions, plans, dreams, desires, hopes, and fears. Yet my knowledge never works against you. Instead, it harmonizes with my love for you, so that I am constantly and faithfully thinking of ways to reward you when your heart and your actions are favorable to me.

"Great and mighty God, whose name is the LORD *Almighty,*
great are your purposes and mighty are your deeds.
Your eyes are open to the ways of all mankind; you reward each person
according to their conduct and as their deeds deserve."

JEREMIAH 32:18–19

WHY DID JESUS HAVE TO DIE?

The crucifixion of my Son wasn't a tragedy,
but a divinely designed plan.

The death of my Son on the cross has been a stumbling block for many people. Even the apostle Paul wrote "the message of the cross is foolishness to those who are perishing" (1 Corinthians 1:18). The world sees the crucifixion as pointless and unnecessary. Two thousand years ago, the cross was viewed as an execution tool for the vilest of criminals—not a messiah. Today the culture at large either ridicules the cross or sees it as a fashion accessory.

But that's not the way you see it. After you received my free gift of salvation, you saw the cross as a symbol of success. It was the pivotal event that allowed sinful humanity to be reconciled to me. The crucifixion of my Son wasn't a tragedy, but a divinely designed plan that satisfied my anger against sin.

Because of your sinful nature, there's nothing you could have ever done to save yourself. Jesus *had* to die in your place as a sacrifice for your sins. Because of Him, my anger was turned away from you, and the punishment you deserved was laid on Jesus. That made it possible for you and me to have a personal relationship, changing our former enmity into friendship.

For what the law was powerless to do
because it was weakened by the flesh,
God did by sending his own Son in the
likeness of sinful flesh to be a sin offering.
ROMANS 8:3

YOUR SPIRITUAL GUIDE

The Holy Spirit walks beside you to keep you in the center of my will.

Do you want to know my will for your life? The answer to that question depends on how you define my will.

If you're thinking of those big moments in your life—where you go to school, the kind of career you choose, the person you marry, the church you attend—then you're probably going to find my will somewhat elusive. Rarely do I give you clear and visible signs for such momentous decisions.

On the other hand, if you view my will more like a mystery novel—where clues are revealed progressively, a little bit here, a little bit there—then you're a lot closer to actually knowing what I want you to do. As much as you'd like to know my will for the big stuff in your life, it's much more a series of small revelations I give you as you walk with me daily, relying on my Holy Spirit as your guide.

"The Lord makes firm the steps of the one who delights in him," the psalmist wrote (Psalm 37:23). That's exactly what my Holy Spirit does: He walks beside you, using my Word, the wise comments of other believers, circumstances, and your own thoughts to keep you in the center of my will.

Since we live by the Spirit, let us keep in step with the Spirit.
GALATIANS 5:25

MY WORD IS SWEET

Every bit of my Word gets sweeter each time you taste it.

Throughout your life you have many teachers. Your parents taught you how to speak, how to perform basic tasks, and how to get along in a family. Your schoolteachers instructed you in the basics of reading, writing, math, and science. Teachers in your church open my Word and tell you about me.

But I am the best teacher you will ever have, because I am able to teach in ways that others cannot. Through my Spirit I can direct my truth to your mind, giving understanding of things you could never know on your own. And I incline your heart to have the will to obey what I say.

When my teaching sinks into your life, it becomes more than head knowledge. My Word becomes fixed in your heart so that your desires are aligned with my will. Over time, your inclination is to keep my commands automatically. As I am faithful to you, so you become faithful to me.

The words of the Bible become so valuable you can't get enough of them. You long to taste them, whether you're reading history, poetry, prophecy, or letters. Each word of each verse of each chapter of each book of my Word gets sweeter each time you taste it. My Word never gets old—it only gets better.

I have not departed from your laws,
for you yourself have taught me.
How sweet are your words to my taste,
sweeter than honey to my mouth!

PSALM 119:102–103

I WANT YOU BACK

I am willing to forgive you and welcome you back home.

How is your life going right now? Are you feeling close to me, or has something come between us?

The only thing that can interfere with our relationship is sin, which takes you off the path I designed for you. In fact, sin takes you in the opposite direction, completely away from me. It's never worth harboring sin. Though you are my child, your sin will keep us apart. Sin turns your back to me, and you shouldn't waste a second in doing an about-face.

I don't care who you are or what you've done—I want you back. Don't stay away from me because you're afraid of what I may do to you. Don't think your sin is so bad that I can't forgive you. Need I remind you that I love you completely?

There's no good you could do to make me love you more, and there's no bad you could do to make me love you less. If you are willing to ask forgiveness and return to me, I am willing to forgive you and welcome you back home.

Return to the LORD your God, for he is merciful and compassionate,
slow to get angry and filled with unfailing love.
He is eager to relent and not punish.

JOEL 2:13 NLT

YOUR SUIT OF ARMOR

I have already prepared an incredible suit
of spiritual armor for you to use.

You are in a spiritual battle, so you need spiritual armor and spiritual weapons. I have already prepared an incredible suit of spiritual armor for you to use. Here's an inventory of the different parts:

The *belt of truth* is the truth of my Word. A Roman soldier's leather belt was the foundation for the rest of his armor. So it is for you with my Word. The *breastplate of righteousness* is like the body armor that protects the vital organs from attack. Because of what my Son did for you on the cross, you are righteous before me, shielded from the assault of your adversary, the devil. The *gospel of peace* will keep you from stumbling, while the *shield of faith* will help you resist temptation. The *helmet of salvation* is your gift by my grace, and the *sword of the Spirit* is your one offensive weapon. This is my Word, which the Holy Spirit will help you understand. Then you can know all I've done for you and can stand strong in battle.

All you have to do is put it on and use every piece.

Therefore put on the full armor of God,
so that when the day of evil comes,
you may be able to stand your ground,
and after you have done everything, to stand.
EPHESIANS 6:13

I DON'T SHOW FAVORITISM

*It's one thing to say you're a Christian,
and quite another to act like it.*

Of all the religions in your world, Christianity is the only one that doesn't have entrance requirements. Many faiths ask you to follow strict guidelines to be included. If you want to go to heaven, you have to perform. Other religions prefer that you have a certain ethnic background. Still others are highly favorable to males.

I don't show favoritism of any kind. My Son exemplified this inclusiveness in His life and teaching. In Christ there are no ethnic, economic, or gender barriers. Anyone who calls on His name can become a Christian (Galatians 3:28).

Though I am generous with those who want to join my family, I do have expectations for my children. It doesn't matter who you are or where you came from, I treat you all the same. Once you put your faith in my Son and you identify yourself with Him, I expect you to live up to the family name.

It's one thing to *say* you're a Christian, and quite another to *act* like it. Pause for a moment and take inventory of your own life: Should I be pleased with the life you're living, or do you need to be more Christlike? Pray and ask me to help you do that.

*"I now realize how true it is that
God does not show favoritism
but accepts from every nation the one who
fears him and does what is right."*

ACTS 10:34–35

I AM THE ONLY WISE GOD

Come to me for wisdom rather than drinking from the world's well.

From a human perspective, the wise person is often seen as the one who is clever or shrewd. He or she sees opportunities others overlook. In this context, having wisdom is an advantage rather than a quality.

But from my perspective, this is the wisdom that comes from the world—and it is foolish when compared to my wisdom (1 Corinthians 1:20–21). That is why I want you to come to me for wisdom rather than drinking from the world's well. Worldly wisdom is tainted; mine is absolutely pure. The wisdom of the world is limited; mine is infinite.

Because I am everywhere and have complete knowledge, I can clearly see everything in your life. And I am able to help you map out a life plan that will leverage your best qualities for your good and my glory.

Though my wisdom is better than any "wisdom" the world can offer, my children often have trouble trusting it. That's because following my wisdom takes faith in what you can't see. I may walk you through some challenges before I reveal my opportunities. Stay with me. Trust me always to have your highest good in mind.

To the only wise God be glory forever through Jesus Christ!
ROMANS 16:27

WHY DID MY SON PERFORM MIRACLES?

Without His miracles, the teachings of Jesus are empty promises.

Many people respect Jesus as a wise teacher, but they snicker at the idea of His miracles. Often, those with the greatest education are the most troubled by my Son's supernatural acts.

What about you? Do you believe in my Son's miracles? Do you know why they're such an important part of His life and work? Furthermore, do you understand that without His miracles, Jesus really is nothing more than a wise teacher?

Every miracle my Son performed had a purpose. By healing the sick, giving sight to the blind, and restoring hearing to the deaf, Jesus fulfilled prophecy concerning the true Messiah. By commanding the wind and waves to be calm, He showed His authority over nature. When He cast out demons, my Son demonstrated His power over the supernatural world, including Satan.

Most importantly, His miracles proved that He had divine authority to forgive sins, something only I can do (Mark 2:7–11). That effectively proved that He was equal to me.

Jesus' teaching about love and salvation are compelling, but without His miracles, they are empty promises.

Say to those with fearful hearts,
"Be strong, do not fear;
your God will come.". . .
Then will the eyes of the blind be opened
and the ears of the deaf unstopped.

ISAIAH 35:4–5

GREATER IS THE ONE WHO IS IN YOU

*The Spirit of Christ in you is greater
than the spirit that is in the world.*

Spiritual warfare is all around you, and it's not just Satan and his demonic forces waging the battle. Satan can only be in one place at a time, and there are only so many demons—so he cleverly influences human beings to do his dirty work. These false prophets, false teachers, and self-proclaimed spiritual leaders are hard at work perpetrating a false gospel.

How do you recognize these people? Here is the most telling sign: If they insist that Jesus was only a man, without supernatural abilities or divine characteristics, they are false. If their goal is to bring Jesus down to your level and convince you that you don't need Him, they are against Christ.

Against this false teaching, you have the truth detector known as the Holy Spirit, who gives you the assurance that Jesus is everything He said He was. You can be absolutely sure of this: the Spirit of Christ in you is greater than the spirit that is in the world.

So be alert! Let your truth detector do His work, and remain steadfast in what you know to be true.

*You, dear children, are from God and have overcome them,
because the one who is in you is greater
than the one who is in the world.*

1 JOHN 4:4

MY WORD GIVES YOU HOPE

*My Word is a cure for your instability
and a depository for your hope.*

Nobody likes instability. Think of a simple table—it's unstable when one of its legs is wobbly. Set something on a table like that, and it isn't long before it collapses.

What about *people* who are unstable in their thinking? Like the table with the wobbly leg, the results are never good.

Instability happens when there's no firm foundation. Regarding opinions and beliefs about me, people who are not solidly grounded in my Word risk becoming unstable due to conflicting thoughts. For example, a person can have a desire to serve me while constantly thinking of things that dishonor or displease me. Such a person is double-minded—swinging back and forth between a desire to serve me and a desire for worldly pleasures.

When from time to time you see this unstable tendency in your life, hate it—because if it isn't corrected, it will be your undoing. To counter double-mindedness, pour my Word into your life. There is no better cure for instability and no more worthy depository for your hope.

*I hate double-minded people, but I love your law.
You are my refuge and my shield; I have put my hope in your word.*
PSALM 119:113–114

Ask Me for Wisdom

I will give you wisdom in generous amounts;
all you need to do is ask.

Everything about me is infinite—my power, my knowledge, my love, my grace, and my wisdom.

You don't have to ask for my love and grace—I've already given these to you in full measure. As for my knowledge, you are capable of knowing only so much this side of heaven. But my wisdom—now there's something I can give to you in generous amounts. All you need to do is ask, and I will give it to you.

I don't usually pass along wisdom in spectacular fashion, so don't expect angels at your door bearing heavenly revelations. But you can definitely expect to find wisdom in my Word—you'll just have to develop some good Bible study habits to unveil it. My Holy Spirit also gives you wisdom if you're just quiet enough to hear His voice.

At some point, everyone tries to make life work according to their own wisdom. It's far, far better to ask for mine. I won't be stingy, and I won't criticize you for mistakes you've made in the past.

If any of you lacks wisdom, you should ask God,
who gives generously to all without finding fault,
and it will be given to you.

James 1:5

IF YOU HELP THE HELPLESS, YOU ARE HELPING ME

The Holy Spirit knows all needs
and is anxious to show you where they are.

A lot of people talk about social justice these days, as if this is a new idea. The way some people glorify the concept, you'd think they consider it more important than me. It's not intentional, but it can easily happen when you don't keep your priorities in line.

Let me explain something very important: anything you put above me—or even alongside me—is an idol. Even a very noble endeavor, like feeding the poor or reducing human trafficking, becomes idolatrous if your focus on the activity supersedes your focus on me.

Don't get caught in this trap. When you're concerned about the injustice done to others (as you should be), simply respond to the leading of my Holy Spirit, who knows all needs and is anxious to show you where they are. Don't wait to join a team or travel around the world before showing mercy to the least of your brothers and sisters.

And remember this: the fewer people who know what you're doing, the better. Don't worry about getting credit. I am the only one who needs to know.

"The King will reply, 'Truly I tell you,
whatever you did for one of the least of these
brothers and sisters of mine, you did for me.' "
MATTHEW 25:40

BEAR ONE ANOTHER'S BURDENS

Use your gifts to help carry the burdens of those who have problems.

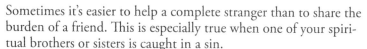

Sometimes it's easier to help a complete stranger than to share the burden of a friend. This is especially true when one of your spiritual brothers or sisters is caught in a sin.

Human beings tend to marginalize people who fail, especially if it's a moral failure. But I don't want you cut them off, even if they've sinned against you personally. My church is a place for healing, not hurting. The law of Christ requires you to do all you can to win back and restore a church member who strays (Matthew 18:15–17). Just be careful you don't fall prey to the same temptation in the process.

As a member of my Son's body of believers, you have been gifted in special ways by my Holy Spirit. Use those gifts to help carry the burdens of those who have troubles and problems. This includes people who have fallen into sin, but also those facing overwhelming obstacles in their lives.

And when *you're* the person who needs help, swallow your pride and allow other members of my family to help you.

Brothers and sisters, if someone is caught in a sin,
you who live by the Spirit should restore that person gently.
But watch yourselves, or you also may be tempted.
Carry each other's burdens, and in this way
you will fulfill the law of Christ.
GALATIANS 6:1–2

I AM ETERNAL

*I created time for your benefit,
yet I also made you for eternity.*

My child, today I want to stretch you once again.

This time, I'll take your thoughts that are fixed on your own mortal world to *my* reality that stretches from eternity past to eternity future. This will not be easy for you, but it's time well spent if you can dislodge yourself from your clock-and-calendar-oriented life to an existence with no boundaries.

Come with me to a place where there is no time—where eternity is like a piece of white canvas stretched infinitely in all directions. Time marks the creation of the universe and the beginning of your existence, but I dwell outside time. I live in the eternal now, with no past and no future. To me, the span of time from Genesis to Revelation is like one event, and I appear as Creator and Finisher simultaneously.

I created time for your benefit, yet I also made you for eternity. Time will continue endlessly when you join me in heaven, where the four living creatures sing, "Holy, holy, holy is the Lord God Almighty, who was, and is, and is to come" (Revelation 4:8). Contemplate these lofty thoughts, my child. Let them carry you to where I am at the edge of eternity.

*Before the mountains were born or you brought forth the whole world,
from everlasting to everlasting you are God.*

PSALM 90:2

JESUS BROKE SATAN'S POWER OVER YOU

*Where you were once Satan's slave to sin,
you are now completely free.*

———————❖———————

My Son shares my eternal nature, yet He made the ultimate sacrifice by leaving our eternal home to break into your world at just the right time to erase the power of Satan and death. The implications of His heroic life should never cease to amaze you. In fact, they should compel you to fall to your knees in worship, crying out, "Worthy is the Lamb, who was slain!" (Revelation 5:12).

By His death, my Son crushed Satan's head (Genesis 3:15), breaking Satan's murderous grip on your soul once and for all. By defeating Satan, Jesus also defeated death, the final enemy.

The realities of this victory are staggering. Where you were once Satan's slave to sin and a sure victim of death, you are now completely free. Your old master still thrashes like a snake whose head has been cut off—but it's only a matter of time before he lies motionless, and you stand triumphant beside your Savior and Lord.

———————❖———————

*Since the children have flesh and blood,
he too shared in their humanity
so that by his death he might break the power of him
who holds the power of death—
that is, the devil—and free those who all their lives
were held in slavery by their fear of death.*

HEBREWS 2:14–15

THE HOLY SPIRIT
DIRECTS YOU TO SERVE

You need always to be ready to hear a call from the Holy Spirit.

I've told you that the Holy Spirit consistently points you to Christ. Indeed, my Spirit is the presence of my Son in your life, reminding you constantly of His love, urging and helping you to imitate His life.

One way my Spirit does this is by directing you into specific Christian service. Now, don't confuse "Christian service" with "vocational ministry." Serving and glorifying my Son should not be a job—it's your joyful duty.

Here's an example of the Holy Spirit's direction: In the early church, some of my followers were seeking me through worship and fasting when the Holy Spirit prompted them to commission Barnabas and Saul (later called Paul) for service. As a team, they would take the Good News of Jesus to many towns and cities. On his own, Paul would spread the life-saving message throughout the known world.

You might not hear such a direct call from my Holy Spirit, but you need to be ready. A call certainly won't come if you're preoccupied elsewhere. It's when you seriously seek me that the Holy Spirit will direct you to do something extraordinary.

*While they were worshiping the Lord
and fasting, the Holy Spirit said,
"Set apart for me Barnabas and Saul for the
work to which I have called them."*

ACTS 13:2

MY WORD GIVES UNDERSTANDING

As you read the scriptures, let the words illuminate your life.

❖

I sincerely hope you stand in awe of my wonderful Word. No other book has such astonishing unity, though it was written by forty men over a period of sixteen hundred years.

Only I could have told such a magnificent story—the story of my creation and my love for you, of your rebellion toward me, and of my exquisite plan to bring you back home through the sacrifice of my Son. And don't forget the end of the book: He is coming back to take you home to a new heaven and a new earth.

My Word is my story, but it's your story, too. I am the author, Jesus is the theme, and you are part of the plot—because it was all written with you in mind.

When you read, study, memorize, and meditate on the scriptures, let the words illuminate your life. They'll enter through your eyes and flood your heart with the Holy Spirit's fire and light. Then, as you give it time and space, my Word will seep into every pore and fiber of your being, giving you understanding and ultimately emerging through your life for all to see.

❖

Your statutes are wonderful; therefore I obey them.
The unfolding of your words gives light;
it gives understanding to the simple.

PSALM 119:129–130

FALL IN LINE

How can I bless what you're doing
when my desire for you is to join what I'm doing?

So many of my followers want to go their own way, making their own plans without giving a thought to what *I* want to do with and through them.

Consider this, my child: you are free to live your life by doing good things for me. You can start a ministry designed to help people find me. You can go to school to become better equipped to teach my Word. You can join a team that spreads my compassion to the dark corners of the world. You are free to create films, write books, compose music, or lead worship—all of this is within your grasp. But unless you are working where I am working, you will not be completely satisfied in your soul.

Here's what I mean: You can do all these things for me, but what if I am working elsewhere? How can I bless what *you're* doing when my desire for you is to join what *I'm* doing?

Rather than focusing on your projects, lift your head and notice what I am doing—then fall in line. I love your passion and I approve of your talents, but if you're not on my path, you'll notice something is missing. I won't necessarily oppose you, but I may not bless you, either.

Consider what God has done:
Who can straighten what he has made crooked?
ECCLESIASTES 7:13

RESIST THE DEVIL

*Don't get into situations where you
are likely to be tempted to do wrong.*

Satan is a nasty character. Though he's already been defeated and knows his fate is sealed, he struggles and strains, using every weapon in his arsenal to attack, tempt, hinder, discourage, and accuse you. For those who are not my children, Satan tries to keep them from learning about my plan of salvation.

So how do you win when Satan is so strong? Here's my advice:

First, realize that Satan knows your weaknesses (1 Peter 5:8–9). He's not omniscient like I am, but he knows your past and will attack you where you are most vulnerable. Second, recognize that Satan is stronger than you (Acts 26:18). You can't conquer him in your own strength, so you need to rely on my supernatural power. Third, don't allow yourself to get into situations where you are likely to be tempted to do wrong. Resist the devil's schemes (James 4:7). Finally, use prayer and my Word to keep the devil from getting a foothold in your life (Ephesians 4:27). When my Son was tempted in the desert, He spoke my Word back to Satan, saying, "It is written." Follow His example.

*Submit yourselves, then, to God.
Resist the devil, and he will flee from you.*

JAMES 4:7

LOVE THOSE WHO OPPOSE YOU

Shock people—in a good way.

———◆———

Here's an idea for your church that will definitely get you noticed. It might even encourage some new people to visit, if for no other reason than to discover what's so different about you. My idea? Love your enemies.

Does your church have enemies? You might be surprised. What about your neighbors who seethe when the church grows and cars spill into the neighborhood as people seek places to park? How about your local government officials, who resent the fact that your church doesn't pay property taxes? What about that local atheist group who meet regularly for fellowship, but would never dream of meeting in a church building?

What if your church offered to meet some financial needs of its neighbors? What if your church made a contribution to a city or county agency that gives aid to the poor? What if you invited the local skeptics to meet in one of your rooms, then provided free refreshments with no strings attached?

What would happen? How would they respond? I know how I would respond. I would be very pleased.

———◆———

"But love your enemies, do good to them, and lend to them without expecting to get anything back."
LUKE 6:35

NATURE TELLS YOU MUCH ABOUT ME

The evidence of my existence is revealed all around you.

I know that placing your faith in me would be much easier if you could actually see me. But believe me, you couldn't handle that just yet. I have intentionally chosen not to reveal myself to you in visible form, in part because my invisibility helps strengthen your faith.

Though you can't see me, proof of my presence is all around you. I designed and fine-tuned the universe—everything in the natural world—to reveal my existence and my character to you.

All of creation proclaims my creativity and power. The expanse of the cosmos and the intricacies of the cells in your body attest to my strength and ability. Whether you use a telescope or a microscope, what you see demonstrates that a supernatural force (that's *me*) has intervened. People may choose to deny the truth, but my existence is obvious. Let the nature I created reassure you of my presence and power.

For since the creation of the world God's invisible qualities—
his eternal power and divine nature—have been clearly seen,
being understood from what has been made,
so that people are without excuse.
ROMANS 1:20

LOOK AT JESUS TO KNOW ME

I sent my Son to earth so you could know me better.

I am not a god who is aloof. I am not a god who keeps distance from his creation. I created you, and I love you, and I desire an intimate relationship with you.

While I know everything about you, you are not able to fully comprehend everything about me. Yet I want you to understand aspects of my character and my nature. That is one of the reasons I sent my Son, Jesus, to earth. Who I am was revealed by Him. To know Christ is to know me.

When you read of Christ's tender mercies, you are learning about me. When you read of His healing power, His passion for justice, and His condemnation of religious hypocrites, you are reading of my character as well. When you have a mental picture of the pain and agony of Christ on the cross, you are discovering the depth of my love for you.

I want you to know me better. That will happen as you know more about my Son.

We know also that the Son of God has come and has given us understanding, so that we may know him who is true.

1 JOHN 5:20

ALL OF MY POWER IS IN MY SPIRIT

The Holy Spirit is all-powerful and is my presence within you.

—————— ❖ ——————

Don't be frustrated in your attempt to understand the complex concept of the Trinity.

Really, there is no tangible example in nature that illustrates the three-in-one relationship of God the Father, Christ the Son, and the Holy Spirit. All analogies fail: the three parts of an egg (the white, the yolk, and the shell) each have a different composition; the three forms of water (liquid, vapor, and ice) have the same source but different characteristics. Not so with the members of the Trinity—we share identical attributes, character, and nature because we are one.

Instead of being perplexed, be reassured and comforted by this. The Holy Spirit who lives in my children is not some abbreviated, downsized version of me. He is *all* of me. With the Holy Spirit in your life, you have all of my power, all of my peace, and all of my wisdom as a resource. Allow my Spirit to have full rein in your life so that my complete nature is released in you.

—————— ❖ ——————

*The angel answered, "The Holy Spirit will come on you,
and the power of the Most High will overshadow you."*
LUKE 1:35

MY WORD TELLS YOU ABOUT YOURSELF

I will use it to bring correction into your life.

The voice of scripture is my voice. So, when the Bible speaks to your heart, that is me talking directly to you.

When I want to communicate with you, my Word is one of my favorite methods. Read it with the understanding that I'm the author—and with the expectation that I have a message to communicate to you.

Much of what you read in my Word is intended to instruct you about my nature and character. But you'll also find things intended to guide you in every aspect of your life. For your benefit, I want you to understand the parameters of godly living.

At times, you'll get off track and I'll use my words in scripture to redirect you. Sometimes it will be a word of encouragement, at other times a matter of a small correction. Occasionally, I might convict you over a major shift you need in your life.

At all times, remember that I tell you these things because I love you and want what is best for you.

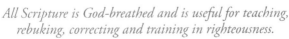

All Scripture is God-breathed and is useful for teaching,
rebuking, correcting and training in righteousness.
2 TIMOTHY 3:16

IT MATTERS WHAT YOU THINK ABOUT

Think about things that are pure and excellent.

You can avoid a lot of trouble in your life if you carefully screen what fills your mind.

Protecting your thought-life is essential because your actions and conduct are the direct result of what you think about. I want your mind focused on things that are godly, moral, noble, and upright, because better behavior will follow. Your words and actions will reflect those characteristics, honor me, and directly benefit you, your family, and your friends.

I'm not talking about a checklist of do's and don'ts. I want to you live in freedom from oppressive legalism. But you can't trust your instinct to "do what is right" if you've filled your mind with thoughts that are immoral, dishonest, and contrary to my nature.

Keep your thoughts on things that are pure, true, and wholesome, because that is the environment in which we can have the best dialogue with each other.

Finally, brothers and sisters, whatever is true,
whatever is noble, whatever is right,
whatever is pure, whatever is lovely, whatever is admirable—
if anything is excellent or praiseworthy—think about such things.
PHILIPPIANS 4:8

DON'T GET CAUGHT UP IN CULTURE'S MIND-SET

I have placed you in the world,
but don't conform to its way of thinking.

If you believe in me and become a child of mine, you have a new inner nature. I have redeemed you and rescued you from the slavery of sin.

You are now at odds with the rest of the world—all those people who do not aspire to a godly life. You will be pressured to fit into their mold, what they deem an "acceptable" life. But don't conform to the world's standard of living.

How can you resist the temptation and appeal of what the world offers? I'm glad you asked. You must always be engaged in the process of renewing your mind according to my teachings. Continually reprogram your way of thinking according to what is right and true.

Don't fall for the world's lies and distorted values. Instead, focus on my principles, those of eternal significance. As you become more familiar with this new way of thinking, the righteous life will become more instinctive to you.

Do not conform to the pattern of this world, but be transformed by the renewing of your mind. Then you will be able to test and approve what God's will is—his good, pleasing and perfect will.

ROMANS 12:2

LIVE IN UNITY WITH MY OTHER CHILDREN

*It is my desire that you live in unity
with your spiritual brothers and sisters.*

It is painful when a good father sees his children in conflict. He wants them to live in harmony with each other—for their own sakes and for the sake of the extended family.

I'm no different. I want to see my children getting along with each other, for their own sakes and for the welfare of the entire faith community.

So I want you to make every effort to live in unity with your fellow believers. You don't all have to think alike—I've given you varying personalities, talents, and spiritual gifts, so I expect some differences of opinion. But I want you to be unified in a commitment to love and honor each other. I want your relationships to be mutually respectful and to reflect the love of Christ.

When that happens, even as you navigate through your differences, your fellowship can be sweet. I will be honored, and your entire spiritual family will benefit.

Don't wait for someone else to take the lead. Step up and do your part now.

---

*How good and pleasant it is
when God's people live together in unity!*
PSALM 133:1

MY KNOWLEDGE IS BEYOND YOUR ABILITY TO UNDERSTAND

I know more about you than you know yourself.

There is nothing I don't know. I know everything that has been. I know everything that will be. I know all about the cosmos, and I know all about you. I hope you are awed by my omniscience, but don't be intimidated by it.

Never make the mistake of thinking that you can hide something from me. That just won't happen. And don't pretend to be someone you aren't. I know who you are—at the very core.

But, my dear child, always remember that I have *always* loved you, no matter what you have done or what you will yet do. I loved you before you were even born. You didn't lose my love when you failed in the past, and my love for you is not at risk if you fail in the future.

I know everything about you—even your innermost thoughts, the ones you can't even articulate. And still, my love for you prevails.

*Such knowledge is too wonderful for me,
too lofty for me to attain.*
PSALM 139:6

JESUS LIVED A BALANCED LIFE

*Faith in me does not require
that you ignore all other areas in your life.*

Consider what Jesus went through as a young adult, growing up as the Son of God. He knew His special divine mission, yet he lived as the oldest brother in a family of mundane circumstances.

I want you to realize that my Son grew up with a balanced life. Though He had a divine birthright, He went through the normal human growth processes—social, physical, and mental. Jesus was well liked and admired by those who knew Him, and He had my full favor.

While my Son was at all times fully devoted to me, He did not ignore the other aspects of His life. Rather, He allowed the spiritual dimension of his life to improve and flavor the social and intellectual components of His life. He was not pretentiously religious in a way that offended others. His relationship and commitment to me was lived in the context of a full and well-adjusted life.

May *your* life be the same. Allow my Holy Spirit, living in you, to make all the dimensions of your life balanced and Christlike.

*And as Jesus grew up, he increased in wisdom
and in favor with God and people.*
LUKE 2:52 TNIV

ALLOW THE HOLY SPIRIT TO BE ACTIVE IN YOUR LIFE

Don't let the work of the Holy Spirit be quenched.

My dear child, I have given the Holy Spirit to you as a gift. He dwells in each and every one of my believers, and He is me living in you.

But the Holy Spirit is a perfect gentleman. He will not force His will on you. Instead, He waits patiently for you to give Him access to your life. Then He sets about to help you flourish through His characteristics of love, joy, and peace.

You can, however, squelch what the Holy Spirit wants to accomplish in and through you. You can shut Him down by allowing sin to take root in your life. While He will never leave you, the Holy Spirit will take a step back if you consciously decide to pursue worldly desires instead of a life that honors and pleases me. You can also suppress the work of the Holy Spirit if you choose to disregard the spiritual gifts He brings into your life for ministering to others.

Don't let defiance or indifference limit the benefit of my Spirit being alive and active in your life.

Do not put out the Spirit's fire.
1 THESSALONIANS 5:19 TNIV

LEARN TO USE MY WORD CORRECTLY

Don't just read my Word; apply it.

I want you to build your life on my Word. But that will only happen when you build my Word *into* your life.

The power and truth of my Word is not revealed when you simply speed-read its pages. Please study it carefully, then meditate on what I say to you in those verses.

Go beyond the words themselves—search for the true meaning of the message. Don't select an interpretation of what *you* want my Word to say, so it conveniently fits your personal desires. Instead, pray that I will use my Holy Spirit to reveal the interpretation of what I actually intend to say to you.

After you finish reading, studying, and meditating on a passage, consider how the truth of the text applies to your life. What changes are you going to make in your life so that it conforms with what I've just said to you in my Word?

Do your best to present yourself to God as one approved,
a worker who does not need to be ashamed
and who correctly handles the word of truth.
2 TIMOTHY 2:15

BECOMING SPIRITUALLY MATURE IS A PROCESS

*Salvation happens in a moment,
but spiritual growth continues throughout your life.*

Your salvation is not the culmination of a spiritual life. It is just the beginning. Your commitment to be a fully devoted follower of mine starts a process of spiritual growth that should last the rest of your physical life.

Spiritual maturity isn't instantaneous. It involves baby steps and building blocks. The process involves studying my Word, finding support and encouragement from other believers, and following the guidance of my Holy Spirit in your life. Gradually you will find my nature and characteristics becoming more prominent in your life. Then begins an ascending spiral of godliness in your character.

You will never achieve perfection in your lifetime, but your life will become a partial reflection of *my* perfection.

*For this very reason, make every effort to add to your faith goodness;
and to goodness, knowledge; and to knowledge, self-control;
and to self-control, perseverance; and to perseverance, godliness;
and to godliness, mutual affection; and to mutual affection, love.
For if you possess these qualities in increasing measure,
they will keep you from being ineffective and unproductive
in your knowledge of our Lord Jesus Christ.*

2 PETER 1:5–8

DON'T TAKE REVENGE

Your goal should be to exhibit the character of my Son—
not to keep score of who did what to you.

You've heard the phrase "an eye for an eye." It's a principle that ensures that punishment is commensurate with a crime.

But you can let the civil authorities take care of criminal sanctions. On a personal level, I don't want you concerned with "getting even" or "settling the score" with *anyone* who does you wrong. Forget about plotting revenge—that will only cause hatred and bitterness to fester in your heart.

Here's the approach I want you to follow when someone has wronged you: forgive them and love them. Abandon all thoughts of revenge. I know, this doesn't come easily to you, and it doesn't feel natural. But that's because it's a supernatural response.

You'll need to rely on my Holy Spirit to guide your reactions and restrain your emotions. But a forgiving and loving response is the Christlike one. Your goal should be to exhibit the character of my Son—not to keep score of who did what to you.

"You have heard that it was said, 'Eye for eye, and tooth for tooth.'
But I tell you, do not resist an evil person. If anyone slaps you
on the right cheek, turn to them the other cheek also."

MATTHEW 5:38–39

Teach and Encourage One Another

*My Word should be used among believers
as a tool for spiritual growth.*

My divine design for your life assumes that you will be part of a faith community devoted to me. I never intended that you, as my child, would live alone, disconnected from a larger family of believers. I have a role for you to play in their lives, and conversely, I want to work through them in your life.

Together in community, I want all of you to use my Word to facilitate each other's spiritual growth. Use my Word to encourage each other in steps of spiritual maturity and godliness. At the same time, use my Word to guide and correct when someone is getting off course.

Don't be defensive when someone seeks to bring correction into your life, because I might be using him or her personally to deal with you. Likewise, check your own motives before you look to correct someone else. Be sure that I am prompting you.

*Let the message of Christ dwell among you richly
as you teach and admonish one another with all wisdom through
psalms, hymns, and songs from the Spirit,
singing to God with gratitude in your hearts.*

Colossians 3:16

CONTINUE TO GROW IN YOUR KNOWLEDGE OF ME

The more you know of me, the more you will love me.

You live in the tension of having a new spiritual nature, but of struggling against your former sinful nature. Although your salvation gives you victory over that old nature, I know the battle going on in your mind and body, of doing what you don't want to do, and failing to do those things you know you should (Romans 7:14–25).

You could call this "spiritual schizophrenia"—and the cure is to have a better and deeper understanding of who I am. When you grow in your knowledge of me, you'll have a deeper love for me, and you'll be more grateful for my love toward you. Instead of obeying me out of fear, guilt, or obligation, you'll be drawn to a joyful obedience that grows from an appreciation of my holiness and majesty. You'll *want* to live a righteous life, not because I demand it, but because you realize that that is an appropriate response for all I've done for you.

It only makes sense—you can't pursue godliness unless you have a knowledge of who I am and how I think.

Live a life worthy of the Lord and please him in every way:
bearing fruit in every good work, growing in the knowledge of God.
COLOSSIANS 1:10

JESUS HAD EMOTIONS

Your Savior knows and relates to your human condition.

In his earthly body, my Son, Jesus, was all God. And, at the same time, He was all human. Don't ask me how I arranged that—it's one of those divine mysteries that just can't be explained simply enough for human understanding.

It is enough for you to know that Jesus exhibited a range of human emotions. Not the sinful ones like jealousy, greed, and hatred, because He lived a sinless life. But the noble emotions, like passion, joy, and grief, were a definite part of His life.

Realize that your Savior was not some impersonal, unfeeling deity, putting in time on planet earth to fulfill some distasteful assignment. Quite the contrary. Jesus volunteered for the mission to leave my presence in heaven, take on human form, and die a torturous, sacrificial death for your redemption and the redemption of the entire human race.

Jesus' heart broke over the lost and sinful condition of humanity. He wept at the thought that many would reject Him. The entire story of Christ is emotional—and His greatest emotion was love.

As he approached Jerusalem and saw the city, he wept over it.
LUKE 19:41

THE HOLY SPIRIT GUIDES YOU INTO ALL TRUTH

The Spirit will illuminate for you the truth that Christ is my Son.

───────◆───────

My Holy Spirit is not flamboyant. Oh, He produces results that are spectacular and dramatic—but He doesn't draw attention to Himself. Instead, His role is to direct attention to my Son, Jesus Christ. The Spirit's most effective means of spotlighting Christ is to guide you and other believers into the truth that I have revealed myself in Jesus.

The tipping point in Christianity is the belief that Jesus Christ is my Son. In fact, Christ and I are one, so He was sinless and holy, as I am. Anything less than that and His death on the cross becomes meaningless. Your salvation is not possible.

You took a step of faith when you believed that Jesus was my Son and your Savior. But now that you are my child, I have commissioned the Holy Spirit who lives in you to confirm this truth to you. He will speak this truth to you as you read my Word and fellowship with me. My Holy Spirit will give you the confident assurance of the truth that Christ is Lord.

───────◆───────

*"But when he, the Spirit of truth, comes,
he will guide you into all the truth."*

JOHN 16:13

DON'T JUST LISTEN TO MY WORD—OBEY IT

Obedience to my Word is a valid indicator of your devotion to me.

Your commitment to me is not properly measured by the time you spend reading my Word. Don't get me wrong: I *want* you reading the scriptures. But when reading is nothing more than a visual exercise, the quantity of time spent is irrelevant, even useless. Yes, I want you to read my Word, but the true test of your devotion to me is the action you take on what you've read.

People who are content to "read only"—without any accompanying action or change in their lives—are fooling themselves. They can't be my true followers if they are indifferent to the commands in my Word, if they are impervious to the truth in scripture, and if there is no action to back up their proclamation of faith.

Never settle for being a *reader* of the Word. Follow your reading with action and obedience, so you'll be a *doer* of the Word.

Do not merely listen to the word,
and so deceive yourselves. Do what it says.
JAMES 1:22

LOVE ONE ANOTHER AS JESUS LOVES YOU

*Your love for other Christians
should have the characteristics of Christ's love for you.*

My Son told His disciples He was giving them a new commandment: "Love one another as I have loved you." Today, I want you to realize the dimensions of this command and what distinguishes it from the "love your neighbor" rule of the Old Testament.

The *new* part of Christ's charge was twofold. First, it is addressed to the love that my followers should have for *each other*. Jesus was talking specifically about the depth of your love toward other Christians. Secondly, He stated that you should love them in the manner that Christ has loved you.

My Son set the bar high. He loved you to the point of absolute self-sacrifice. And that is the degree of love I want *you* to display to my other children, your Christian brothers and sisters. Love in this degree will prove to the world that you are a follower of my Son.

*"A new command I give you: Love one another.
As I have loved you, so you must love one another.
By this everyone will know that you are my disciples,
if you love one another."*

JOHN 13:34–35

WALK HUMBLY WITH ME

What pleases me? It is really rather simple.

This may surprise you, but I'm not very interested in religion. So don't put on a big religious performance for my sake. I won't be impressed.

But I will be very pleased if you endeavor to walk humbly with me.

"Walking" means that we are traveling together, headed in the same direction. When we walk together, you proceed down the path of a godly life. While you will occasionally stumble on the way, we can remain in great conversation with each other. Our relationship will flourish as we walk together.

Your attitude should be one of humility. Have reverence and respect for the fact that I am God and you are not. Never be arrogant about your salvation, because you did nothing to earn it—you are saved by my grace. On the other hand, don't give in to self-contempt—you have value because I choose to love you.

Let's walk together today.

And what does the LORD require of you?
To act justly and to love mercy and to walk humbly with your God.
MICAH 6:8

REMEMBER MY SON AND WHAT HE DID FOR YOU

Communion commemorates the death of Christ on the cross.

I know you would never say it out loud. But there are times when you catch yourself thinking, *God, what have you done for me lately?*

Satan certainly plants thoughts like that in your mind, but your own forgetfulness and ingratitude can bring you to such a question without demonic prompting.

My love for you is without question. I allowed my Son to suffer a brutal death for your sake. I allowed Him who was holy to become sin so you could be saved from yours (2 Corinthians 5:21). I don't want you to forget my love. I don't want you to forget my Son's sacrifice.

That's why I tell you to commemorate Jesus' death and resurrection through communion. Do it to remember. And do it with a grateful heart.

The Lord Jesus, on the night he was betrayed, took bread,
and when he had given thanks, he broke it and said,
"This is my body, which is for you; do this in remembrance of me."
In the same way, after supper he took the cup, saying,
"This cup is the new covenant in my blood; do this,
whenever you drink it, in remembrance of me."

1 CORINTHIANS 11:23–25

I AM RIGHTEOUS

I am just and fair in all my dealings with everyone.

I know there are times when you read my Word and have questions—serious, heartfelt questions—about how I operate. You wonder about the people who lived and died without ever hearing of salvation through my Son: Have they missed a chance at eternal life? Is that fair? Or you see conduct and behavior condemned in my Word that seems entirely acceptable in your culture today. Is it fair to impose seemingly antiquated standards on your contemporary generation?

I know you'll have such heartfelt questions about my principles of sin and salvation. Deeper study of my Word will give you some answers, but some matters will remain a mystery as long as you live on this earth. For those, take comfort in the fact that I am righteous. I am just and fair and equitable in all my dealings and judgments. This is the natural expression of my holiness.

Though you may not understand all my ways, you can trust that they are fair and proper.

He did it to demonstrate his righteousness at the present time,
so as to be just and the one who justifies those who have faith in Jesus.
ROMANS 3:26

233

JESUS WAS WITHOUT SIN

That fact alone demands your attention—and your reverence of Him.

The Jewish religious leaders of Jesus' day hated Him. They wanted to discredit my Son by any means possible. Yet His greatest critics and archenemies could not point to a single sin in His life.

Of course, that came as no surprise to me, because like me, my Son was, is, and always will be sinless.

This sinlessness of Christ should have been a clue to those Jewish leaders that Jesus was exactly who He said He was—my Son. But their hearts were prejudiced against Him by their own self-interest.

How about you? How do you respond to my Son? Does His sinless life convince you of His deity? Doesn't that qualify Him to be a role model in your life? Does it give Him the credentials that make His teachings worthy of consideration?

Don't take a cavalier attitude toward Christ. He is the only Person ever to have lived without sin. That fact alone demands your attention—and your reverence of Him.

"Can any of you prove me guilty of sin?
If I am telling the truth, why don't you believe me?"
JOHN 8:46

THE HOLY SPIRIT CONVINCES YOU THAT YOU NEED ME

You were so lost in your sin
that it took my Spirit to snap you out of it.

What persuaded you of your need for a Savior?

I know exactly what it was. It wasn't a brainstorm on your part. It wasn't a great sermon you heard. It wasn't even a calamity in your life that brought you running to me. The bottom line is this: you were so lost in your sin that you couldn't even think straight about me.

But then my Holy Spirit set about His work to convince you of your sinfulness and need of me. He is the cause of your salvation. He convinced you of the disparity between your depravity and my righteousness.

Don't think you were spiritually perceptive to realize your need of me. You were rebelling against me until the Holy Spirit penetrated your life.

"When he comes, he will prove the world to be in the wrong
about sin and righteousness and judgment: about sin,
because people do not believe in me."
JOHN 16:8–9

DON'T BE FOOLED BY THOSE WHO TWIST THE TRUTH

If anyone is adding to or subtracting from my Word,
it is a distortion.

My Word contains all you need to know about me, about yourself, and about how to live in godliness (2 Peter 1:3). Now, I'm not saying you can disregard this Sunday's sermon as superfluous. Preachers and books can certainly assist you in understanding my Word. But I want you to guard against anyone who teaches a "gospel" that perverts the clear truth of my Word.

False teachers say what they say out of ignorance or selfish ambition. They claim "new revelations" or say that certain biblical principles no longer apply. When you hear these kind of teachings, run in the opposite direction.

You need to be perceptive in these matters. And the way to do that is to know and understand my Word. It's easy to spot counterfeit teaching when you are totally familiar with the genuine article.

I am astonished that you are so quickly deserting the one who
called you to live in the grace of Christ and are turning to a
different gospel—which is really no gospel at all.
Evidently some people are throwing you into confusion
and are trying to pervert the gospel of Christ.
GALATIANS 1:6–7

BE TRANSFORMED BY THE RENEWING OF YOUR MIND

Refresh your mind daily with my principles.

You're my child, so I want what's best for you. Sometimes that means telling you something you don't want to hear.

Here goes: you aren't tough enough to be godly while you live in the world. Your culture will eat you alive if you try to live a pure and righteous life without my supernatural help.

Living a Christlike life takes the continual renewal of your thinking. You must purge your mind of the world's attitudes and adopt *my* way of thinking. And I'm not talking about some annual thing—this must happen daily.

Each day, spend time in my Word and in conversation with me to transform your thoughts, attitudes, and actions. You won't succeed unless you learn to think and evaluate life from my perspective. Your personal transformation is dependent upon your mind's renewal.

Do not conform to the pattern of this world,
but be transformed by the renewing of your mind.
ROMANS 12:2

DON'T LOVE THE WORLD

You can't have it both ways.
If you love the world, then you don't love me.

I welcome your declaration of love for me—but I don't determine the authenticity of your love from your expressions. I can tell how you genuinely feel about me by examining your heart.

If I find you harboring a love for the ways of the world, then I know you aren't sold out for me. Loving me involves *despising* the sinfulness of the world. It's not enough that you abstain from the impure activities of the world if you still have affection for worldliness in your heart. Even those sinful cravings must be removed from your life. If you allow them to remain, it's a sign that you love the world more than you love me.

Love me and the things that are important to me. Purge your heart of anything that is contrary to my character.

Do not love the world or anything in the world.
If anyone loves the world, love for the Father is not in them.
1 JOHN 2:15

YOU HAVE BEEN GIVEN A SPIRITUAL GIFT

Discover it so you can use it for the benefit of others.

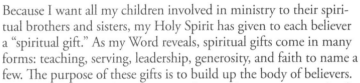

Because I want all my children involved in ministry to their spiritual brothers and sisters, my Holy Spirit has given to each believer a "spiritual gift." As my Word reveals, spiritual gifts come in many forms: teaching, serving, leadership, generosity, and faith to name a few. The purpose of these gifts is to build up the body of believers.

And I haven't left *you* out. You have at least one spiritual gift, a supernatural ability and sensitivity that will facilitate my ministry in some way. As with any gift, it would insult the giver if you ignored it and left it unwrapped. So work toward discovering your own gift.

Read in my Word the description of the spiritual gifts. Ask other believers if they have a sense of what your spiritual gift may be. Look for areas of ministry that appeal to you, because your gift will benefit others.

But don't worry about the power to engage your gift—that's what my Holy Spirit is for.

We have different gifts, according to the grace given to each of us.
ROMANS 12:6

YOU CAN KNOW ME, NOT JUST KNOW ABOUT ME

You have personal, firsthand knowledge of me.

There's a big difference between knowing *about* someone and actually *knowing* the person.

When you know about someone, you have secondhand information. A third party has relayed details to you; the facts may be true, exaggerated, or completely fabricated. You can't be sure if what you know *about* the person is reliable. But it's totally different when you actually, intimately *know* the person.

Many pontificate about me, but they speak from mere speculation. My dear child, you know so much more about me—and what you know is true—because you actually *know* me. You have no need to listen to pointless guesses about my nature and character. You know my attributes from personal experience. You are part of my proof of who I am.

And guess what? I know you. We can enjoy each other's company because we are not strangers. We are the heavenly Father and his spiritual child.

*I write to you, dear children,
because you know the Father.*

1 JOHN 2:14

BECAUSE HE WAS TEMPTED, JESUS CAN SYMPATHIZE WITH YOU

Christ can relate to your struggles because He endured them, too.

You do not have a Savior who is indifferent to your struggles. Though many kings have no idea what life is like for their subjects, Jesus will never dismiss or diminish the tension you feel living in a fallen world. He *knows* what it's like to be tempted by all the world has to offer.

In my Son, you have a Lord and Savior who understands your struggles. He can sympathize with your trials. He Himself withstood the full force of Satan's temptation, and He endured the agony and pain of the world's sin. There is no one better to seek in the time of your need.

Jesus is eager to comfort and minister to you. Tell Him about your hardships, not because He's unaware but because I want you to initiate the dialogue that will follow. In the context of that conversation, you will find peace, comfort, and guidance. He has gone through what you face now.

Because he himself suffered when he was tempted,
he is able to help those who are being tempted.
HEBREWS 2:18

THE HOLY SPIRIT
PRAYS ON YOUR BEHALF

When you don't know what to pray for,
the Holy Spirit steps in for you.

Parts of your life are easy, but a lot of it is tough—very tough. I hope you know that I'm eager for you to turn to me in prayer. But I know that you're sometimes reluctant to discuss your problems, even to me—because the turmoil in your life seems so overwhelming. You would pray if you could, but you can't—because you don't even know what to say. You want my will to be done, and you desire my help—but you lack the energy and focus to talk through the problems.

Don't despair, my child! Let the Holy Spirit pray to me on your behalf. The Holy Spirit knows the mess you are in. He knows my will for your circumstances. And He knows how to talk with me about it.

When you are beaten down, when you can do nothing more than utter a groan or a sigh, the Holy Spirit can articulate your feelings to me. Be confident that the Spirit and I work together on your behalf. Prayers are being spoken for you, and those prayers are in the process of being answered.

In the same way, the Spirit helps us in our weakness.
We do not know what we ought to pray for, but the Spirit himself
intercedes for us through wordless groans.
ROMANS 8:26

TEACH MY WORD TO YOUR CHILDREN

Make my commands a natural part of your daily conversations.

It pleases my when you read my Word. But I am even more delighted when my Word becomes an integral part of your life. I know that the principles of my Word—if made part of your daily routine—will provide you the basis for a righteous and godly life.

And I know that's the kind of life that you want for your own children.

So model the process by which that will happen. Don't make your time in study of my Word a private affair—make it a family event. Look for every opportunity to explain the principles of my Word in the context of your everyday activities. Let my precepts fill your conversations.

Do these things, and you will embed my Word in your children's hearts.

*These commandments that I give you today
are to be on your hearts. Impress them on your children.
Talk about them when you sit at home and when you walk
along the road, when you lie down and when you get up.*
DEUTERONOMY 6:6–7

NOTHING CAN SEPARATE YOU FROM MY LOVE

You can never go beyond the reach of my love.

Your life is filled with things that fail. Finances, relationships, health, jobs, marriages, plans—really, what can you count on? Only this: my love for you.

My love is eternal. I have loved you since before time began, and I will continue to love you for the rest of eternity.

Nothing can separate you from my love. It reaches far and wide, and you can never run beyond its reach. Its depth is unlimited—no matter how deeply you're buried by human troubles and sorrows, my love will be with you. No human can steal my love from you; no power of Satan can sever it. Not even *you*, by your own faults and failings, can cause me to withdraw my love.

My love for you is everlasting.

For I am convinced that neither death nor life,
neither angels nor demons,
neither the present nor the future, nor any powers,
neither height nor depth,
nor anything else in all creation, will be able to separate us
from the love of God that is in Christ Jesus our Lord.
ROMANS 8:38–39

GIVE TO THOSE IN NEED

Your giving should be characterized by generosity and humility.

Allow me to be very personal with you for a moment. I created you, so I feel I'm entitled.

Let's focus on your money: not on the portion you keep for yourself, but on the amount (and method by which) you give to the poor.

I have blessed you more than many others, and I want you to use your abundance for the sake of others in need. But when you do so, watch your motives. I want your giving to be truly charitable, which means that you're doing it for another person's welfare. Don't look for benefits in return, other than the joy of helping others. Charity that is pure and true does not care whether a gift is tax deductible, and it abhors publicity.

When you give help to the poor, it is as if you are giving to me. Let your charity be an act of worship. Do it enthusiastically, with bold generosity, and in humility.

"But when you give to the needy,
do not let your left hand
know what your right hand is doing,
so that your giving may be in secret."
MATTHEW 6:3–4

DON'T NEGLECT YOUR SPIRITUAL GIFT

Your spiritual gift doesn't benefit anyone if you fail to use it.

I have given each of my children at least one spiritual gift. This is a gift *to* you, but it is not solely a gift *for* you. All spiritual gifts are given for the purpose of building up the body of believers.

So you must realize that this is not a gift to be set on a shelf for periodic admiration like a trophy. You have a spiritual gift because I intend for you to use it. That means you must be engaged in ministry to others.

Obviously, there is learning involved. You'll try several different areas of ministry and service before you get a sense of exactly how I have gifted you. But I don't want you sitting on the sidelines, planning to use your gift only after you have fully researched all of its theological ramifications.

Really, I will only reveal the nature of your spiritual gift while you are in the midst of ministry. So get out there, get busy serving others—and your spiritual gift will be revealed.

Do not neglect your gift. . . . Be diligent in these matters;
give yourself wholly to them, so that everyone may see your progress.
1 TIMOTHY 4:14–15

I Do Not Change

I offer you stability that you can rely on.

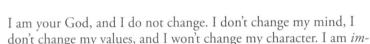

I am your God, and I do not change. I don't change my mind, I don't change my values, and I won't change my character. I am *immutable*—meaning that it is impossible for me to change.

Think about it: the nature of change is that it makes something better or worse. But I am perfect in all my ways, so there is no change that could improve me. My perfection prohibits a change that would diminish me.

My immutability benefits you. While, from time to time, you want a change of scenery, a change of diet, or a change of routine, change is not a good thing when it comes to the ruler of the universe. Know that I will never change the rules on you. I will never vacillate in my feelings for you, loving you today but rejecting you tomorrow.

My plan for the redemption of humanity, for the restoration of fellowship between me and my children, was set in place before the creation of the world—and it will remain the same for all eternity.

Every good and perfect gift is from above,
coming down from the Father of the heavenly lights,
who does not change like shifting shadows.

JAMES 1:17

JESUS IS THE MEDIATOR BETWEEN YOU AND ME

He is the only one who can bridge the gap that divides us.

A chasm exists between humanity and me. It is an abyss as wide as eternity is long. It is a separation that finds me in my holiness on one side, and humanity in its sinfulness on the other.

There is only one Person who can bridge that rift. There is only one who can serve as a master mediator and resolve the sin-caused conflict that divides us. Peace and fellowship between us is only possible through my Son, the God-man Jesus, who shares my holiness and who bore the death penalty for humanity's sinfulness.

I loved you in your sinful condition, but an intimate fellowship between us is only possible through the work of Christ. He is the one who has brought us together. And for that reason, He deserves your love and devotion.

*For there is one God and one mediator
between God and mankind, the man Christ Jesus.*
1 TIMOTHY 2:5

YOU CAN RESIST THE HOLY SPIRIT

When you reject the guidance of the Holy Spirit,
you are ignoring me.

There are many ways that I choose to communicate with you—through nature, through my Word, through the counsel of other believers. But the most direct and clear line of communication between us is when my Holy Spirit speaks to bring guidance, correction, encouragement, and comfort to your life. When you feel Him in your heart or sense His presence in your thoughts, that's me speaking to you.

Remember this arrangement the next time you sense my Holy Spirit prompting you—but your inclination is to ignore it. You are certainly free to disregard the guidance of the Holy Spirit in your life. But when you resist Him, you are rejecting my efforts to transform and improve you from the inside out. I am set on guiding you to a godly and righteous life, and my Holy Spirit is the change agent for this assignment.

Don't give in to the temptation to resist my Spirit's efforts. Instead, follow His leading—it will inevitably deepen the fellowship between you and me.

"You stiff-necked people! Your hearts and ears are still uncircumcised.
You are just like your ancestors: You always resist the Holy Spirit!"

ACTS 7:51

MY WORD WILL GIVE YOU COUNSEL

Your resource for instruction in the godly life is my Word.

I am giving you an assignment. It's the same as the one I gave to the disciples who came before you and to the children of Israel who came before them: I am instructing you to live a pure and righteous life in the midst of a fallen and depraved world.

Is that possible? Yes.

Is it easy? No.

How can it be accomplished? By following the precepts in my Word.

Meditate on my Word until it saturates the fiber of your being. Allow its wisdom and instruction to penetrate your mind and your heart. Conform your life to its commands. Recall its comfort in times of trouble. Rejoice in its description of my attributes. Above all else, read it as if it is my personal message to you about my plan of redemption and restoration—because that is exactly what it is.

How can a young person stay on the path of purity?
By living according to your word. I seek you with all my heart;
do not let me stray from your commands. I have hidden your word in
my heart that I might not sin against you.

PSALM 119:9–11

REJOICE IN YOUR SUFFERINGS

I have the perspective that sees the benefit of it all.

You've already learned this: I will not spare you from suffering just because you are my child. In fact, some of the suffering and tribulation in your life is *because* you are my child.

When you're in the middle of struggles, it's difficult for you to see any advantage to them. But let me reassure you that there is a spiritual benefit when you go through difficult things.

Your crisis will cause you to rely on me in deeper ways. You will find that *my* strength allows you to endure the hardship. The ability to persevere under pressure refines your character in many respects, developing the patience to live according to my time-table. Your patience will then allow you to trust me, and your confidence in my control will give you hope in the future.

So don't despair in suffering. Rejoice in it, because it is evidence that I am alive and active in your life.

Not only so, but we also glory in our sufferings,
because we know that suffering produces perseverance;
perseverance, character; and character, hope.

ROMANS 5:3–4

THE WORLD HATED JESUS, SO IT'S GOING TO HATE YOU, TOO

Your devotion to my principles makes you the enemy of the world.

You won't win any of the world's popularity contests if you claim allegiance to my Son. Face it: being a follower of Christ puts you at odds with others in the world. They have a different value system; they live for themselves according to beliefs that contradict mine.

So for you to follow my Son and His teachings, you are expressly rejecting all that the world stands for. And you are viewed as a threat who seeks to undermine the world's philosophies by proclaiming my Gospel.

Don't worry about the animosity the world has toward you. Whatever flack you take for your faith, remember that my Son was hated more. He endured hatred to the point of the cross, all the while *loving* those who persecuted Him.

Follow Jesus' example. Respond to personal attacks in a Christlike manner. Let others see Christ's character in you.

Understand that their hostility is not really directed at you. They are opposing me because they don't want to submit to my sovereignty.

"I have given them your word and the world has hated them, for they are not of the world any more than I am of the world."

JOHN 17:14

BE ONE WITH EACH OTHER AS I AM ONE WITH CHRIST

As I love my Son, so you should love each other.

You and the rest of my children are a diverse group: of different nationalities, different cultures, and different styles of worshipping me. And that's speaking from a global perspective. On the local level—in your own church—there is also diversity: different age groups, different personalities, and different opinions about worship styles.

I know these differences create a challenge for my children to live in harmony with each other. But I desire it nonetheless. In fact, I have high expectations in this regard. I want all of you to live in the same unity and harmony I share with my Son.

There is no greater degree of mutual love than is shared between me and Jesus. Together, we are one. And that same kind of love and respect I want you to have with your spiritual brothers and sisters.

Don't just tolerate others, love them. Love them with the love that I have for my Son.

"I will remain in the world no longer, but they are still
in the world, and I am coming to you. Holy Father,
protect them by the power of your name, the name you gave me,
so that they may be one as we are one."
JOHN 17:11

I OWN EVERYTHING

Everything in creation belongs to me.

———————◆———————

My dear child, please remember that I created all things. The undeniable consequence of this fact is that everything belongs to me. I own the innumerable cattle on earth, and I own the countless hills on which they graze (Psalm 50:10). Everything under heaven is mine (Job 41:11). And to make this personal, everything you have is a gift from me.

Because I own everything, I have the ability to give you anything—or everything. But that would not be good for you.

So when you're tempted to worry about your finances, simply rest in the comfort of knowing that I have the ability and resources to provide everything you need. When you're enjoying financial blessings, don't be prideful and think your accumulation is the result of your own effort—instead, be grateful and acknowledge the source of all you have.

And whatever your situation, be generous to others. I want what I own to be used through you for my glory.

———————◆———————

*Yours, LORD, is the greatness and the power
and the glory and the majesty and the splendor,
for everything in heaven and earth is yours.*

1 CHRONICLES 29:11

JESUS IS THE ONLY WAY TO ME

There is only one way,
but it is available to everyone.

My Son was absolutely correct when He said that He is "*the* way" for humanity to connect with me. Notice that He is not merely one of multiple ways for people to reach me. No, He is the *one and only* way to me.

Don't be deceived into believing that a single way of salvation—Jesus—is too limited or narrow. Many espouse a philosophy that says it's not fair for a loving god to restrict salvation to a single method. What nonsense!

First of all, I am God, and it is my character to be just and fair. But I can also be gracious and merciful. My fairness and justice demand that a death penalty be paid for sinfulness; my grace and mercy allowed my Son to pay that price for all sinners. Accordingly, there is no way of salvation other than Christ.

But salvation through Him is an offer extended to everyone. "The way" of my Son applies equally to all people. There is nothing narrow or restrictive about that. And aren't you glad?

Jesus answered, "I am the way and the truth and the life.
No one comes to the Father except through me."
JOHN 14:6

THE HOLY SPIRIT GUIDES YOU THROUGH MY WORD

My Spirit will make my Word come alive for you.

I know you sometimes read my Word without any sense of my presence. You often find it dry, mundane, and irrelevant.

Let me assure you that the problem is not with the *content* of scripture, because it is powerful and as sharp as a sword, able to cut to the core of your soul. Your obstacle to finding the passion and truth of scripture is your own attitude. Too often, you read my Word in a clinical fashion, looking only for information. Instead, you should read scripture for the purpose of your own transformation.

Approach my Word with an open heart, expecting my Spirit to use the written Word to bring necessary correction and rebuke into your life. Let Him guide and encourage you in godly living through the verses you read. Open my Word with the confident expectation that you will be supernaturally strengthened in the spiritual dimensions of your life.

I want you to become more like Christ—and I'll use my Word and my Spirit to make that happen. There is nothing boring or mundane about that.

All Scripture is God-breathed and is useful for teaching,
rebuking, correcting and training in righteousness,
so that the servant of God may be thoroughly equipped
for every good work.

2 TIMOTHY 3:16–17

MY WORD DRAWS YOU BACK TO ME

Read my Word when you feel you are disconnected from me.

I am always with you. So if I seem distant, it is a matter of your perception—because I haven't gone anywhere. And I haven't turned my back on you: I'm facing you, arms extended, waiting to embrace you.

This separation anxiety is often caused by unconfessed sin in your life, and the solution to that is simple: repent so that our fellowship can be restored. At other times, though, you feel disconnected from me because you've forgotten what you already know of me. You need to remember my attributes, the qualities that drew you to me in the first place. So return to my Word. Scripture reveals my character, describes the sacrifice of my Son, and explains the power available to you through my Spirit.

Fall in love with me, all over again, each time you read my Word.

May my cry come before you, LORD;
give me understanding according to your word. . . .
I have strayed like a lost sheep. Seek your servant,
for I have not forgotten your commands.
PSALM 119:169, 176

CHOOSE WHOM YOU ARE GOING TO SERVE

Your faithfulness to me is always your choice.

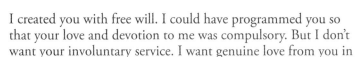

I created you with free will. I could have programmed you so that your love and devotion to me was compulsory. But I don't want your involuntary service. I want genuine love from you in response to who I am.

But I knew there would be a consequence to the free will I gave you: you can choose to follow and serve someone else. Though everyone else pales in comparison to me, I seem to have one major competitor for your devotion: you.

The choice—whether you'll follow me or live for yourself—is yours to make. And it presents itself every day. You make the decision of whether I am worthy of your allegiance or whether you'll concede to your own self-centeredness. But this is not a choice between equal alternatives. The distinction is clear.

Whom do you really wish to serve?

"But if serving the LORD seems undesirable to you,
then choose for yourselves this day whom you will serve,
whether the gods your ancestors served beyond the Euphrates,
or the gods of the Amorites, in whose land you are living.
But as for me and my household, we will serve the LORD."

JOSHUA 24:15

LOOK FOR ME—I WILL BE FOUND

I am not hiding from you.
I am eager to reveal myself to you.

I did not create the universe with the thought of concealing my existence. In fact, I left clues all around you as evidence of my presence. These signs are obvious even to a casual observer. Beyond that, I have given you my Word as a written record of who I am. And, greatest of all, I sent my Son to earth as the physical representation of me. How much more proof should you need?

However, knowing that I exist is not the same as knowing me personally. Satan and his demons know *of* me, but we're not close friends. So it's my desire that all humanity progress from an academic knowledge of my existence to a personal relationship with me. And for those who want to make that journey, I will reveal myself. For humans who sincerely desire to find me, I will make myself known to them.

"You will seek me and find me when you seek me with all your heart.
I will be found by you," declares the LORD.
JEREMIAH 29:13–14

I LOVE IT WHEN YOU GIVE TO ME CHEERFULLY

*I want you to give from a generous spirit,
not a sense of obligation.*

Everything in the world belongs to me. If you have anything, it is a gift from me. So I don't need your money at all.

But I want you to give back to me—through ministries that advance the spread of my Gospel and that care for the disadvantaged—because you need to acknowledge my priority in your life. It is one thing to say that you love me; it is another thing to show it on your bank statements.

I'll still accept your money if you give it grudgingly, but that's not how I want to receive it. I want you to give from an overwhelming feeling of charity for those who are in need. I'm hoping you'll give out of a sense of gratitude for what I have given to you—for all that I've done for you.

Be generous with what I have given to you. Be charitable to others for my sake.

*Each of you should give what you have decided in your heart to give,
not reluctantly or under compulsion, for God loves a cheerful giver.*
2 CORINTHIANS 9:7

BE STILL AND KNOW THAT I AM GOD

You can hear me best when you aren't on the run.

My dear child, you are too busy, scurrying about in life. Your days are hectic and overcrowded with activity. You have innumerable demands on your time, and your family and friends—even your entertainment sources—are all screaming for your attention. This cacophony drowns me out.

To get your attention, I could blare from heaven in a voice that shakes the world. But that is not how I want to speak with you. Often, my preference is to use a gentle whisper (1 Kings 19:12).

I want you to listen for my voice. I want you to hear it. So carve out some time each day to sit quietly before me. Stop multitasking for a while. Remove the distractions. Unplug and shut down everything except your mind. Take a deep breath. Focus your thoughts on me. When you do, you'll be amazed at the clarity with which you can hear my voice.

"Be still, and know that I am God;
I will be exalted among the nations,
I will be exalted in the earth."

PSALM 46:10

JESUS IS COMING BACK

Let the imminent return of Jesus
be your hope and your motivation.

You have the privilege of understanding the mystery that confounded my prophets from ancient times. They spoke of the coming of the Messiah, but they described Him as both a suffering servant and a triumphant conqueror. They didn't realize what you now know: the Messiah would come twice.

My Son's first visit to earth was as a sacrificial lamb, slaughtered for the sins of humanity. But at some future time, known only to me, He will return to earth as a triumphant king. At that time, He'll initiate a sequence of events that leads to the final conquest of Satan and the restoration of order and perfection to earth.

In view of that certainty, I want you to redeem your time. Live in the knowledge that Christ will return. Don't waste the time that remains. Pursue a godly life and promote my message. Let the imminent return of Jesus be your hope and your motivation.

"So you also must be ready,
because the Son of Man will come
at an hour when you do not expect him."
MATTHEW 24:44

THE FRUIT OF THE SPIRIT IS LOVE, JOY, AND PEACE

My Spirit will produce my character qualities in you.

You inherited certain characteristics from your biological parents. Some of them relate to your appearance; some pertain to your personality. Some are positive; others are less desirable.

In a similar way, I as your heavenly Father expect to see some of *my* traits in your life. These definable qualities—all of which are desirable—are "inherited" by you from me through the transformative power of my Spirit who lives in you.

The influence of my Spirit will produce His "fruit" in you—including love, joy, and peace. While even nonbelievers experience these emotions from time to time, the substance of Spirit-induced love, joy, and peace is supernatural. With my love in your life, you can overcome self-centeredness and direct your devotion to me. My Spirit will give you a genuine joy that transcends difficult and tragic circumstances. And you will realize a true and steadfast peace that results from the confident reassurance of my sovereignty.

These are the characteristics of my Son, and I want you to be like him.

But the fruit of the Spirit is love, joy, peace.
GALATIANS 5:22

BE QUICK TO KEEP MY COMMANDS

I want you to follow my precepts
out of love, not obligation.

We both know it: I am God, and you are not. That ultimate reality means that I've got an advantage over you. It's my omnipotent, all-powerful leverage. Bottom line: I could *force* you to do whatever I want. But that's not how I want the relationship between us to be.

I will never coerce you into following my principles. I'll encourage and implore you to do so, but I won't compel you. If you won't follow on your own, the bad consequences of your rebellion may still bring you around. Just ask the prodigal son (Luke 15:11–24).

I don't want you to obey my commands from a sense of obligation. I want your obedience to be motivated by love. And to fully know what I desire, you'll need a hunger and thirst for my Word.

May your passion be for acquiring my wisdom through intimacy with me.

You are my portion, LORD; I have promised to obey your words.
I have sought your face with all my heart; be gracious to me according
to your promise.
I have considered my ways and have turned my steps to your statutes.
I will hasten and not delay to obey your commands.

PSALM 119:57–60

DON'T WORRY ABOUT YOUR DAILY NEEDS

Trust me. I'll take care of them.

I want you to be free from the mundane worries of life so that you can worship and serve me without distraction. Here, I refer particularly to your basic needs of food, clothing, and shelter. You might not consider these necessities minor or mundane, but they are. They shouldn't cause you any anxiety, because I've got them covered.

My dear child, don't you realize how important you are to me? If I carried a wallet, your picture would be in it. I am not going to abandon you in a time of need. I will always make a way to provide for your life.

Never despair over basic necessities. I will provide for your care and your safety.

"Therefore I tell you, do not worry about your life,
what you will eat or drink;
or about your body, what you will wear. Is not life more than food,
and the body more than clothes? Look at the birds of the air;
they do not sow or reap or store away in barns,
and yet your heavenly Father feeds them.
Are you not much more valuable than they?"
MATTHEW 6:25–26

THERE ARE DARK FORCES ALL AROUND YOU

Satan and his demons are not fictional.
Beware of them, but don't fear them.

Beware, my child: demonic forces are all around you. Don't be misled by Satan's publicity campaign; the media blitz that portrays him as a harmless, silly creature in a devil costume with little horns, a pointy tale, and a pitchfork. That's the image he *wants* to you see whenever you think of him. In reality, he is the embodiment of evil. Satan and his army of demons are a powerful force intent on your destruction.

But don't be afraid. As my child, you are under my protection. Though Satan can wreak havoc in the circumstances of your earthly life, he has no power to affect your eternal destiny. Realize that the more committed you are to following me, the more you'll provoke Satan's wrath. So be on guard. Stay strong and alert in the power of my Word and the strength of my Spirit.

For our struggle is not against flesh and blood,
but against the rulers, against the authorities,
against the powers of this dark world and against the spiritual forces
of evil in the heavenly realms.
EPHESIANS 6:12

CONFESS YOUR SINS TO ONE ANOTHER AND PRAY FOR EACH OTHER

*There should be mutual accountability and support
among the community of believers.*

You can't fool me. I know you sometimes try to dodge accountability to me by slipping out of fellowship. You think (mistakenly) that I won't notice your backsliding if you can manage to avoid personal interaction with me. Well, it doesn't work. Just because I'm invisible doesn't mean I'm absent.

I knew all along that you would need an in-your-face alternative for the sake of accountability. That's why I always intended for you to be part of a community of believers who provide spiritual reinforcement, guidance, and adjustment for each other.

You might think that you can avoid me. But it's much more difficult for you to avoid a blatant question like "How is your walk with the Lord?" from a spiritual brother or sister. You *need* other believers who can encourage and correct you—so develop strong Christian friendships for mutual support and protection.

*Therefore confess your sins to each other
and pray for each other so that you may be healed.
The prayer of a righteous person is powerful and effective.*
JAMES 5:16

I REWARD THOSE WHO SINCERELY SEEK ME

Your pursuit of me is rewarded by a relationship with me.

I am many things too awesome for you to fully comprehend. I am omniscient, omnipresent, and omnipotent. I am the Creator of the universe, transcendent above all that I have made—and my sovereignty places me in control of it all. I am the God Almighty.

It is fitting and appropriate for you to revere me. But do not be intimidated by me. For among my other attributes, I am loving and approachable.

I desire that our relationship be one in which I can call you "my child," and you can call me "Father." I want to be known by you. I want us to share a relationship that flourishes as you mature in your love and understanding of me. So seek me while you have the time (Isaiah 55:6). I'll reward you for doing so. Your efforts will not be in vain. I will reveal myself to you and welcome you into fellowship with me.

And without faith it is impossible to please God,
because anyone who comes to him must believe that he exists
and that he rewards those who earnestly seek him.

HEBREWS 11:6

JESUS WILL GIVE YOU ABUNDANT LIFE

A life overflowing awaits you in Christ.

My Son has promised you eternal life through the salvation He offers. But this is not just a promise of a future home in heaven. True, it is a guarantee of spending eternity with me, but it is not just for the future. Your "eternity" began at the moment of your salvation.

This promise of eternal life is also here and now. You have the divine privilege of a relationship with me at this very moment, one that continues through the remainder of your earthly life, and then far, far beyond.

But there is still more. The eternal life offered by Jesus is no routine, bland, humdrum experience. He offers you an abundant life, a flourishing life, a life that greatly exceeds your expectation or imagination.

Don't underestimate what I want to do in your life. If you will allow me to lead, hang on for an amazing ride.

"The thief comes only to steal and kill and destroy;
I have come that they may have life, and have it to the full."
JOHN 10:10

THE HOLY SPIRIT POURS MY LOVE INTO YOUR HEART

He will empower you to love those
you can't seem to love on your own.

My Son taught that all of my commands could be summarized into two: love me with all your heart, soul, and mind, and love your neighbor as yourself (Matthew 22:37–40). And He told His disciples to love each other the same way that He loved them (John 13:34–35). These are not archaic ideas. They remain my commandments to you today.

But, practically speaking, how can you love me with full intensity? How can you love that neighbor who drives you crazy? And how can you love those obnoxious brothers and sisters in your church in any way that resembles how I love them?

The candid answer is that you cannot—at least not in your own abilities. But you can through the strength of my Spirit. He will empower you to love those that you consider unlovable. Each one is a soul that I love—and through my Spirit, you will begin to see others through my eyes.

Follow my Spirit's prompting, and love others.

And hope does not put us to shame,
because God's love has been poured out into our hearts
through the Holy Spirit, who has been given to us.

ROMANS 5:5

MY WORD WILL REMIND YOU OF MY STEADFAST LOVE

*The more you read my Word,
the more you'll be drawn to my love.*

I know you are busy and your schedule is hectic. I know you have many demands on your time. Yet I'm giving you another one: read my Word every day.

Stop rolling your eyes—don't think that I'm laying some tedious, monotonous chore on you. It's just the opposite. I want to infuse your mundane world with a glimpse of the supernatural.

Your life will be much more stable and enjoyable when you have a confident reassurance of my love. That happens as you spend consistent time in my Word. Let the passages of scripture reveal my character to you. Let the verses speak to you of my love and care. Allow me, through my Word, to deepen your love and understanding of me.

Our relationship will grow deeper as you hunger for my Word each day.

*Your hands made me and formed me;
give me understanding to learn your commands.
May those who fear you rejoice when they see me,
for I have put my hope in your word. . . .
May your unfailing love be my comfort. . . .
Let your compassion come to me that I may live,
for your law is my delight. . . .
May I wholeheartedly follow your decrees,
that I may not be put to shame.*

PSALM 119:73–74, 76–77, 80

271

KEEP WATCH: YOU DON'T KNOW WHEN JESUS IS COMING BACK

The specifics are unknown to you,
so don't commit yourself to a single timetable.

You've heard it said that my Son, Jesus, will return to earth. He will gather you and the rest of His saints to Himself, and the grandest reunion the universe has ever known will begin.

But it won't be a party for everyone: a phase of judgment will also be involved. The joyful celebration of some will be countered by the sadness and torment of others. So it is that Christ's return will be both a celebratory and a somber event.

It is important you know this because there are ramifications for how you spend your time now. You only know the "how" of my plan—you don't know the "when." Don't make the mistake of thinking I will come so soon that you can quit your job and camp on a hilltop watching for my Son's arrival in the clouds. On the other hand, don't believe that Christ's return will delay for centuries, giving you plenty of time to put your life in order.

Be diligent in your service, as if my Son will return at any minute. But serve me with patience and endurance as if His return is far off.

"Therefore keep watch,
because you do not know on what day your Lord will come."
MATTHEW 24:42

I WON'T LET YOU ENDURE MORE THAN YOU CAN HANDLE

I'll help you escape any temptation.

In my Son, you have a Savior who knows about human temptation. He knows the pull of it, and He knows the power that is required to resist it. That's important, because Satan is constantly setting traps for my children, hoping they will be caught in his sinful snares.

Dear child, the power of my Spirit within you can overcome anything that Satan puts in your path. And through my Spirit I will provide you a way to escape the entanglement of any temptation that is too much for you to resist.

But don't try to abuse this privilege. Don't ever get cozy with sin because you think I'll snatch you out of the jaws of enticement. My Spirit's power applies in circumstances when you do your best to avoid the temptation—not jump into it.

If you rebel against me and go looking for trouble, I'll back off and let your desires run their natural course. The best choice is always to turn from temptation—but if you are unexpectedly seized by it, I'll orchestrate a way of escape.

No temptation has overtaken you except what is common to mankind.
And God is faithful; he will not let you be tempted
beyond what you can bear.
But when you are tempted, he will also provide a way out
so that you can endure it.

1 CORINTHIANS 10:13

273

IF SOMEONE AMONG YOU WANDERS FROM THE TRUTH, BRING HIM BACK

Don't live disconnected from other believers.

Jesus told His disciples to love each other in the same way that He loved them (John 13:34–35). Shortly after that statement, He revealed the extent of His love for them by dying on the cross. My Son demonstrated that love among believers should be sacrificial, putting the welfare of others ahead of your own preferences.

Don't live disconnected from other believers. Be involved in the lives of Christians—ministering to each other. While society tells you to "mind your own business," I want you to take the risk of confronting and restoring fellow believers who have abandoned their faith in the pursuit of immorality. I know this is difficult and awkward for you, but it is an act of love.

Be careful, though—proceed as Christ would. I don't want you to be guilty of pride or unkindness in your efforts. If you succeed, you will have rescued a fellow believer; if not, you will have honored me in the effort.

Brothers and sisters, if someone is caught in a sin,
you who live by the Spirit should restore that person gently.
But watch yourselves, or you also may be tempted.
GALATIANS 6:1

I AM CAPABLE OF JEALOUSY

I am jealous for you because of my desire to protect you.

I am a jealous God. Make no mistake about it: I demand your total allegiance.

You must not worship any other god than me (Exodus 20:3). You should worship and serve me only (Matthew 4:10). But never think I'm egotistical, arrogant, self-absorbed, or envious. I am *jealous*, but not in the way you typically use the word.

I am jealous *for* you. I have an intense desire to protect you from harm. I know that your attraction to anything other than me will lead you down a path to destruction. So it is for your own good—for your own eternal benefit—that I demand your loyalty.

I am your protective heavenly Father. I am jealous for you, my child. I do not want anything or anyone in your life that will interfere with our relationship—that will jeopardize your spiritual safety.

Do not worship any other god, for the LORD, whose name is Jealous, is a jealous God.
EXODUS 34:14

JESUS IS YOUR EXAMPLE

Model your life after the way my Son lived.

I call on you to live a godly and righteous life. And I recognize that what I expect of you is counterintuitive to your experience.

Your natural instincts are usually the opposite of the thoughts and actions I want in your life. That's why I've give you an instruction manual (my Word), and a model to follow (my Son). I sent Jesus to earth so that humanity would have a physical, visible image of me. My Son's life serves as a representation of the godly life.

When I tell you to be "Christlike," I don't expect you to gather disciples, wear sandals, and perform miracles on a hillside. In fact, you don't need to worry about copying any specific assignment that I gave my Son. Rather, you should follow His teachings.

Emulate Jesus' passion for me and His love for all people. Have a heart of humility like He displayed. Be as eager to serve and care for the disadvantaged as He was. When you follow the example of Christ, you will be living a godly and righteous life.

Whoever claims to live in him must live as Jesus did.
1 JOHN 2:6

THE HOLY SPIRIT LIVES WITHIN YOU

*Wherever you go and whatever you do,
you take the Holy Spirit with you.*

A tenant has the use and enjoyment of an apartment, but that tenant has no right to damage or desecrate the landlord's property. And so it is with you.

As my child, you have my Spirit living in you. Your body is no longer yours—I bought you at the cost of my Son's life. Yes, I have given you freedom, but that is the freedom from enslavement to sin. You are now free to live a life that honors *me*.

Those who say that my salvation allows them to live in whatever sinful way they desire are people who are still enslaved to sin. If they truly belonged to me, the thought of pursuing immorality would be repulsive to them.

Your conduct should always reflect the fact that your body is the dwelling place of my Spirit. Don't drag Him into places where He wouldn't want to go.

*Do you not know that your bodies are temples of the Holy Spirit,
who is in you, whom you have received from God?
You are not your own; you were bought at a price.
Therefore honor God with your bodies.*

1 CORINTHIANS 6:19–20

MY WORD IS YOUR LAMP AND YOUR LIGHT

Scripture will light the path for you.

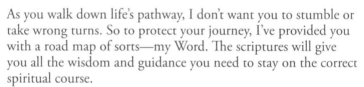

As you walk down life's pathway, I don't want you to stumble or take wrong turns. So to protect your journey, I've provided you with a road map of sorts—my Word. The scriptures will give you all the wisdom and guidance you need to stay on the correct spiritual course.

The dangers on your journey are the snares of the devil and the potholes of your own poor judgment. There are also the distractions of false prophets and teachings. But if you integrate the principles of my Word into your life, you can always stay on the right path.

Rely on my laws, depend on my precepts, and follow my wisdom. Then you will never veer off course as you proceed toward the godly life that pleases me and benefits you.

Your word is a lamp for my feet, a light on my path.
I have taken an oath and confirmed it,
that I will follow your righteous laws. . . .
Though I constantly take my life in my hands,
I will not forget your law. . . .
Your statutes are my heritage forever; they are the joy of my heart.
My heart is set on keeping your decrees to the very end.

PSALM 119:105–106, 109, 111–112

I WON'T LISTEN IF YOU ARE HARBORING SIN IN YOUR LIFE

I am eager to listen,
but only if you are speaking my language.

You don't want to listen to deceitful and hypocritical people. Neither do I. And that is why I am not inclined to listen to *you* if you're only pretending to be "spiritual" with me—while living with sin in your life.

I want to be in fellowship with you at all times. But that can't happen if you are actively engaged in sinful behavior. I am holy, and your unrepentant sin is a barrier between us.

But the moment you acknowledge and truly repent of your sin—demonstrating the sincere intention to abandon it and leave it behind—our fellowship can be restored immediately.

My vocabulary is entirely of godliness and righteousness. If you are entrenched in sin, you aren't speaking my language. Confess your sin so we can communicate with each other.

Surely the arm of the LORD is not too short to save,
nor his ear too dull to hear. But your iniquities have separated you
from your God; your sins have hidden his face from you,
so that he will not hear.

ISAIAH 59:1–2

I'M LEAVING YOU IN THE WORLD

But I'm not leaving you alone or defenseless.

On your particularly difficult and discouraging days, you've often wondered why I don't take you to heaven the moment you surrendered control of your life to me.

Without a doubt, heaven is a place you'll want to be—just wait until you see it and enjoy my presence, up close and personal. But in the meantime, I have a purpose for you on earth. You are my mouth, my hands, and my feet in the mission of proclaiming my love and serving those in need of care and comfort.

I know this assignment is difficult—but remember that I am always with you. I have not forgotten or abandoned you. Satan and his demons do not have authority over you. You are mine, and you have my almighty protection.

Yes, you remain *in* the world, but you are no longer a part *of* the world. You are a child of mine, filled with my Holy Spirit and under my constant love and security.

"My prayer is not that you take them out of the world but that you protect them from the evil one."

JOHN 17:15

DON'T TIRE OF DOING GOOD FOR OTHERS

When you are serving them,
you are serving me.

As you minister to others, keep in mind that you are doing it for *me.*

If you let your focus drift, and labor with the expectation of gratitude, you are going to be disappointed. By and large, humans are an ungrateful and unappreciative lot. No one knows that better than me.

Sadly, this is also true—sometimes especially true—of my own children. You might find that they are particularly difficult to deal with, and exceptionally unthankful.

I know you're tempted to quit at times. The task of ministering to others can make you weary. But persevere, whether or not you see the kind of results you'd like, and whether or not people express gratitude. Remember that you are working for the sake of my kingdom.

Be motivated by your love for me. I appreciate your work and rejoice in seeing you serve others. You have *my* thanks—and that should be enough.

Let us not become weary in doing good,
for at the proper time we will reap a harvest if we do not give up.
Therefore, as we have opportunity, let us do good to all people,
especially to those who belong to the family of believers.
GALATIANS 6:9–10

YOUR REBELLION GRIEVES ME

Behind every sin is a spirit of defiance.

People try to categorize sin by severity: a "white lie" isn't as bad as filing a fraudulent tax return. . .immoral thoughts aren't as bad as the act of adultery. . .and anger isn't as bad as murder. Don't fall into that trap! If you try to rank sins from least to greatest, you're going to think I'm not bothered by the "minor" ones. That's simply not true—every one of your sins grieves me.

All sin, of whatever nature, represents your rebellion against my will. Any action or thought that is opposed to my values is a defiance of me. If you choose to live for yourself and your own pleasures and reject the principles I established, you are acting against your own best interests.

Life your way, on your terms, lived for momentary pleasure, interferes with our relationship. So don't be cavalier about sin, even those sins you consider insignificant. The defiant attitude that prompts sinful behavior is never trivial to me.

How often they rebelled against him in the wilderness
and grieved him in the wasteland!
PSALM 78:40

JESUS ENDURED THE PAIN OF BEARING YOUR SIN

The pain of sin was far worse than the physical pain of His torture.

I had to turn away when my Son was crucified. I could not look upon the horror of it all.

It wasn't the blood and brutality or his anguish that made me avert my eyes. It was the sin that came upon Him: your sin, and the sins of all humanity.

Of all the cruelty inflicted on Christ at Calvary, the greatest pain He suffered was bearing the sins of the world. The weight of those sins was heaped upon my Son as He died a substitutionary death that paid the price rightfully owed by every sinner. So that you could be saved, I laid your guilt on my Son.

He was bruised, tortured, and killed for your wrongs. He was disfigured and murdered for your sins. He was like an innocent sheep being slaughtered.

It was my will that all of this occur, and He was willing to endure it. Jesus loves you that much.

God made him who had no sin to be sin for us,
so that in him we might become the righteousness of God.

2 CORINTHIANS 5:21

THE HOLY SPIRIT INSPIRED MEN TO WRITE THE SCRIPTURES

What they wrote were my words, not theirs.

When you read my Word, that is exactly what you are doing: reading *my* words. They are *my* thoughts, *my* pronouncements, and *my* precepts. The words in scripture were not derived from human wisdom. Quite simply, my Word is not man made.

Now, of course, I did use about forty men in the transcription process. But I didn't turn them loose, alone and unsupervised. Instead, each of them was filled and guided by my Spirit. The Holy Spirit was the author and producer of the work. My Spirit spoke through these men, using their personalities and vocabulary, to compose and pen the truth I wanted to disclose.

Their original texts were without error. The writers recorded my Word just the way I wanted it said. Read the Bible with the reverence you would show if I was speaking directly to you—because that is exactly what I'm doing.

Above all, you must understand that no prophecy of Scripture came about by the prophet's own interpretation of things. For prophecy never had its origin in the human will, but prophets, though human, spoke from God as they were carried along by the Holy Spirit.

2 PETER 1:20–21

IF YOU ASK ME, I WILL TEACH YOU MY WORD

Learn to apply my Word to your circumstances.

It is important for you to read my words. It is more important for you to know the truth of my Word, and how to apply my Word to your life situations.

If you ask me, I will give you discernment—the ability to know how and when to apply scripture to your circumstances. Your faith will intensify when you discover how my principles and precepts relate to the occurrences of daily life. My discernment will give you wisdom in dealing with conflict and crisis. The ability to apply my Word will help you minister to others; rather than giving them your own feeble words, you will be equipped to extend my comfort to those who are hurting.

I want to give you understanding of my Word. Ask for it, then read scripture with the clear expectation that I will speak to you.

*Deal with your servant according to your love
and teach me your decrees. I am your servant;
give me discernment that I may understand your statutes.*

PSALM 119:124–125

IF YOU CONFESS YOUR SINS, I WILL FORGIVE YOU

I don't require perfection,
but I do expect confession.

Salvation comes to those who confess their need of a Savior and invite me to reign in their lives. But, as you are painfully aware, salvation is not immediately followed by perfection. That's all right—I don't require perfection. But I do expect confession.

People who genuinely love and follow me don't want to revel in sin. They regret and repent each time they give in. When I see that attitude, I am glad to forgive your transgressions. If my children are willing to acknowledge and confess their sin, I am quick to forgive. But your repentance must be authentic and heartfelt.

My dear child, do not ignore your sin. Don't think I am unaware of it or that you can hide it from me. I am eager to restore our relationship through forgiveness, but you must initiate the process. How? With the admission of your sin and a clear intent to refrain from it in the future.

If I had cherished sin in my heart, the Lord would not have listened;
but God has surely listened and has heard my prayer.
PSALM 66:18–19

FLEE FROM IDOLATRY

Don't just turn from it;
run away from it.

I know you don't have little statues of "gods" on your shelves. But never think you are immune from the snares of idolatry.

You would never trust a piece of carved wood or a clay figurine for your well-being. But you sometimes struggle with placing your trust in a job, your checkbook, or your retirement account. Putting your hope for security on anything other than me is idolatry.

Whenever my Spirit convicts you that you are worshipping something other than me, you need to make a correction. Make changes and make them fast.

Money and power have a strong pull on people. You know that I won't allow you to be tempted beyond what you can resist (1 Corinthians 10:13), but this promise applies to those situations in which you're trying to avoid the temptation. Never allow yourself to flirt with finding security in anything other than me.

These worldly things are not necessarily evil in themselves—but they become so if they gain a priority in your life that rightfully belongs to me.

Therefore, my dear friends, flee from idolatry.
1 CORINTHIANS 10:14

BE CONTENT WITH WHAT YOU HAVE

If you have me,
you have everything you really need.

I deserve to be acknowledged as your sole source of contentment. After all, every good thing in your life comes from me (James 1:17). You should be thankful to me for all that you have.

Except for me, everything in your life is transitory—so here is the bottom line: I am all that you have, and I am all that you need. I hope you can grow in your spiritual understanding to the point where I am all that you want. Then you will have true contentment.

When you are discontented, you are either ungrateful for what I've given to you or suspicious and skeptical of my plan for your life. You need to realize that I will provide all that you *need*, whatever is appropriate for you to have. When you learn to love *me* more than the other things in your life—when you trust me totally as your source of supply—you will have reached the essence of faith in me.

Then, regardless of what you have, you'll be truly content.

But godliness with contentment is great gain.
For we brought nothing into the world,
and we can take nothing out of it.

1 TIMOTHY 6:6–7

I LOVE WITH AN EVERLASTING LOVE

Even your sin does not terminate my love for you.

I designed the relationships in the human family as a metaphor of my relationship with humanity. So when I call you "my child," you can have a better understanding how I love you as a father.

Use your knowledge—or your hope—of a loving father when you think about *our* relationship. A father still loves his toddler even in the midst of the child's tantrum. When a teenager is punished for breaching the rules, the father's love is not diminished.

And so it is between you and me. Your sin has consequences that interrupt our intimacy—but upon your repentance and my forgiveness, we are immediately restored to close fellowship. And all the while, my unconditional, everlasting love for you continues.

"In a surge of anger I hid my face from you for a moment,
but with everlasting kindness I will have compassion on you,"
says the LORD your Redeemer.
ISAIAH 54:8

JESUS MADE IT POSSIBLE FOR YOU TO BE MY FRIEND

*He was the agent of reconciliation
that allows us to be together.*

Here was the problem: I was holy and could not associate with sin in any manner—you were completely sinful and deserved to be punished. Your sin made us enemies.

But my Son, Jesus, was the solution: He bridged the gap between us by offering His holy life as the sacrificial payment for your sin.

Christ's work on the cross—His death and resurrection—performed an act of reconciliation between you and me. Because of His death and suffering, you and I can be as close as a father and child. We can now fellowship together for all eternity.

You are saved because Christ became the reconciliation between sinful humanity and the holy God—me.

*For if, while we were God's enemies,
we were reconciled to him through the death of his Son,
how much more, having been reconciled,
shall we be saved through his life!
Not only is this so, but we also boast in God
through our Lord Jesus Christ,
through whom we have now received reconciliation.*

ROMANS 5:10–11

THE HOLY SPIRIT RESTRAINS SIN

My Spirit keeps the world from falling apart.

I laugh—and yet I am saddened—when I hear human beings proclaim that society evolves to a higher level with each generation. That is laughable because it is so preposterous. The tragic reality is that the human race is in a downward spiral of depravity. And Satan is hard at work behind the scenes to promote the decay and destruction of your human race.

For the time being, things are holding together. But it's not your politicians, universities, scientists, or think tanks that keep the ship afloat. You owe it all to the Holy Spirit.

My Spirit is restraining the power of Satan that would otherwise throw your world into total anarchy. But the Holy Spirit's restraining role will not continue forever: at some point, He'll step aside and allow Satan unbridled freedom for a while. Expect chaos to ensue—until Jesus steps in to make all things right.

For the secret power of lawlessness is already at work;
but the one who now holds it back will continue to do so
till he is taken out of the way. And then the lawless one will be
revealed, whom the Lord Jesus will overthrow with the breath
of his mouth and destroy by the splendor of his coming.
2 THESSALONIANS 2:7–8

MY WORD HELPS YOU IN YOUR DISTRESS

Find comfort in my scriptures.

When your circumstances are devastating—when it seems you have no one on your side—turn to me. And when the noise of your distress seems to drown out my Spirit's voice, turn to my Word. I can speak to you through scripture. As you read my words, you can hear my voice in every verse.

You will find reassurance and comfort in the truth of my promises. I have vowed to care for your every need, and I have never broken an oath I've made. Since my Word conveys a sense of my majesty and magnitude, you can see the size of your troubles in the context of my ability to handle them.

Scripture contains eternal truths. Your life on earth is transitory, just a moment in time compared to the eternity you will spend with me. Read my Word and be refreshed with a view of your everlasting hope.

Though I am lowly and despised, I do not forget your precepts. . . .
Trouble and distress have come upon me,
but your commands give me delight.
PSALM 119:141, 143

WHEN YOU PRAY,
ASK ACCORDING TO MY WILL

If you pray, I will answer.

I am interested in what happens in your life—even more than you are. And I want to talk with you about your concerns, hopes, desires, and worries. Please realize, my child, that when you pray to me, I'll be listening. And I will answer your prayers, if you're following my rules.

First, for me to hear your prayers, you have to live according to my precepts. You can't be harboring unconfessed sin.

Secondly, you must pray according to my will. This means that, ultimately, you are asking for what I want. This is the tricky part: you can be very specific about what you desire, but you must acknowledge that I know what is best for you—and that you will trust my judgment. The bottom line is that you may have a preference, but you are really asking within the context of wanting *my* will, even if I have something else for planned you.

Be assured that I always hear and answer such prayers.

This is the confidence we have in approaching God:
that if we ask anything according to his will, he hears us.
1 JOHN 5:14

FAITH WITHOUT WORKS IS DEAD

Genuine faith is revealed by your actions.

You salvation is by my saving grace. You did nothing to earn it.

As far as obtaining salvation is concerned, your actions are irrelevant. But your conduct does matter when it comes to determining the authenticity of your faith.

I am omniscient, so I have no problem knowing whether your belief in me is genuine. But when you question yourself about the sincerity of your own faith, you can use your actions as a barometer. Are you pursing a godly life? Are you living according to my principles? Has your behavior changed from what it was before you were saved? Do you keep returning to the same sins with little feeling of regret or repentance? Are you consistently reading my Word and spending time with me in prayer? Are you part of a community of believers and active in ministering to others?

None of these activities can earn you salvation. But if your life lacks them, your claim to being my child might be nothing more than pretense.

In the same way, faith by itself,
if it is not accompanied by action, is dead.
JAMES 2:17

YOUR SPIRITUAL HEALTH COMES FROM CORRECT TEACHING

Sound doctrine leads to right living.

My Word gives you everything you need to know for godly living (2 Timothy 3:16). I want you to carefully study the scriptures so you build sound doctrine in your life. Similarly, I want you involved in a community of believers where the truth of my Word—not human wisdom—is taught.

Don't be impressed with oratory that sounds good but lacks spiritual content. Don't settle for a well-packaged sermon that contains nothing more than worldly platitudes. Self-improvement advice should not be confused with scriptural truth.

I want you to be grounded in the principles of my Word. Accordingly, make sure you are exposed to sound teaching of the truths of scripture. The more you know of my Word, the easier it will be to spot teaching that comes up short.

He must hold firmly to the trustworthy message as it has been taught, so that he can encourage others by sound doctrine and refute those who oppose it.

TITUS 1:9

I HAVE COMPLETE KNOWLEDGE OF YOU

I use that knowledge in providing for your care.

You can run from me, but you can never hide. Literally.

When you think about running, I already know the "where" and "how" of your plans. And I know everything else about you, too—your successes and failures, your fears and hopes. I know you inside and out, from birth to death.

I want this to be an *encouragement* to you, my child. As for your past, nothing that you've done could ever dissuade me from loving you. As for your future, nothing you could do would make me love you less. I love you in spite of who you are—because I love what my Son has done for and through you.

Take comfort by the fact of my intimate, omniscient knowledge of you. It allows me to protect and provide for you. My love can be specifically tailored to *your* needs.

For your ways are in full view of the LORD,
and he examines all your paths.
PROVERBS 5:21

THE RESURRECTION OF JESUS ENSURES YOUR RESURRECTION

Eternal life is the inheritance of every believer.

When you put your faith and trust for salvation in my Son, you received a new nature. Your old, sinful nature was put to death, and you were "born again" (John 3:7) into my family.

As a child of mine, even during your earthly life, you can have direct fellowship with me. And no matter how tough your life seems, you have the confident optimism that this life is not your final experience.

Because there is much more. The resurrection of Jesus assured your resurrection, as well. Your life does not end with your physical death—your soul is eternal. And by reason of your spiritual rebirth, you will spend eternity with me.

You have already been resurrected from a decaying life to one that is imperishable. Your eternal life and accompanying companionship with me were made possible by my Son's death and resurrection. His resurrection assured yours.

Praise be to the God and Father of our Lord Jesus Christ!
In his great mercy he has given us new birth into a living hope
through the resurrection of Jesus Christ from the dead,
and into an inheritance that can never perish, spoil or fade.

1 PETER 1:3–4

LET THE HOLY SPIRIT FILL AND CONTROL YOU

Let my Spirit influence and flavor every aspect of your life.

You can allow all sorts of things to influence your life. I want your life to be influenced by my Spirit.

Just as wine affects your thinking, your emotions, and your behavior, I want my Spirit to fill and control you. I want His love, joy, peace, patience, gentleness, and goodness to color your thinking, your emotions, and your behavior. I want your reactions and responses to be based in His character.

Unlike wine, which affects you temporarily, my Spirit is always with you. But He will not force Himself on you—you must voluntarily relinquish control to Him. There is a direct relationship in your life between your submission and His control. The only way to have more of Him is to allow Him to have more of you.

Do not get drunk on wine, which leads to debauchery. Instead, be filled with the Spirit.
EPHESIANS 5:18

MEDITATE ON MY WORD

*Extracting all my Word has to offer
takes discipline, time, and repetition.*

When you call out to me, I want you to use more than your
mouth. Draw deep from your well of emotions, crying out to me
with your heart. You don't have to pretend—I already know what's
troubling you. I just need to hear it from you with all humility
and sincerity.

To get to that place of raw openness, go to my Word. There
you will find an inexhaustible source of wisdom, encouragement,
and truth. But its riches aren't always in plain view. You will have
to dig deep, like a miner looking for precious gold.

In your own life, nothing of value ever comes easily. So it is
with my Word. Extracting all it has to offer takes discipline, time,
and repetition. Reading a passage through one time will give you
a shot of energy, but dwelling on it deeply will give you lasting
nourishment.

*I call with all my heart; answer me, LORD,
and I will obey your decrees. . . .
My eyes stay open through the watches of the night,
that I may meditate on your promises.*

PSALM 119:145, 148

I AM CONFORMING YOU TO THE IMAGE OF MY SON

You are in the process of being made Christlike.

The prize of your salvation is not a ticket to eternity in heaven. That's just an extra benefit.

The true reward of salvation is much greater: your transformation to Christlikeness (Philippians 3:10). You will never become *Christ*, because you are not God—you are a created being. But it is my goal that you always move toward becoming *like* Christ.

While you are on earth, this work of transformation can progress. But it will never be complete. You will continue to stumble into sin, though ideally less and less often. Later, when you reach heaven—when sin has been finally and fatally conquered—you will truly be like Jesus.

Know that you are my work in progress. I don't expect perfection from you, but I am pleased to find you walking closely with Christ. Then you know Him better and imitate Him more accurately.

For those God foreknew he also predestined to be
conformed to the image of his Son,
that he might be the firstborn among many brothers and sisters.
ROMANS 8:29

WHO ARE YOU TO JUDGE YOUR NEIGHBOR?

Replace your judgment with discernment.

There is only one true Judge, and it is not you.

No, I am the sole adjudicator of whether a person is saved or lost. So when it comes to your family, friends, and neighbors, let *me* be responsible for determining whether they are my children or not. As for your role in their lives, I've given you only one primary command—and it is not to judge them. I just want you to love them.

But don't abandon your spiritual discernment while you live up to this truth. My Word is filled with principles and precepts that pertain to godly living and a righteous life. Scripture identifies conduct that pleases me, and conduct that constitutes sin. Learn to take a stand against sinfulness, without being critical of the person.

Jesus was always loving to sinful individuals, though He never condoned their behavior. He spoke out against their conduct while displaying affection for them personally. Follow His methods, and leave the judgment to me.

> *There is only one Lawgiver and Judge,*
> *the one who is able to save and destroy.*
> *But you—who are you to judge your neighbor?*
> JAMES 4:12

WHEN YOU GATHER, WORSHIP ME

You are a participant in every worship service you attend.

Going to church to be entertained is going for the wrong reason.

Your primary role at church is not to critique the sermon, the music, or the décor. You have a specific function at church: you are a participant in the worship service. Remember that you aren't the audience—I am.

When you think the preacher and the musicians are solely responsible for worship, you are mistaken. I am eager to be worshipped by *you*. And though you don't select the songs, it pleases me to hear you join in the singing. Even the worst vocalist makes a joyful noise for me.

In the same way, if you're not preaching the sermon, I am still worshipped when you listen intently to the teaching—and I am pleased with you consider how you will conform your life to the principles of scripture you're learning.

Be filled with the Spirit, speaking to one another with psalms, hymns, and songs from the Spirit. Sing and make music from your heart to the Lord, always giving thanks to God the Father for everything, in the name of our Lord Jesus Christ.
EPHESIANS 5:18–20

I AM EVERYWHERE

Anywhere you go, I am there.

I am omnipresent. That means that I am everywhere—all at the same time.

No other being can make that claim, not even Satan. He seems ubiquitous (meaning he gets around), but he can only be in one place at a time.

Think of the ramifications of my omnipresence: I am always wherever you are. I will never be away from you. If another child of mine needs me somewhere else, I can be with that child and still be by *your* side.

When I promised that I would never leave nor forsake you, I knew I could fully keep that promise. You are never beyond my reach. You will never wander away from me. No road can take you to a place where I can't extend my hand to you.

Where can I go from your Spirit? Where can I flee from your presence?
If I go up to the heavens, you are there;
if I make my bed in the depths, you are there.
If I rise on the wings of the dawn, if I settle on the far side of the sea,
even there your hand will guide me,
your right hand will hold me fast.

PSALM 139:7–10

JESUS IS THE TRUTH

Not only did my Son speak the truth,
He is the truth.

When my Son walked the earth, He was the embodiment of me. My character was revealed in the things He said and did. He conveyed my truth accurately in the lessons He taught and the sermons he preached. But more than just communicating truth, He *was* truth in human form.

In your experience, you've never met anyone who is totally truthful. Even if you did, that would merely mean the person had never lied or exhibited deceit. The truth of Christ, however, goes beyond mere truthfulness. The nature of His truth means that His teachings and principles are reliable, upright, and without fault or flaw. Christ's truth was righteousness incarnate.

The truth of Christ is proof that He is God. You can follow His teachings and model your life after Him because of this reality.

Jesus answered, "I am the way and the truth and the life.
No one comes to the Father except through me."
JOHN 14:6

THE HOLY SPIRIT HELPS YOU IN YOUR DISTRESS

*When you are in too much agony to pray,
my Spirit will pray for you.*

I am not a God who is a disconnected from your reality. My own Son suffered in ways that are far beyond anything you will ever endure, so He can relate to your misery. And I know that there are times when the pain of your circumstances is so great that you cannot even verbalize a prayer for help. In those cases, my Spirit is able and willing to pray on your behalf.

You'll have times of prayer when you can do nothing more than sob. You'll be overwhelmed in situations that leave you speechless. Don't abandon prayer merely because you can't articulate your thoughts.

Instead, come to me and let my Spirit pray *with* you and *for* you. I will hear His prayers and—because we speak the same divine language—I will catch all of His passion and nuance.

I love to hear you pray—but when you can't, the Holy Spirit is your very capable prayer advocate.

*The Spirit helps us in our weakness.
We do not know what we ought to pray for,
but the Spirit himself intercedes for us through wordless groans.*
ROMANS 8:26

MY WORD WILL GIVE YOU COMFORT

When you feel the heat of opposition,
you can depend on my Word.

Do you have enemies? Not those who oppose you in business or for some personal reason, but people who hate you because of your faith in me?

Before you answer, let me tell you a secret. If you don't have *any* spiritual enemies, you aren't serving me with your whole heart—and you don't love my Son to the fullest. If you were completely committed to me, you would upset some people—maybe enough for them to actively oppose you.

When you do experience opposition and persecution because of your allegiance to me and my Son—obeying all that my Word tells you even when its principles go against the grain of culture—then you have reason to be thankful. People are noticing you because of your faith.

As you feel the heat of opposition, you can depend on my Word for comfort. When culture insults me and treats your brothers and sisters with contempt, my Word will give you hope. And when you learn of members of my family suffering for my sake in other parts of the world, pray for their comfort. Pray that they will have access to my Word.

Many are the foes who persecute me,
but I have not turned from your statutes.
PSALM 119:157

I WILL FINISH WHAT I STARTED IN YOU

*Take comfort in the security of knowing
that I'll never quit working in you.*

Salvation—becoming a child of mine—happens quickly, the moment you acknowledge Christ as your Lord and Savior. But the process of sanctification—becoming Christlike—is a much longer project, beginning at the point of salvation and continuing through your earthly lifetime.

You are a construction project of sorts. The work that I began *for* you commenced when my Son died on the cross to pay the penalty for your sin. That was a "once and one time only" event that covered the sin of all humanity.

In contrast, my work *in* you began centuries later, when you received my gift of salvation—and it is a lifelong process. Through my Spirit, the scriptures, and the ministry of other believers, I am transforming you to be a reflection of my Son. Transformation moves at different speeds, but it will be perfected for you (and all other believers) when Christ returns to earth. Then we'll all be brought together face-to-face.

I never leave a job unfinished, so I'll be working in you daily. Just be aware of what I'm trying to accomplish in you.

*Being confident of this, that he who began a good work in you
will carry it on to completion until the day of Christ Jesus.*

PHILIPPIANS 1:6

BE MY WITNESS

Just tell others what you know about me.

The command I gave to those who followed my Son is the same command I give to you: be a witness for me. Tell the people who haven't heard of my love for them or of my desire to be reconciled with them.

"Witnessing" is quite simple, though I know it can seem intimidating. So keep these principles in mind: I'm not asking you to *save* others—that's my job, for which you are not equipped. Don't feel that you need to be an expert in all theological concepts—I'm just telling you to share your story of our relationship. And remember that I'm not leaving you on your own with this assignment—I'm equipping you with my Spirit who will guide your thoughts and direct your conversation.

Sharing reports of what I've done for you should become a normal part of your life. If my presence is a vibrant part of your life, I'll become an integral part of your life's story.

*"But you will receive power when the Holy Spirit comes on you;
and you will be my witnesses in Jerusalem, and in all Judea and
Samaria, and to the ends of the earth."*

ACTS 1:8

CARE OF THE POOR

I have given you resources to be shared with others.

I have already bestowed blessings on you, and there are more where they came from. Some blessings have been spiritual, others more tangible. Some have been for your own personal benefit—others were given that you might bless the people around you.

As far as financial resources are concerned, I never intended for you to stockpile wealth for your own personal plans. I want your sense of security to come from your trust and faith in me.

When I choose to bless you financially, it's for the purpose of ministering to others who are in need. I give to you so that you can give to others.

There is a divine inefficiency at play here—I'm going through you as a middleman—but you will gain blessing in addition to that experienced by the people who receive your gifts.

There were no needy persons among them.
For from time to time those who owned land or houses sold them,
brought the money from the sales and put it at the apostles' feet,
and it was distributed to anyone who had need.

ACTS 4:34–35

I AM GOOD

*My goodness means I am
kind and benevolent to all people*

Many people, when they were children, recited this little prayer: "God is great, God is good, let us thank Him for our food." I like that prayer because it highlights two very important qualities of mine—my greatness and my goodness.

Adults tend to see one of those qualities as superior to the other, as in "She used to be just *good*, but now she's *great*!" But as those qualities apply to me, superiority is a misconception. My greatness and goodness are different, but neither is inferior to the other.

When you say, "Great is the Lord," you are making a statement about my omnipotence, my righteousness, and my holiness. My greatness should inspire awe and respect. By comparison, when you say, "The Lord is good," you are commenting on my kindness and benevolence to all people. To be sure, I am a God of justice—but I am also inclined to be kind to all.

The problem is that you sometimes have trouble *accepting* my goodness. You lived in rebellion for so long that you are uncomfortable with my being nice to you. Like an abused animal, you sometimes cower even when approached by a tender hand.

Don't be afraid. My goodness is genuine, and it's for your benefit.

Taste and see that the LORD is good.
PSALM 34:8

JESUS IS PREPARING A PLACE FOR YOU

Your heavenly home has been custom designed just for you.

Your heart is easily troubled, my child. Sometimes you live under a cloud of uncertainty so heavy that you don't see yourself ever breaking through. Around the world, my children wonder how they are going to make their next house payment, or deal with illness, or live through the heartbreak of a rebellious child.

I did not design your heart to bear such grief. That's why my Son has already taken your sorrow upon Himself, promising you a future when there will be no more heartache. Your existence in the valley of tears is temporary—it's like you are living in a tent. But Jesus is preparing a permanent place for you in my heavenly house.

This is no empty promise. In fact, I've already seen your room, and I can say with certainty that it's been custom designed just for you. So take heart. Trust my Son. Someday He will take you home.

"Do not let your hearts be troubled.
You believe in God; believe also in me.
My Father's house has many rooms;
if that were not so, would I have told you
that I am going there to prepare a place for you?
And if I go and prepare a place for you,
I will come back and take you to be with me
that you also may be where I am."

JOHN 14:1–3

THE HOLY SPIRIT DRAWS YOU TO MY SON

Nobody embraces my Son as Savior
unless my Spirit paves the way.

As compelling as my Son is, people are not naturally attracted to Him.

Oh, some are drawn to the person they *think* Jesus is: non-judgmental, accepting of all, lowly, meek, and mild. But for the most part they back away from who my Son really is: the holy and righteous one who came to save sinners.

That's why I sent the Holy Spirit—to draw people to the *real* Jesus in saving faith. Most people are fine with Jesus as a sage, but nobody embraces Him as Savior unless my Spirit paves the way.

The problem is that people are in the dark spiritually—not for lack of light, but for their inability to see. As my Son said to Nicodemus, "No one can see the kingdom of God unless they are born again" (John 3:3).

In other words, the only way to overcome your spiritual blindness is for you to be born again by the Holy Spirit. But you can't be born again unless the Holy Spirit draws you to my Son. When that happens, both your eyes and your understanding open, so you can see Jesus for who He really is—and accept him for what He has done for you.

"No one can come to me unless the Father who sent me draws them."
JOHN 6:44

MY WORD WILL GIVE YOU PEACE

The common denominator for all people at peace is my Word.

Do you recall a time when you met a person who was truly at peace?

I don't mean someone who has died and now "rests in peace." I'm describing living people at peace with me because they are saved. . .at peace with themselves because their conscience is clear and their destiny secure. . .at peace with others because they are generous to all. . .and at peace with the world because things always seem to work together for their good.

Where does that kind of peace come from? Why are some people at peace while others experience constant turmoil?

The common denominator for all people at peace is my Word. Those who love my Word put themselves under its authority— and they do so without equivocation. They don't negotiate with my Word, they simply obey it. Of course, this doesn't mean they automatically understand everything they read—but they trust me completely for the ultimate outcome.

What a contrast with those who love the world more than my Word. They are confused, because the wisdom of the world causes them to stumble. But those who love my Word have peace, because the wisdom of my Word keeps their footing sure.

Great peace have those who love your law,
and nothing can make them stumble.

PSALM 119:165

Week 44
FRIDAY
Your Life

SUBMIT TO ONE ANOTHER

Like my Son did, I want you to set aside your "rights" in order to serve others.

You have always had a problem with submission. It's a characteristic of your fallen nature, to resist submitting to others, especially those you consider inferior or wrong. But you need to put your resistance aside and follow my desire for you.

I want you to submit to your brothers and sisters in my family—not because you are inferior, but because it brings your character in closer conformity to my Son.

If you think submitting to others is beneath you, consider what my Son did for you: though He is equal to me in every way, Jesus submitted to my will (Matthew 26:39) and humbled Himself by becoming obedient to death—for you (Philippians 2:8).

Like my Son did, you should set aside your "rights" in order to serve others. It's all about bearing people's burdens, and is beautifully pictured in marriage. A wife should willingly follow her husband's leadership, and the husband must put his interests aside in order to care for and love his wife.

Don't fight submission. This healthy relationship with one another begins your submission to me.

Submit to one another out of reverence for Christ.
EPHESIANS 5:21

THE FRAGRANCE OF MY SON

The aroma of my Son will please some and offend others.

As my child, you have unique qualities. Because you have the Holy Spirit in your life, you have the mind of Christ, giving you special insight into my Word and wisdom that the world does not understand. You also have a certain fragrance that is very pleasing to me. It's the aroma of my Son in your life, like a priceless perfume poured over your head. This aroma is so strong that others who don't yet know my Son will sense it as you share His life and message with them. Often you don't even have to use words—simply your life will do.

But you need to know that the aroma of my Son will not please every person you encounter. In fact, to some people, you'll stink—though it won't be because the aroma has changed. The difference is with the receiver: while the aroma of my Son through your life is heavenly to those who seek me, it offends those who want nothing to do with me. To them, it is the smell of death—their own death—rather than the smell of life.

For we are to God the pleasing aroma of Christ among those who are being saved and those who are perishing. To the one we are an aroma that brings death; to the other, an aroma that brings life.

2 CORINTHIANS 2:15–16

STOP QUARRELING AND START PLANTING

Stop fighting, concentrate on planting and watering, and leave the rest to me.

Here's a sign that you are an immature believer: you take sides with certain preachers, teachers, and writers, usually over Bible doctrine, then argue with your brothers and sisters about who's right.

It is completely correct to have concern for important issues. That shows maturity. But you are acting like a spiritual baby when you take sides, supporting the teacher you agree with, condemning the teacher you disagree with, and then arguing with people who follow the teacher you oppose. Ridiculous! You and your opponents are like children in a sandbox, quarreling over who gets to play with a toy. You are embarrassing yourselves and bringing shame to the church.

You don't need to agree on everything. But you should all understand your role—as well as the roles of Bible teachers and writers in the body of Christ. You are all spiritual farmers. With your words, you plant seeds in the soil of unbelief, and you water the seeds with your life. That's as far as you can go. I am the only one who can actually make the seeds grow.

So stop fighting and concentrate on planting and watering. Leave the rest to me.

So neither the one who plants nor the one who waters is anything, but only God, who makes things grow.

1 CORINTHIANS 3:7

I SPEAK THROUGH YOUR THOUGHTS

I am the "still small voice" in your head that guides you.

Never forget that I created you in my image. That means you bear my imprint—you are my personal design, fashioned in my likeness.

That doesn't mean you *look* like me, but you can *think* like me. I planted in your heart a sense of my eternal kingdom (Ecclesiastes 3:11), and I have placed a knowledge of me and the ability to contemplate me in your mind (Romans 1:19). Because of sin, Satan has clouded your thinking (2 Corinthians 4:4), but when you are reborn by a work of my Spirit, your mind is renewed as you are transformed from darkness to light.

As your mind grows ever more conscious of me, I enter your thoughts, giving you increased wisdom and understanding. Essentially, I speak to you through your thoughts. Think of me moving through your mind with a lamp, illuminating the corners of your consciousness. I am the "still small voice" in your head that helps you in decisions and prompts you to carry out my will.

My instruction today is to keep this beautiful channel open. Give me room in your mind by fixing your thoughts on me (Philippians 4:8).

The human spirit is the lamp of the LORD
that sheds light on one's inmost being.
PROVERBS 20:27

MY SON ENDURED TERRIBLE PAIN

Jesus suffered and died for one simple reason:
so you and I could have a relationship.

To appreciate how much my Son has done for you, it is very important that you know how much He suffered for you.

Jesus' death by Roman crucifixion was the ultimate in humiliation, agony, and pain. Though Jesus is fully divine, He is also fully human—and He knew the shame and the pain He would have to endure. So He asked me if there was any other way to accomplish your salvation (Matthew 26:39). At the same time, my Son knew the cross was the only way—so He willingly went like a sheep to the slaughter (Isaiah 53:7).

First Jesus was blindfolded and beaten. Then, stripped of His clothing, He was tied to a post and flogged without mercy by Roman soldiers—who then mocked my precious Son by putting a robe on His shoulders and a crown of thorns on His head. Desperately weakened, Jesus carried His own cross toward Golgotha, where the Romans hammered spikes into His hands and feet. Then He hung on that cruel cross for hours until he took His last breath, crying, "It is finished."

My Son died that day, but it wasn't in vain. His suffering and death were for one simple reason: so you and I could have a relationship. The pain was great, but the payoff was even greater.

*"My soul is overwhelmed with sorrow to the point of **death**."*
MATTHEW 26:38

MY SPIRIT IS EVERYWHERE

Wherever you go, my Holy Spirit is there,
helping you and reminding you of my Son.

If you have any question that the Holy Spirit is equal to me in every way, let me settle it for you: though He is a distinct Person, the Holy Spirit is *all* that I am.

One proof of this truth is that the Holy Spirit is everywhere. You can't go anywhere my Spirit can't follow. When you're at home with your family, He is among you. When you go to work, my Spirit is in your office. When you visit distant places, my Spirit travels with you. Whether in heaven (where He reflects my glory) or on earth (where He imparts my power), the Holy Spirit is there, helping you and reminding you of my Son.

But there's another dimension where my Spirit dwells—and that's in the inmost parts of your mind. He is your active conscience, convicting you against sin and directing you to purity. He is your foolproof guide, granting you wisdom when you need it.

Considering all the benefits of having Him as your constant companion, I advise you to give my Spirit full access to your heart and mind. Don't shut Him out by your own worthless mental wanderings. Invite Him to fill your life with *His* thoughts.

Where can I go from your Spirit?
Where can I flee from your presence?
PSALM 139:7

THE BOOKS OF MOSES

The first five books of my Word
reveal much about my character and purposes.

My Word is more than a collection of sixty-six different books written by forty authors. The Bible is *one* book with *one* story—*my* story.

Through thousands of events, characters, and places, my glory, my love, and my plans for you and all humankind are explained with dramatic clarity. When you read my Word as my story, you will see there is one purpose through its pages and through the ages: I want you to come back to me, and I've paid the ultimate price to make that possible.

The first five books of my Word (which some call the Pentateuch) reveal much about my character and purposes. I am spirit, not material. . .I am present, not absent. . .I am the supernatural Creator, the forgiving Savior, ever faithful to my promises and altogether holy.

Don't skip these five books. Read and study them to learn of my extravagant creativity and exquisite care in making a perfect home for you. See how I rescued humans when sin almost led to their complete destruction. Pore over the way I personally directed my chosen people out of enslavement to a new hope.

Most encouraging of all, you will find that my plan to save you has never for one second gotten off track. What I started in Genesis, I will be faithful to complete.

"I am the LORD your God,
who brought you out of Egypt, out of the land of slavery."
EXODUS 20:2

Don't Speak with Contempt

*If you show bitter animosity to another believer,
you are subject to judgment.*

I've noticed a disturbing trend among my children: too many of you hold your fellow Christian brothers and sisters in contempt.

It's an easy trap to fall into. Somebody makes a derogatory comment about you, but rather than turning the other cheek, you return fire. You criticize them just as they criticized you, only more intensely.

And here's another way you show contempt: A political or church leader takes a position you strongly disagree with. So you respond with a condescending disapproval, tinged with disgust, not face-to-face with the leader but to whomever is within earshot. With your modern technologies, it doesn't take much to broadcast your contempt to people around the world.

Listen: this is *not* the way you are to act. When you show this kind of bitter animosity—even if the person you target never knows about it—you are subject to judgment. The satisfaction you may get from your criticism just isn't worth the risk.

*"But I tell you that anyone who is angry with a brother or sister
will be subject to judgment."*
Matthew 5:22

BE STRONG AND COURAGEOUS

*You can move forward by faith
because I have gone before you.*

Confidence is an enviable character quality. The confident person usually accomplishes more than one who is uncertain.

I want *you* to have confidence in all you do, but it can't be a confidence based on human ability or achievement. I despise a prideful confidence where the effort and results depend on you alone. To find true success in every dimension of your life—personal, professional, emotional, mental, and spiritual—you need to place your confidence in me. Indeed, the very word *confident* comes from a word that means "with" (*con*) "faith" (*fide*). The highest confidence you can have is to place your trust in me through faith.

So here's my word of confidence for you today: with me above you, me below you, and me beside you, there is nothing to fear and no reason to be discouraged. No matter where you go today, no matter who you talk with, no matter how big the task ahead of you, you can move forward with faith because I have gone before you.

So be encouraged! Go through this day confidently because you trust me fully.

*"Have I not commanded you? Be strong and courageous.
Do not be afraid; do not be discouraged, for the Lord your God
will be with you wherever you go."*

JOSHUA 1:9

BE READY TO GIVE AN ANSWER

I want my children to be ready
to answer the questions the world is asking.

Your church is both a sanctuary and a school. No matter where you meet with your brothers and sisters in Jesus, you can rest under the shadow of my wings. When you gather, whether in a magnificent cathedral or an ordinary home, you are set apart unto me in a sacred space for worship, for the observance of my sacraments, and for service.

Your church should also be like a school where you learn to follow me more fully. My desire for you is that you grow in both character and mind: in character so those in the world will want to know more about the hope you have; and in mind so when they ask, you will be ready to give a reasonable explanation for why your faith in me is true. How do you know I exist? Why do you believe I created the universe? Who is Jesus and why does He matter? Is there an answer to the suffering in the world? These are the questions the world is asking. I want my children to know how to answer them, and my church is an ideal place to learn.

But in your hearts revere Christ as Lord.
Always be prepared to give an answer to everyone who asks you
to give the reason for the hope that you have.

I PETER 3:15

323

I Don't Want Anyone to Perish

I know everyone won't turn to me,
but I want them to. And you should, too.

Because I am compassionate, merciful, and slow to anger, I am giving the world more time for more people to turn to me.

The downside to my patience is that, with more time before my Son returns, there is also more time for suffering, both from natural disasters and human cruelty. But the upside outweighs the negative: the longer I wait to close the door on sin and suffering, the greater the number of people who will be in my kingdom.

I want as many as possible to be saved. In fact, my desire is for *none* to die in their sins. Knowing this, you should feel compelled to match my desire with your prayers for the souls of those around you. Do you want everyone in your neighborhood, your workplace, or your school to be saved? Do you want all the politicians, entertainers, and professional athletes to turn to me? Do you want every atheist and agnostic to know the truth?

If you do, you'll pray and witness with passion and purpose. I know everyone won't turn to me, but I want them to. And you should, too.

This is good, and pleases God our Savior,
who wants all people to be saved
and to come to a knowledge of the truth.

1 Timothy 2:3–4

JESUS WAS ABANDONED

*This is what Jesus feared
when He prayed to me in the garden.*

This is one of the most difficult messages I could ever give you. It concerns the death of my Son, something that tore at my heart. But even His death—terrible as it was—did not compare to the agony of separation that afflicted my Son and your Savior.

Throughout His public ministry, Jesus knew what it was like to be rejected. He met opposition wherever He went. But with the events leading up to His crucifixion, the rejection and abandonment intensified. First, all His disciples deserted Him and fled (Matthew 26:56). Then Peter, His close friend and loyal follower, denied Him three times (Mark 14:66–72).

But none of this could match the pain Jesus felt when, as the sins of the world fell on Him, *I myself* abandoned Him. This is what Jesus feared when He prayed to me in the garden (Matthew 26:39). The physical torture was excruciating, but when I turned away from my Son—because of the sin He bore—He was utterly alone. Yet it was necessary for Jesus to die twice, once physically and once spiritually, so you would *never* have to experience eternal separation from me.

*About three in the afternoon Jesus cried out in a loud voice,
"Eli, Eli, lema sabachthani?" (which means
"My God, my God, why have you forsaken me?").*
MATTHEW 27:46

DO NOT BELIEVE EVERY SPIRIT

Knowing the truth is the best way to detect what is false.

Because Satan masquerades as an "angel of light" (2 Corinthians 11:14), he is very adept at imitating my words and work. But there's always a clever twist. One of Satan's primary methods is to use false teachers and fake prophets to proclaim a message that *sounds* close to the truth, but is in fact very far from it.

You need to know how to spot these false messengers and their counterfeit "gospel," because—as you know—a counterfeit of anything is completely worthless. In the case of a false gospel, it's actually quite dangerous—because its victims believe they are following truth, when in fact they are buying into a lie. It's not a pile of worthless money that's at stake, but people's eternal souls.

Practice spotting counterfeit gospels. When you hear a message or read a book, test the spirit behind it. Stay in tune—intimately—with my Holy Spirit, who will help you know the true Gospel backward and forward.

Knowing the truth is the best way to detect what is false.

Dear friends, do not believe every spirit,
but test the spirits to see whether they are from God,
because many false prophets have gone out into the world.
1 JOHN 4:1

THE BOOKS OF HISTORY

*If you want to see how I interact
with my handpicked leaders, read these books.*

Much of the Old Testament is narrative, or story. Not only that, it's a history of my personal interaction with humanity.

After I delivered my people from slavery through the leadership of Moses, I gave them my law as a guideline for living. The time was 1400 BC, and my people were about to enter the land I promised them. As much as I loved Moses—he was one of the few people in history to meet me "face-to-face"—I chose Joshua to lead my people into the Promised Land. Joshua foreshadowed Yeshua, or Jesus, who will someday lead you into the heavenly land I promised you.

These Old Testament history books—from Joshua to Esther—record the lives and faith of some very familiar characters: Samson, Ruth, Samuel, Saul, David, Solomon, Ezra, Nehemiah, and Esther. If you want to see how I move with action and compassion, judgment and mercy, interacting with my handpicked leaders, read and study these twelve books. The way I have worked in history is a great reminder of how I act and move now.

*"Keep this Book of the Law always on your lips;
meditate on it day and night, so that you may be careful
to do everything written in it."*
JOSHUA 1:8

FOR SUCH A TIME AS THIS

*No problem is too big for the person
who is willing to trust me completely and follow me fully.*

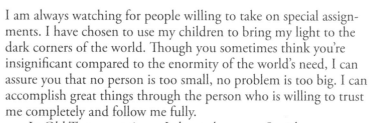

I am always watching for people willing to take on special assignments. I have chosen to use my children to bring my light to the dark corners of the world. Though you sometimes think you're insignificant compared to the enormity of the world's need, I can assure you that no person is too small, no problem is too big. I can accomplish great things through the person who is willing to trust me completely and follow me fully.

In Old Testament times, I elevated a young Jewish woman named Esther, who was willing to follow my plan, to the position of queen. Then I used her to prevent the certain annihilation of my people.

In the eighteenth and nineteenth centuries in England, a young man by the name of William Wilberforce followed my leading and worked tirelessly to abolish slavery.

In America of the nineteenth century, an uneducated shoe salesman named Dwight Moody responded to my call and became an evangelist who introduced countless people to me.

What about you? Are you willing to do something great for such a time as this? I don't need your skills—all I want is your obedience.

*"And who knows but that you have come to your royal position
for such a time as this?"*
ESTHER 4:14

The Right Way to Give

*Give what you have,
not what you don't.*

When it comes to sharing what you have with others—whether with individuals or ministries—there are three ways you can give: you can offer up your time, your talent, or your treasure. Sometimes you'll share in one area; at other times you'll give all three. But more important to me than the size of your gift is the attitude of your heart.

I want you to be wise about your giving. No matter how worthy the cause, don't give more than you have. Don't give so much time that it hurts your relationships. Don't exhaust your talents so that those who depend on you are disappointed. And most of all, don't give money you don't have.

Here's a simple principle to follow: give in proportion to what I have given you. Never hold back when you see a need—but don't overgive to the detriment of yourself and others.

*Whatever you give is acceptable if you give it eagerly.
And give according to what you have,
not what you don't have.*
2 Corinthians 8:12 nlt

MAKE DISCIPLES OF ALL NATIONS

*It's only a matter of time—perhaps in your lifetime—
before the whole world hears.*

All three Persons of the Trinity are involved in your salvation—but the Holy Spirit alone marks you as one of my children and one of Christ's co-heirs.

On the Day of Pentecost, the Holy Spirit descended upon all believers and the church was born. Immediately these believers, now anointed and infused with my Spirit's power, fanned out to every corner of the known world in obedience to my Son's Great Commission. The apostle Paul ministered throughout the Roman Empire. Doubting Thomas, energized by the power of my Son, faithfully took His life-changing message to India and China.

Those early disciples were told to make *more* disciples and baptize all nations—because baptism unites all believers, regardless of ethnicity, gender, or geography. Today the Good News of Jesus continues to go out to every nation and nearly every people group. It's only a matter of time—perhaps in your lifetime—before the whole world hears.

What are you doing to carry out my Son's commission? How willing are you to make disciples of all nations?

*"Therefore go and make disciples of all nations,
baptizing them in the name of the Father
and of the Son and of the Holy Spirit."*
MATTHEW 28:19

LOVE ME WITH EVERYTHING YOU HAVE

The reality of your love for me shows that your faith is genuine.

A lawyer once asked my Son what he needed to do to inherit eternal life. Now, I love lawyers because they are trained to seek the truth—and if you are honest with them, they will almost always respond to your questions with honest answers.

Jesus answered this particular lawyer with another question: "What does the Word of God say?" The lawyer correctly answered, "Love the Lord your God with all your heart, soul, strength, and mind." Jesus affirmed this answer because it was right on the mark. It still is.

If you want to please me, you need to love me from the center of your being—sincerely, without reservation. I want that eternal part of you to embrace me as the only one who will satisfy your soul.

Put some muscle into your love. Don't just *say* you love me; *prove it* by your actions. And engage your mind as you pursue me. The more you know me, the more you'll love me.

Will this love alone save you? My grace toward you and your faith in my Son is what saves—but your real love for me shows that your faith is genuine.

"Love the Lord your God with all your heart and with all your soul and with all your strength and with all your mind."
LUKE 10:27

331

MY SON WAS AN INCREDIBLE TEACHER

Jesus is your teacher. Learn all you can from Him.

We've already discussed what happens when you view Jesus as no more than a wise teacher. In that case, faith is useless—because a mere teacher doesn't perform miracles as Jesus did. A teacher doesn't forgive sin as Jesus did. And a teacher can't save you as Jesus did.

Still, though He was much more than a teacher, my Son was indeed a teacher. In fact, He was the greatest and most revolutionary teacher in history.

My Son was born into a culture where an oppressive government enslaved people, where women and children were second-class citizens, and where the poor and afflicted were exploited and cast aside. When Jesus declared, "Blessed are those who are persecuted" (Matthew 5:10), people were astonished that I actually cared for the downtrodden. When He said, "Love your neighbor as yourself" (Luke 10:27), He extolled the concept of serving others, regardless of who they are. My Son treated women as equals and invited children to come to Him (Luke 18:16). And, most scandalously of all, He was the friend of sinners (Luke 7:34).

Jesus is *your* friend, Jesus is *your* Savior, and Jesus is *your* teacher. Learn all you can from Him.

They were amazed at his teaching, because his words had authority.
LUKE 4:32

THE HOLY SPIRIT HELPS YOU LOVE

As good as you think you are at love,
you need help.

From all I have told you, from all you have read in my Word, you should have no question that *love* is your highest calling—and my greatest desire for you.

You can have all the success in the world, but if you don't love, you're a failure. You could have every spectacular spiritual gift, but if you don't love me and your neighbor with all your heart, soul, strength, and mind, your gifts are empty. You could even have more faith than anyone else, but without love, that faith is futile.

Love isn't something you manufacture. You can't fake loving someone. And you certainly can't fool me. Love must come from your core and it must be other-, not self-, serving.

As good as you think you are at love, you need help. So I've given you the Holy Spirit, to make you better at loving. Give my Spirit full access to your life, let Him guide your intentions and actions, and He will show you how to love. Your response will be natural and from the heart.

When you follow His lead, your love will do even more: it will show the world that you are my follower, and I am your God (John 13:34–35).

This is how we know that we live in him and he in us:
He has given us of his Spirit.

1 JOHN 4:13

THE BOOKS OF POETRY AND WISDOM

My Word contains some of the most magnificent poetry ever written.

Throughout the ages, poets have expressed their thoughts and feelings of life, love, heaven, and earth in ways both intimate and majestic. Great literature—in particular, poetry—has the ability to capture the imagination and stir the emotions like little else. Is it any wonder, then, that my Word—the greatest piece of literature ever written—should contain some of the most magnificent poetry ever written? I am the ultimate source of creativity and imagination, and the Bible is *my* book.

In the middle of the Old Testament are the five books of poetry and wisdom, containing some of the world's most memorable verses. People are drawn to these books again and again because they express what you often think and feel about your life—and about me.

The book of Job tells you how to deal with suffering without losing faith; the Psalms describe me and our relationship; the book of Proverbs teaches you to do the right thing; Ecclesiastes shows that ultimate meaning is found in me; and the Song of Songs proves that I am love.

When you feel down and need a lift, go to my books of poetry and wisdom. They will do wonders for your soul.

I lift up my eyes to the mountains—where does my help come from?
My help comes from the LORD, the Maker of heaven and earth.

PSALM 121:1–2

I CARE ABOUT SEX

You honor me with your body
when you run from sexual temptation.

One of the strangest things anyone can say about me is that I don't want my children to enjoy sex.

Do you realize how ridiculous that is? Who created the sexes—male and female—so they would complement one another and enjoy each other in all dimensions of their being? Who made their bodies so they would be attracted to each other? And who designed sex itself, so it would not merely be a way to propagate the human species but an intensely pleasurable experience? Of course, I myself am the answer to all these questions.

I care about sex, but I care about you even more. That's why I designed sex to be enjoyed in the framework of marriage, when a husband and wife are so deeply committed to one another that their bond is a picture of the relationship between Christ and the church.

You honor me with your body when you run from sexual temptation. This includes sex with your eyes, not just sex with your body. When you commit yourself to sexual purity before marriage and sexual fidelity through marriage, you show that your body is not yours alone. It also belongs to me.

The body, however, is not meant for sexual immorality
but for the Lord, and the Lord for the body.

1 CORINTHIANS 6:13

I HAVE CHOSEN THE POOR TO BE RICH IN FAITH

Because they are at such a disadvantage,
I go out of my way to honor the poor.

It grieves me to see how the poor are treated. It's always been this way, in every culture, a consequence of the sin that infects the entire human race.

The corruption of the human spirit means the poor will always be the object of scorn and pity. Those who have very little will always be exploited for the little they have. It's a shameful attitude, and I hate it—not just for what it does to the poor, but for what it does to you.

Because they are at such a disadvantage, I go out of my way to honor the poor. I may not give them material things, but my tendency is to pour spiritual riches on them. Some of my most enthusiastic and dedicated followers are those who live in deep poverty.

You shouldn't be surprised at this. Prosperous people generally put their faith in material things—including their ability to make money. On the other hand, those who have very little are more likely to focus on me. There's not much else in their lives competing for my attention, so once they find me they tend to be very faithful.

Poor people, as viewed by the world's standards, are rich beyond measure in my eyes.

Has not God chosen those who are poor in the eyes of the world
to be rich in faith and to inherit the kingdom
he promised those who love him?

JAMES 2:5

Always Show Respect

You may be convinced that you are absolutely right,
but don't come across that way.

When you share your faith, whether it's one-on-one or in front of a group, I want you to be humble.

Because you have the truth on your side, any argument you offer is going to be very compelling. But don't be condescending to the opinions of others, even if they discount your argument. It's enough that you operate from a position of truth. You don't need to ridicule your opponents.

And when you're the one *being* ridiculed, don't respond in kind. Even an atheist who vehemently denies my existence deserves respect. Respond to others' angry tone with gentleness.

You may be convinced that you are absolutely right, but don't come across that way. Say things like, "It is reasonable to believe," or "This is what I have found to be true." Give your opponents room to be wrong on their terms, not yours. Let your words speak for themselves—and, even more, let your *life* tell the story. Then even your harshest critics will be moved to hear what you have to say.

Always be prepared to give an answer to everyone
who asks you to give the reason for the hope that you have.
But do this with gentleness and respect.

1 Peter 3:15

IT IS IMPOSSIBLE TO PLEASE ME WITHOUT FAITH

*Putting your faith in me
means that you believe certain things about me.*

There's only one way for you to begin and continue a relationship with me: by faith.

But what does that mean? It's not a leap in the dark, that's for sure. It's more like a leap into the light—because the most important thing about faith is its object. If you have faith in me, your belief is washed in light and anchored to the surest of all realities, defined by these fundamental truths:

I am the self-existent God in three Persons, the Creator of all. Jesus is my Son, fully divine and fully human, sent to provide a way for you to have a relationship with me. This salvation comes to you by trusting in the life, death, and resurrection of my Son. My Holy Spirit is the presence of Jesus in your life, and the Bible is my inspired Word and your authoritative guide for everything on which it speaks.

Putting faith in me means you believe these things about me—and trust that I will reward you for your sincere belief.

*And without faith it is impossible to please God,
because anyone who comes to him must believe that he exists
and that he rewards those who earnestly seek him.*

HEBREWS 11:6

THE RESURRECTION OF MY SON

If Jesus was not raised from the dead,
your faith is useless.

As important as the death of my Son is for your salvation, it would be meaningless without His resurrection.

If Jesus had not been raised from the dead, your faith would be useless. You would still be under the penalty of sin (1 Corinthians 15:17). If there was no resurrection, there would be no chance for you to go to heaven. In fact, without a living Christ, you would have no hope whatsoever (1 Corinthians 15:19).

Ah, but your sins have been forgiven, you do have a future in heaven, and you possess a glorious hope—all because Jesus *is alive* and sitting at my right hand.

But humans often ask, *How do I know the resurrection actually happened?* For one thing, the tomb that held Jesus is empty—and there were hundreds of eyewitnesses who saw Him after His death and burial (1 Corinthians 15:1–6). These truths, coupled with the testimony of a multitude of transformed believers through the centuries, are a witness to the power and presence of my Son in your life.

What more compelling proofs do you need?

"I am the resurrection and the life.
The one who believes in me will live,
even though they die; and whoever lives
by believing in me will never die."

JOHN 11:25–26

THE HOLY SPIRIT HELPS YOU UNDERSTAND ME

My Spirit gives you something the unbeliever doesn't have.

Sometimes you wonder why unbelievers don't see me the way you do. You don't understand everything about me, but you know enough to follow me with confidence. Believing my Word and joining my family are perfectly sane options for you.

But unbelievers conclude you're living in a fantasy world.

Put yourself in a skeptic's shoes for a minute: because he doesn't have the Holy Spirit in his life, he knows nothing of the spiritual connection you and I have. Jesus dying for your sins? The Holy Spirit living inside you? Having a conversation with me like you would talk to a friend? Hoping for the return of my Son? It all sounds pretty far-fetched to someone in the natural human state.

But you do have the Holy Spirit, my presence in your life, who gives you understanding. The unbeliever lacks both, unless my Spirit is actively convicting him of sin, convincing him that he needs me.

That's why you should pray for your unsaved friends. Pray that the Holy Spirit will begin His work in them.

*The person without the Spirit does not accept the things
that come from the Spirit of God but considers them foolishness,
and cannot understand them because
they are discerned only through the Spirit.*

1 CORINTHIANS 2:14

BOOKS OF PROPHECY

There is much in these books that will show you my character.

The seventeen books of Old Testament prophecy are among the most important—but least read—in my Word. I understand that these books have an aura of mystery, and that the prophets who wrote them seem eccentric and countercultural. That's by design.

I chose prophets like Daniel to speak for me because he was willing to reject his pagan culture whenever it conflicted with his commitment to me. I picked Isaiah because he was skilled in writing about me in a majestic, visual style. Jeremiah spoke for me from the midst of a declining kingdom, doing so without complaint—because faithfulness was more important to him than success. Hosea endured an adulterous marriage so he could describe what it's like for me to have a relationship with a rebellious, unfaithful people.

It's true that there are many predictions in these prophetic books. Your faith will be strengthened as you see for yourself how many of these have been fulfilled to the letter, mostly by my Son, the Messiah. But don't focus on the prophecies alone—there is much in these books that will show you my character and instruct you on how to live uprightly before me.

The LORD is good, a refuge in times of trouble.
He cares for those who trust in him.
NAHUM 1:7

LOSE YOUR LIFE TO FIND IT

Are you willing to pay the price required to follow my Son?

Following my Son is not easy. It is life changing and eternally rewarding, but it is a difficult way for one simple reason: to follow my Son, you must be willing to lay your life down in service to Him.

The great deception of your time is that following Jesus is easy, requiring very little of you. Accept my Son as your personal Savior, the idea goes, and you will have a happy life. You don't have to give up anything or radically change the way you live. Jesus suffered and died, but you won't have to.

Sadly, people buy into these lies, perpetuated by Satan to draw them away from the truth. Then they wonder why their life in Christ is so empty.

Jesus is honest about what you can expect: you will suffer, the world will hate you, and it is possible you will die for the cause of Christ. This is the reality and the cost of being a follower of my Son. Are you willing to pay the price? That's something you need to decide.

"For whoever wants to save their life will lose it,
but whoever loses their life for me and for the gospel will save it."
MARK 8:35

THE WORLD DOESN'T KNOW ME

The darkness is ignorance of the truth,
and the light is understanding.

Do not be surprised if the world doesn't "get" me—because the world doesn't know me.

Those in the world are like blind men and women stumbling in the dark. Though they'll deny it, they know in their hearts that I exist—but their understanding is obscured by the darkness of the world. So they live as if I don't exist, or they come up with their own ideas about who I am and how I work. All the other religions and belief systems in the world were born in this dark ignorance.

But you have seen the light because you've seen my Son—who is the light of the world. His light gives life to everyone. It breaks through the darkness, and there's nothing in your sinful world that can extinguish His light.

The darkness, of course, is ignorance of the truth, and the light is understanding. The world doesn't know me, but Jesus does—and you know Jesus. You are a child of light, and the darkness can never overcome you.

"Righteous Father, though the world does not know you,
I know you, and they know that you have sent me."

JOHN 17:25

JESUS IS THE VINE

As long as you remain attached,
you will produce much fruit.

Today I'll give you a beautiful image of what it means to be a member of the body of Christ.

Picture a lush vineyard brimming with grapes, such as is commonly found in the Middle East. My children are the branches (from which the spiritual fruit grows) and my Son is the Vine (from which the branches grow). As a branch, you are of the same substance as the Vine—you have the same kind of body as the body of my Son, but you are completely dependent upon Him for nourishment and growth. Indeed, He is the source of your salvation and your eternal life with me.

Apart from the Vine, you can't do anything. But as long as you remain attached, you'll produce much fruit. Now, don't ever think that you are useless. To the contrary, as a branch you'll produce fruit the church wants and the world needs. When you recognize that everything a healthy branch requires comes from the Vine, you will more fully appreciate the other branches around you. You'll never think you're better than anyone else but always produce fruit together for the good of my church and my ultimate glory.

"I am the vine; you are the branches.
If you remain in me and I in you, you will bear much fruit;
apart from me you can do nothing."

JOHN 15:5

WITH ME ALL THINGS ARE POSSIBLE

*The impossible happens
because nothing is too difficult for me.*

There are so many distractions in the world. You face so many opportunities, responsibilities, and worries.

People with a lot to lose—those with an abundance of material possessions—have more on their to-do list than others, and are less inclined to sincerely seek me. Those who are building careers don't give me time because their jobs demand so much of them. Then there are those caught up in the ideas and attractions of the culture—everything about their lives is defined by the music they listen to, the movies they enjoy, the technology they use, and the friends they have. Some are interested in "spirituality," but they don't want to be confined by the content of my Word.

So how do any of these people—the rich, the driven, and the distracted—come to a place where they recognize a need for me in their lives? On the surface, it would seem impossible. And, in fact, it is.

Nobody preoccupied with earthly cares voluntarily turns his or her heart toward heaven unless I get involved. But once I do, the impossible happens—because nothing is too difficult for me. No heart is too hard for my love.

*"With man this is impossible,
but with God all things are possible."*
MATTHEW 19:26

MY SON CONQUERED DEATH FOR YOU

Because of Jesus, death does not have the final say.

My dear child, the worst thing about life on earth is death. Your life can be wonderful one moment as you enjoy all the blessings I provide for you—then, in an instant, your world is shattered by the unexpected news that someone you care for deeply has fallen into the black hole of death.

It may be happen in an instant through an accident or a heart attack, or the news may be that a deadly disease is in the process of taking your loved one's life. Death is agonizing, horrifying, and—even for the strongest person—utterly distressing. Even my Son wept when confronted with the news that a close friend had died (John 11:34–37). Death is no respecter of persons, and no one escapes.

Yet because my Son was raised to life three days after His own death, he demonstrated that death could not hold Him. And His death and resurrection give you and everyone who believes in Him victory over death. Because of Jesus, death does not have the final say.

Your physical death is but a temporary interrupter. You need not fear, because you have my promise that eternal life awaits you.

"Where, O death, is your victory? Where, O death, is your sting?"
. . . Thanks be to God! He gives us the victory
through our Lord Jesus Christ.
1 CORINTHIANS 15:55, 57

MY SPIRIT HELPS YOU DO MY WILL

*When you immerse yourself in my Word,
my Spirit will merge my will with yours.*

Knowing my will for you isn't difficult, but it does take time and effort.

Resist the temptation to take shortcuts. Never take a fortune cookie message as my will, even if it coincides with a decision you're about to make. And don't play the game where you close your eyes, open the Bible, and point to a verse at random. I don't use parlor tricks to convey my will to you. I speak through people, through thoughts, and most often through my Word.

When you're in tune with my Word, you are aligned with my will—because the Holy Spirit illuminates your understanding. In fact, when you immerse yourself in my Word, my Spirit, through His intercessory work on your behalf, will merge my will with yours. In other words, your desire to do something will coincide with my desire for you.

It's no coincidence when that happens. It's the work of the Holy Spirit in your life.

*And he who searches our hearts knows the mind of the Spirit,
because the Spirit intercedes for God's people
in accordance with the will of God.*

ROMANS 8:27

347

THE GOSPELS TELL THE STORY OF MY SON, JESUS CHRIST

*The Gospels of Matthew, Mark, Luke, and John
are biographies of my Son.*

You know I want you to be like my Son, Jesus. But how will you imitate Him if you don't know the kind of man that He was?

The fact is, you must learn of Him if you are to be like Him. Fortunately for you, I have provided you with a thorough and trustworthy record of my Son's earthly life, covering the time from His miraculous birth to His death, resurrection, and ascension. This sacred biography is set forth in the first four books of the New Testament—Matthew, Mark, Luke, and John.

These Bible books, named for their authors, are referred to as the *Gospels* because they proclaim the "Good News" that my Son came to earth to provide salvation for humanity. They explain the means by which sinful people can be reconciled with me. Immerse yourself in these Gospels. Examine the things that Jesus did. Reflect on what He said. Notice how He interacted with the people He met. Heed His instructions to His disciples. Absorb His principles into your life so that you may emulate Christ.

*Jesus performed many other signs in the presence of his disciples,
which are not recorded in this book. But these are written
that you may believe that Jesus is the Messiah, the Son of God,
and that by believing you may have life in his name.*

JOHN 20:30–31

MAKE MY KINGDOM YOUR TOP PRIORITY

My kingdom is both earthly and heavenly.
It is "already" and "not yet."

You'll find topic of my kingdom often in my Word. My Son spoke about this kingdom more often than anything else, which indicates just how important it is.

Many wonder what my kingdom is all about. Is it eternity future when I rule over all in a perfect world? Or is it now, when all my children enjoy my presence through the work of my Son and the fellowship of my Spirit? In reality, my kingdom is both earthly and heavenly. It is "already" and "not yet."

This is what Jesus meant when He prayed, "Our Father in heaven, hallowed be your name, your kingdom come, your will be done, on earth as it is in heaven" (Matthew 6:9–10). You should anticipate a future kingdom when you'll dwell with me in perfect love and justice, but you must also do my will on earth, letting me use you to bring love and justice to a world desperately in need of both.

In fact, make my kingdom your top priority.

"But seek first his kingdom and his righteousness,
and all these things will be given to you as well."
MATTHEW 6:33

TELL THE WORLD ABOUT MY KINGDOM

You must share what you know with those who are dying.

My kingdom is both a future and a present reality. My kingdom has come to earth because of my Son, who has saved you, and my Spirit, who is transforming you. They work together to build a body of followers tasked with taking the Good News of my kingdom to the world. Indeed, advancing my kingdom is at the heart of my Son's Great Commission (Matthew 28:19).

As you live in the world, I want you to think of ways you can tell others about my kingdom. Why wouldn't you? If a friend was dying of a disease and you had the only cure—had once experienced the cure's life-saving effects yourself—you would eagerly share your knowledge with your friend. To hold back would be inhumane.

In the same way, it's inhuman—and very much against my will—to withhold knowledge of the spiritual cure for the fatal disease of sin. Listen! You *must* share what you know with those who are dying. That is my will and your mission.

"And this gospel of the kingdom will be preached in the whole world as a testimony to all nations, and then the end will come."

MATTHEW 24:14

MY CHURCH IS INDESTRUCTIBLE

Because the church is built on the life and work of my Son,
I will not let it fail.

The body of Christ is indestructible. Since the founding of my church on the Day of Pentecost (when the Holy Spirit came upon the believers in power), Satan has tried his best to destroy it. The opposition started immediately with a fierce persecution, resulting in the death of many of my faithful followers. These early saints refused to turn from their faith in me—and they paid a dear price for their belief.

It's been like this through the centuries. Satan continues to assault my church, and where He doesn't attack directly, he tries to cause division. It grieves me to see my children fighting with one another, usually over minor points of doctrine—since that sows seeds of confusion in believers and unbelievers alike.

Despite what you see—examples of both persecution and division—don't be discouraged. Don't give up. The church is my idea and the bride of my Son. Because it is built on the life and work of my Son, I will not let the church fail—even if all the fury of hell comes against it.

"I will build my church,
and all the powers of hell will not conquer it."
MATTHEW 16:18 NLT

I AM YOUR LIGHT

There is no darkness or shadow of turning in my being.

There is an enormous contrast between darkness and light, and it's not just in the scale of brightness. Light has a quality that darkness can never duplicate.

In the physical world, light is life giving; darkness is not. Light enables plants to grow and produce oxygen for the air you breathe; darkness fosters dormancy. That is why my first command in creation was, "Let there be light" (Genesis 1:3). The universe could not exist without the light of the sun, the moon, and the stars.

Light in the spiritual world, where I dwell, is an element of glory, purity, holiness, wisdom, joy, and beauty. As the source of light, all spiritual life and growth depends on me. My Son, who is one with me in substance, is Light of light. In His entire being, Jesus is the very brightness of my glory.

The darkness of the world dissipates when I approach because there is no darkness or shadow of turning in my being. And because you bear my image, you *reflect* my light. Walk in my light and let it shine wherever you go.

This is the message we have heard from him and declare to you:
God is light; in him there is no darkness at all.

1 JOHN 1:5

JESUS BRINGS YOU CLOSE TO ME

My Son has made it possible for you to draw near to me.

How I long to tell you the awesome privileges you have because of your faith in my Son. Without Him and all that He's done for you, you would be lost, without hope. With Him, you gain the opportunity to flourish in life during your years on earth. Then you have the sure prospect of eternal life with Him in heaven.

Here's the best part about your life now: you don't have to wait for heaven to enjoy my presence. It begins here and now! In the days of the Old Testament, only the high priest could come into my presence in the temple's "holy of holies." Everyone else was shielded from me by a curtain. But the death of my Son tore the curtain in two (Matthew 27:51), giving you direct access to me.

So, my dear child, take every opportunity to draw near to me. Jesus has made that possible. Don't squander the gift you've been given—and never forget the price that's been paid.

*Therefore, brothers and sisters, since we have confidence
to enter the Most Holy Place by the blood of Jesus, by a new
and living way opened for us through the curtain. . .
let us draw near to God with a sincere heart
and with the full assurance that faith brings.*
HEBREWS 10:19–20, 22

THE SPIRIT OF PROMISE

*My Holy Spirit is your guarantee
that I will deliver what I have promised.*

You couldn't live day to day if people didn't keep promises. Relationships function best when people follow through on their commitments. Your employment succeeds because you agree to do what's required for the paycheck you expect. You make business transactions based on the integrity of contracts.

And yet, because you're a flawed person dealing with flawed people, these promises, commitments, and contracts are occasionally broken.

In the most important relationship and covenant you could ever have—between you and me—you can be absolutely sure that I will keep my word, following through in every detail. My word is enough, because my ways are perfect—but I want you to have corroborating testimony. So I've given you my Holy Spirit, who is your guarantee that I will deliver what I have promised.

Through His inner witness, my Spirit is my signature that our agreement is binding, that your spiritual inheritance is secure, and that you are my child—forever.

*When you believed, you were marked in him with a seal,
the promised Holy Spirit, who is a deposit guaranteeing our
inheritance until the redemption of those who are God's possession—
to the praise of his glory.*
EPHESIANS 1:13–14

THE ACTS OF THE APOSTLES

Scripture tells how my followers matured and thrived through the power of my Spirit.

After His resurrection but before He ascended to heaven, my Son challenged His followers to proclaim His name throughout the world. They were a ragtag band of believers, few in number—yet within a few decades they had established flourishing communities of believers throughout the Roman Empire. Their efforts to spread the Good News of Jesus changed the world—and have now reached you.

Don't think those early believers achieved such things through their own bravery and strength. At first, they were hesitant and bewildered. But when they relied on the power of my Spirit within them, they proclaimed my Gospel message with great boldness.

Read of their adventures in my Word, in the book of Acts. You'll be inspired when you see how *my* Spirit in *my* followers produces supernatural results and brings my Son's story to the nations.

"But you will receive power when the Holy Spirit comes on you; and you will be my witnesses in Jerusalem, and in all Judea and Samaria, and to the ends of the earth."

ACTS 1:8

PERSPECTIVES ON SUFFERING AND EVIL

*I allow evil and suffering
so you can grow closer to me in dependence and trust.*

That there is much suffering and evil in the world is a source of great disappointment and heartbreak to you. But don't be discouraged. And don't give up on me.

I know it's difficult to confront evil and suffering without losing faith in me, or worse, blaming me. So I'm going to offer you a new perspective on the problem of evil.

The vast majority of evil in the world is caused by sinful people doing bad things to each other. Because I am incapable of wrongdoing, I cannot *cause* evil, nor can I make people do evil things. Still, because I am sovereign, I *allow* suffering and evil. That's a problem for many, until they realize some of the reasons I do.

For one thing, I allow evil and suffering so you can grow closer to me in dependence and trust. I can also use evil for your benefit as I did for Joseph when he was sold into slavery. And finally, though I will one day deal with evil once and for all, I am currently delaying so more people will turn to me.

*"You intended to harm me, but God intended it for good
to accomplish what is now being done, the saving of many lives."*
GENESIS 50:20

NATURE IS GROANING

There are occasional hiccups in nature,
but most of the time it functions beautifully.

As I've told you, most of the suffering and evil in the world is caused by sinful people doing sinful things to one another. But what about the suffering caused by natural disasters? Hurricanes, earthquakes, floods, fires—all of these contribute to human misery and destruction.

So where am I in all these things?

My first response is to remind you that I created the natural world and set it up to run according to laws I designed for maximum functionality. Then sin entered the world like a bomb, throwing shrapnel into the perfection of both human relationships and the natural order.

Because of my grace, the human race has continued with relative civility, and nature still functions with amazing precision. Yes, there are occasional hiccups in nature, but most of the time the natural world embraces and supports you with beauty and benevolence.

When the world itself suffers because nature is groaning, remember that it won't always be this way. I have plans for a spectacular new earth, in which everything will be perfect once again. And I can't wait for you to see it!

We know that the whole creation has been groaning
as in the pains of childbirth right up to the present time.
ROMANS 8:22

357

JESUS WILL NEVER LOSE YOU

You belong to your precious Savior as a sheep belongs to its shepherd.

The Holy Spirit is your guarantee that I will fulfill all my promises to you—and my Son is the reason you are secure.

Jesus does not work independently of me, nor do I work apart from Him. My Son came to do my will, and He obeyed me to the point of death so *you* could have eternal life. Jesus, the living Word, has always been with me and has always been equal to me (John 1:1). Yet, as a unique and distinct Person, my Son came down from heaven as life-giving bread—voluntarily setting aside His divinity and taking on full humanity—to satisfy the spiritual hunger of all who taste of Him.

My Son came for one purpose—to do my will. And my will is that not one person I have saved through my Son will be lost. You belong to your precious Savior as a sheep belongs to its shepherd. You can trust Him completely to keep you, taking you to your ultimate and eternal home with me.

"All those the Father gives me will come to me,
and whoever comes to me I will never drive away.
For I have come down from heaven not to do my will
but to do the will of him who sent me."
JOHN 6:37–38

I WILL BE YOUR LIGHT IN HEAVEN

You will see me as I am,
for you will be in my presence and will see my essence.

Because I am spirit, no one has ever seen me. Yet you long to see me, which is only natural.

Those brought from death to life want to see the one who has saved them. That's why I sent Jesus—so you could view, in a visible form, the one who redeemed you (John 14:9).

Though I am invisible, I have an essence—my literal and unchanging nature, the real me. You can *sense* this now, but when you come to your final home in heaven, in the presence of your Father and my Son, the Lamb, you finally be able to gaze upon my very essence.

You see, though you are redeemed, you are not yet pure in heart—and only the pure in heart can see me (Matthew 5:8). When you are glorified in heaven and your heart has been purified, you will behold my radiant glory and beauty.

In heaven, there will be no darkness, nor will there be any need for light—because I'll be your light. And you will see more than simply an image: you will see me as I am, my very essence.

There will be no more night.
They will not need the light of a lamp or the light of the sun,
for the Lord God will give them light.
And they will reign for ever and ever.

REVELATION 22:5

JESUS IS YOUR KING

*My Son's kingdom is eternal,
populated by those He has redeemed.*

Human beings have a fascination with kings and kingdoms, and that's all right. But there is a problem when your desire for an earthly king overrides your allegiance to me.

That's what happened to my people in Old Testament times. I was their king, but they wanted a king like other nations had (1 Samuel 8:4–9). They were rejecting me, but I accommodated them—though I knew they were in for disappointment. Earthly kings can be capricious and cruel, building their kingdoms on the backs of their subjects.

I am nothing like that—and to prove it, I sent my Son to be your King. Jesus did not come in power, as one of your rulers would, but instead as a servant and sacrifice. Standing before Pilate on the day He was crucified, Jesus clarified the nature of His kingdom. It is not a corruptible, temporary, earthly kingdom, but a perfect eternal kingdom populated right now and forever by those He's redeemed.

As one of my children, you belong to this kingdom. Jesus is your King!

*Jesus said, "My kingdom is not of this world.
If it were, my servants would fight to prevent my arrest by the Jewish
leaders. But now my kingdom is from another place."*
JOHN 18:36

Let Me Strengthen You

*Let go and let me do my work
in you and through you.*

If you let me, I will accomplish some wonderful things in your life.

We're not just discussing a life that is personally satisfying to you. I also want to use you as a mighty witness to the people I put in your path. If you let me work, you'll do things you could have never imagined before.

Because they insist on maintaining control, so many of my children live in mediocrity. You'll never do those good things I planned for you if you hold on to the reins of your life. But if you trust me and give yourself to my Holy Spirit, you will have all the power you need to do what pleases me (Philippians 2:13).

Listen! You have access to my unlimited resources. Take advantage of my power, available to you through my Spirit. Don't be too practical, too self-absorbed, too worried what others will think. Let go and let me do my work in you and through you. I promise, your life will go from mediocre to extraordinary.

*I pray that out of his glorious riches he may strengthen you
with power through his Spirit in your inner being.*
Ephesians 3:16

THE LETTERS OF PAUL, PETER, JOHN, AND JAMES TELL YOU HOW TO LIVE

*The epistles teach you the practical application
of a spiritual life in a fallen world.*

I realize that your living a Christlike life would be much easier if I had transported you to heaven at the moment of your salvation. But I want you living like Christ *in* the world—being my witness and influence in a lost and fallen place. I understand that your new spiritual nature makes you feel like an alien in a foreign culture, at odds with the values and principles of the people around you. But I have not left you without help on handling this assignment.

All of the New Testament epistles address these issues. Each of these letters was written to believers living in the first generation following my Son's ascension. Following Christ at that time often involved persecution, even torture, by the Roman authorities—so the authors of those sacred letters knew their readers were desperate for practical instruction, spiritual encouragement, and divine guidance.

That's exactly what you'll find as you read the epistles. Few of my followers will ever face execution for their faith—but these themes of faithful living in difficult times will resonate with your soul and refresh your spirit.

*What you heard from me, keep as the pattern of sound teaching,
with faith and love in Christ Jesus.*

2 TIMOTHY 1:13

BE LIKE JESUS

Everything my Son is,
you should want to be.

My highest goal for you is to be like my Son.

Oh, I know you will be never be *just* like Him while you're still in your mortal body on earth. But you can make progress on your spiritual journey, a journey that is taking you from where you are to where He is.

In your everyday life, you naturally want to emulate the people you admire. In your spiritual life, I want you to do the same thing—only don't imitate other people, no matter how spiritual they seem to be. Set your sights higher—on my Son. Everything He is, you should want to be. On your own it's impossible, but with my help, you can do it.

As you continue on your journey of spiritual growth, keep this very important thought in mind: your progress on earth will never be complete, but when my Son returns, your transformation will be final. Think of it! Not only will you see my Son in all His beautiful glory, but you will also share in that glory. You will finally be like Him.

Dear friends, now we are children of God,
and what we will be has not yet been made known.
But we know that when Christ appears, we shall be like him,
for we shall see him as he is.

1 JOHN 3:2

HELP THE HELPLESS

If you have true faith,
you will have a heart for people on the margins of society.

There are two ways to keep yourself from being corrupted by the world.

One is *negative*: Avoid worldly activities. Now, this doesn't mean you withdraw from the world—I want you to be salt and light so the world will get a flavor and a sense of me. Even my Son associated with people who didn't share His values, though He never participated in the things that reflected their values. And that's what I want you to do: be in the world but not of it.

The other way to keep yourself from being corrupted by the world is *positive*: Help the helpless. Among the most helpless of all are widows and orphans. They are not the only ones on the margins of society, but they represent all who are. If you have true faith, you will have a heart for such people—and in serving them you will not only put my Word into practice. You will also be in step with my own heart (Deuteronomy 10:18).

Religion that God our Father accepts as pure and faultless is this:
to look after orphans and widows in their distress
and to keep oneself from being polluted by the world.
JAMES 1:27

SILENCE THOSE WHO DECEIVE PEOPLE

*Be alert and know my Word
so you can detect their destructive teaching.*

There have always been false teachers in the church, evil people who deliberately deceive others. Please realize: these are not members of the true church for the simple reason that they oppose true faith.

But they can work their way into your midst, trying to convince you that there is more to salvation than Jesus. In the first century, the false teachers' extra requirement was circumcision. If you weren't circumcised, they said, you weren't saved. Today, the added-on requirement is often extra work, such as helping the poor. If you aren't *doing* certain thing, the false teachers tell you, you aren't saved.

Some of these false teachers are simply confused or ignorant of correct doctrine. Try to bring these people back to the truth. But others are outright deceivers, pretending to be my faithful followers but really in pursuit of financial gain. These people need to be silenced for their deliberate deception.

Be alert and know my Word so you can detect their destructive teaching.

*For there are many rebellious people,
full of meaningless talk and deception. . . .
They must be silenced, because they are disrupting whole
households by teaching things they ought not to teach—
and that for the sake of dishonest gain.*
TITUS 1:10–11

YOU CAN ONLY IMAGINE

Words cannot express how magnificent your life with me will be.

Oh, my dear child, if only you could see, or hear, or even imagine what I have waiting for you!

When you and I are united, face-to-face in heaven, the splendor of the home my Son has prepared, the incredible beauty and wonder of the new heaven and new earth I'll create for you, the unimaginable bliss of being in my presence forevermore. . .well, words cannot express how magnificent your life with me will be.

And yet, even this is not so foreign that you cannot conceive—at least in part—what you will one day experience. I have revealed my goodness and grace to you through the inner witness of my Holy Spirit, so that even in the midst of your mortal life on earth, you can taste the immortal life waiting for you in heaven.

You and I have a real connection, one that inspires and encourages you any time my Spirit brings you into my presence. Keep this link active and continue to grow in your love for me. Set your thoughts on things above, while doing your duty to take my Good News to people below.

You're on the way to heaven. Try to bring many people with you.

"No eye has seen, no ear has heard, and no mind has imagined
what God has prepared for those who love him."

1 CORINTHIANS 2:9 NLT

KEEP YOUR EYES ON MY SON

No one knows you better, has done more for you,
or loves you as much as Jesus.

As you live out your life on earth, awaiting the return of my Son, you have two choices. You can wait in a way that frustrates you or in a way that fulfills you.

The frustrated life comes from wanting to do things on your own, rather than depending on me for wisdom and direction. I'm not saying your life will be free of difficulty when you trust me fully—but you'll certainly add to your problems by holding on to habits and sins that tie you up in knots.

Listen—you don't have to live that way! With me teaching you through my Word, my Son praying for you at my side, and my Holy Spirit strengthening you from the inside, you can experience an *abundant* life.

My child, as you live daily in total dependence on me, keep your eyes on Jesus. You're running a marathon, and my Son is at your side—cheering you on, giving you living water as you race toward the finish line.

No one knows you better, no one has done more for you, and no one loves you as much as Jesus.

Let us throw off everything that hinders
and the sin that so easily entangles.
And let us run with perseverance the race marked out for us,
fixing our eyes on Jesus, the pioneer and perfecter of faith.
HEBREWS 12:1–2

Week 52

WEDNESDAY

The Holy Spirit

MAKE A HOME IN YOUR HEART

*My Spirit will show you the extravagance
of my Son's love for you.*

Never take your life of faith for granted. This isn't like any other reality in your existence.

Though you can't experience me with any of your five senses, your heart feels and your mind knows that I'm your God—who was, and is, and is to come. I am the loving Creator who has connected with you personally and lovingly through my Word, my Son, and my Holy Spirit.

This is not a fairy tale, and there's nothing ordinary about it. Your relationship with me is more real than anything else in your life. It can and should be the most extraordinary experience you have.

But you can't just sit and hope your life of faith will suddenly explode into significance. You should actively make a home in your heart for my Spirit, who will show you by His inner witness the extravagance of my Son's love for you.

That's what your life is all about—so dive in. Know for yourself how vast the reservoir of Jesus' love really is.

*Then Christ will make his home in your hearts as you trust in him.
Your roots will grow down into God's love and keep you strong.
And may you have the power to understand, as all God's people
should, how wide, how long, how high, and how deep his love is.*
EPHESIANS 3:17–18 NLT

THE REVELATION OF JESUS CHRIST

If you read and obey this book,
I promise to bless you.

Most of my children spend their greatest time in my Word reading the letters.

I'm very pleased that you do. These New Testament letters, also called *epistles*, were written to Christians who were experiencing the same challenges, frustrations, and temptations you do.

In these difficult days, be sure to read the *last* book of the Bible, too—the book of Revelation, or more properly, the Revelation of Jesus Christ—which actually contains seven letters to seven churches. You can see if world events are lining up with the prophecies of Revelation. . .and you can judge for yourself if the Second Coming of my Son is near.

No human knows when Jesus will return to earth, but this much I can tell you: Revelation is all about my Son, and you are wise to learn all you can from this book. In fact, if you read it and obey what it says, I promise to bless you (Revelation 22:7).

If you want to know my Son better—if you want a glimpse of His coming in glory—spend time in the Revelation of Jesus Christ.

"I am the Alpha and the Omega,"
says the Lord God, "who is, and who was,
and who is to come, the Almighty."

REVELATION 1:8

369

I WILL WIPE AWAY EVERY TEAR

What is good in your life will be magnified,
and all that is bad will disappear.

❖

Your life now is composed of moments of joy, interrupted by periods of sorrow. Such is the experience of redeemed people.

The apostle Paul endured more hardships, persecutions, and calamities than anyone—yet he kept his eyes on my Son, who had suffered even more. Paul knew his strength came from his weakness, the realization that I was working in his life.

The hardships you face in life—illnesses, tragedies, broken relationships—are hard, sometimes almost unbearable. But I want you to imagine a future that will obliterate every vestige of sorrow and sin from your life. All your troubles and all their effects will be washed into the abyss as you come into my glorious presence.

You will no longer feel pain, not even the smallest amount. You will never again shed a tear for something done or someone lost. Nothing—and I mean *nothing*—will be the same. What is good in your life will be magnified, and all that is bad will disappear.

❖

And I heard a loud voice from the throne saying,
"Look! God's dwelling place is now among the people,
and he will dwell with them. They will be his people,
and God himself will be with them and be their God.
'He will wipe every tear from their eyes.
There will be no more death' or mourning or crying or pain.
REVELATION 21:3–4

ANYONE WHO CALLS ON MY SON WILL BE SAVED

*My plan, conceived even before I made the world,
is centered on Christ alone.*

Everybody wants to go to heaven—but not everyone chooses to get there the way I've prescribed.

Through the ages people have tried to negotiate the terms of my solution to the problem of sin. I require nothing except faith in my Son, sent for the salvation of all who are lost and without hope. My plan, conceived even before I made the world, is centered on Christ alone—and all I ask is that you believe in Him.

There is no plan B. There is no other way. There is no other truth. There is no other source of eternal life. Just as there is only one way to be born, there is just one way to be born again. Jesus is the only way, the only truth, and the only life.

All the other plans formulated by humans—sometimes parts of religions, often the product of their own dark thinking—are false. They don't hold water, and they hold no hope.

When you believed in my Son for your salvation, you became my child. Those still trying to negotiate the terms of my plan are lost. But they can call on the name of Jesus—He is mighty to save, and *ready* to save.

*"There is salvation in no one else!
God has given no other name under heaven
by which we must be saved."*

ACTS 4:12 NLT

THE CHURCH TRIUMPHANT

*All who have believed in me by faith
will live with me and with my Son forever.*

As part of my eternal family, you are like a bride waiting for the glorious day that she will be united with her beloved. And never has any bride waited for a man who loves her as much as my Son.

This bride is not any individual, but all those I've called out to be my witness and presence in the world. This bride is the *church*, existing in the Old Testament as people chosen by me, and in the New Testament as those who have been baptized by my Spirit into the body of my Son.

Everyone who has believed in me by faith—whether anticipating the Messiah to come or longing for Christ to return—will be gathered by my Spirit to live with me and my Son forever. Can you hear my voice? It's a quiet stream now, but soon it will be a mighty torrent of life-giving water, refreshing you in every part of your being forever and ever. Amen!

*"I, Jesus, have sent my angel to give you
this testimony for the churches.
I am the Root and the Offspring of David,
and the bright Morning Star."
The Spirit and the bride say, "Come!"
And let the one who hears say, "Come!"
Let the one who is thirsty come;
and let the one who wishes
take the free gift of the water of life.*
REVELATION 22:16–17

ABOUT THE AUTHORS

Bruce Bickel is an attorney, but he hopes he doesn't have to stay that way. Bruce and his wife, Cheryl, live in the Seattle area.

Stan Jantz was involved in Christian retail for twenty-five years before venturing into marketing and publishing. Stan and his wife, Karin, live in Ventura County, California.

Bruce & Stan have cowritten more than fifty books, including the international bestseller *God Is in the Small Stuff.* Their passion is to present truth in a correct, clear, and casual manner that encourages people to connect in a meaningful way with the living God.

Be sure to check out Bruce & Stan's website:
www.Christianity101online.com.

Bruce & Stan are cofounders of ConversantLife.com, a content and social media online experience designed to promote conversations about faith and culture. They encourage you to check out this site for stimulating blogs, videos, podcasts, and news.

If you have questions or comments, you can connect with Bruce & Stan at

info@Christianity101online.com

SCRIPTURE INDEX